"I have just joined this forum. Yo~~ would love~~ to read your book if it i celebrated my mom's one month : hoping that your health is still goi

*

"It has been a while since you sent me your book. I have read it over and over. Your style of writing and wit is refreshing. Would you be so kind as to send me the second part?"

*

" I read your post about your book on the PKD Chat support boards. I had a transplant in 2005. I would love to read your book."

*

"When I was facing transplant, I searched for just such a book. Fear of the unknown was the worst thing I faced through the whole thing, and a book giving me some idea of what to expect would have been a good thing. I also lost my mom to this disease. I kept a detailed diary about my kidney failure and the transparent process while I was going through it.

Maybe your publishers are right that this book won't appeal to the masses, but perhaps it could be marketed to a medical publisher – one who could put the book into the hands of the nephrologist's offices, who could then recommend the book to their patients facing transplant.

Congratulations on keeping your kidney to 17 years - and many more!"

*

"I read the following post on a PKD board. I am having a transplant in one week and have been trying to learn all I can. I would love to get the information you have put together if you don't mind sharing! Thanks"

*

1

"I would like to read it, I am close to needing to join those on dialysis treatment. Thanks for the good read so far."

*

"Thank you. I am looking forward to reading your book. (My sister) truly enjoyed your style of writing. I'm sure that I will too. It is nice to meet you. Keep in touch."

*

"My sister wants to read your book. ..... She went through a lot with me. Feel free to e-mail. She told me to pass on her e-mail address."

*

"Just finished reading it all. Incredible. .... I wish I would have had a chance to read this before or right after my transplant. In this wonderful age of the Internet, most of the information I got about my kidney disease and transplant information was sugarcoated (most were sponsored by the various drug companies).

I would like your permission to forward your story to fellow kidney patients. One in particular has had two transplants like you have had. Another friend has a husband that is doing dialysis and is getting all the necessary testing done to be listed. I could go on and on about people I know that could benefit from your story. I have contacted the local kidney foundation about a support group for my area.... I'm the type of girl that likes it when things are from one's heart and not through the eyes of someone else. I love history but not unless it is told through the eyes of someone who lived it. You have inspired me as well as others I have come in contact through the Internet. I think we can all do our part to provide others with hope and inspiration. Whether it is writing a book, starting a foundation, a support group, etc... Educating others can help us all LIVE with our diseases and treatments. Your humour and wit really made it an easy read for me. Thank you once again for your story. I like the links you've provided at the end. Feel free to run anything by me. Please keep in touch. Finding a fellow kidney patient is like finding a lost friend! Take care."

"I'm sorry I'm sending you so many e-mails. Your story is wonderful. I did not get much done today. Every time I walked by my computer I had to stop and read more."

*

"I am ready for the second half. I love your sense of humour. You have captured the transplant experience and put it into words. I would have loved to find a book to read like yours before my transplant. You certainly haven't sugar coated anything. People seem to think you just stuff the new kidney in and you are cured."

*

"I just finished chapter 2. It is a gorgeous afternoon and I'm sitting in front of the computer. I have already laughed and cried. Some of your story mirrors mine. I really have to tear myself away and try to get some of my weekend work done. I truly hope you can get published. So many people suffering from kidney disease need hope and inspiration."

*

"I read your story on the National Kidney Foundation's Message Boards. I think you are doing a wonderful thing... I don't have as much experience in dealing with chronic kidney disease as you do. I discovered the problem in the spring of 2005 and had my transplant in June 2006. I would like to read what you have written. I am guessing, but I might be wrong, you are from Europe? I live in the United States. I just recently began contacting people dealing with kidney problems. It is wonderful to share stories and know you are not alone. Take care."

*

"Mike, my son had a transplant four years ago. I would love to read your story."

*

"Finished it last week, at least the first half, and can't wait to get the other half. Promised to try to post back the first half of this week if I get it together! Fascinating so far. Thanks"

*

"I am a home haemodialysis patient had just been forwarded your article "Passing Failure" which I read with great interest. I would be really keen to read your book if he would be happy to e-mail it to me. Your experiences of studying whilst in kidney failure particularly resonated with me as I went into renal failure aged 14 which was eight years ago, so I went through school on dialysis and am now studying full-time Sociology and Economics at the London School of Economics whilst dialysing at home four times a week. I had one transplant which failed within a few days so I am not planning to go down that route again for a while!

I think that despite what the publishers say they should be a market for this sort of book because surely it won't only be of interest to dialysis patients? It could provide a helpful insight to those in the medical profession as far as understanding what a renal patient goes through in trying to have a normal life outside of the hospital routine. I look forward to reading it. Best wishes."

*

"Hi Michael. Thank you so much for sharing parts of your book with us at the National Kidney Foundation. It looks like it will be a marvellous book! Once you get a book published and it is available to the public, let us is know, and we can put it on our website. In the meantime, good luck, and congrats on your successful kidney transplant! Please let me know if there is anything else I can do for you."

*

"Thanks for that Michael. I have started to read Chapter 1 and I experience a lot of déjà vu. I particularly like the "kidneys in gravy" on the hospital menu, as after my transplant I was offered "steak and kidney pie" I'm starting to think that this may be the hospitals chef's little joke. I might check the liver ward next time I visit my local just to see if "liver and onions" is on the menu. Anyway please send me chapter 2. Thanks"

"I have recently read your extract in the BAKPA News and was very inspired by it. I have had similar experiences myself and reading about others coping with in these debilitating circumstances gives me hope for the future. At the age of 23 I was put on the transplant list (as a result of kidney failure since the age of 3) and after three attempts at how the fistula formation was formally put on the haemodialysis a year later. After a year on dialysis my Auntie donated a kidney to me. I battled for six weeks with severe rejection but eventually left Southmead Hospital with a functioning kidney. Having my transplant has enabled me to work again and I now work full-time as a Home Care Organiser of the Social Services. I had just celebrated my 28th birthday and in lived a "normal" life with a transplant for two and a half years. I've often considered writing about my experiences but, apart from fellow renal patients, was not sure anyone would be interested in reading about them. However, I feel this is a human interest subject which is affecting more people every year and so may be more popular than I originally thought. I wish you the best of luck with your book and would be very interested to read it. Best wishes"

**

"TELL ME IF THIS HURTS"

By Michael O'Sullivan

In Memory of Mum and Dedicated to Dad

And thanks to all NHS staff who have kept me alive.

Working Kidney Quota: Mum two; Dad two; me two (WKQ: 2+2+2= 6) – Read on! All will be revealed!

Quotes I recall:

"I 'd rather be dead than be on a kidney machine" - A taxi driver when I needed transport to get to my dialysis session when I was ill.

"Self inflicted injury" - The small print explaining why my Dad, who had given me a kidney, could not claim on his health insurance policy so he could recover from the operation.

"Rachel O'Sullivan" - The name I spotted on the top of the hospital sheet while I was on a trolley on the way to the operating theatre.

CONTENTS

....

"That which does not kill us makes us stronger"

Friedrich Nietzsche

CHAPTER ONE: DETERIORATION BY DEGREE

"One, two, three, four, five, six, buzz, eight, nine, ten, eleven, twelve, thirteen, buzz, fifteen, sixteen, buzz, eighteen", thud. You probably recognise this playground game of buzz: cannot say anything with a seven in or divisible by seven .It was during one of these games a dinky car arrived in our sitting circle and I picked it up and threw it outside the circle and then carried on with the game. The one part of the game that was new was being kicked at the number nineteen by the car owner. At first I felt nothing and when the school bell went I stood up and became aware of a sickly feeling in my right side. Before that day I did not even know where the kidneys were located or even what their function was.

Before going into class for my least favourable Friday morning test which I usually did not do particularly well in, I went to the toilet for a pee but what came out was thick, bright red, fresh blood. I then went into class to take the test – where I got my best ever mark - when it was over I became more aware of the sickly feeling again. I explained this to the teacher and what had happened. I had to do a performance pee-, which was to be the first of many- because he apparently did not believe me. Then an ambulance was called.

I ended up in hospital for a month and missed school (yippee!) I had to lie flat on my back 24 hours a day, as that appeared to the doctors to be the best way of trying to get my kidneys to stop bleeding. I had to do everything (that's everything) lying completely flat. For instance I had to be fed lying flat and to drink one of the nurses slowly lifted my head each time I wanted a sip.

I remember that my uncle brought in an Airfix model kit of a plane. It was very difficult gluing all the bits together when it was already in mid air but occasionally it lay on my stomach having crash-landed due to my aching arms. Putting the little man in, who I understood was the pilot, was tricky. After resting my arms I lifted the plane up into view and could see his bottom staring at me but at least he was now in the cockpit. To avoid any complaint from the Civil Aviation Authority I needed to secure him to his seat pretty fast in time for his first solo flight. Peering directly upward up with glue in hand and at risk of a glue dollop raid at twelve o'clock I persevered. In this ward it was difficulty getting much sleep with all the other children, some crying for their mother and others moaning in pain. I needed shuteye but with the noise, it was more likely, with the glue directly above me, I may get the wrong type.

Suddenly there was a lot of commotion. A boy was trolleyed in to a bed bay and the curtains were quickly whished around him. I heard screaming for about 20 seconds. What's he done? Is it some kind of punishment? Did he wet the bed or something? If so I might be in real trouble as I was still not allowed to leave mine. Then slowly all the attendants left his bed, the curtains were drawn back revealing a boy who I later learnt had broken his leg and had to have it put back in place.

I remember thinking thank god I am only here for a little kidney problem.

After about three weeks I could lift my head and rest it on my elbow and sip drinks by myself and then eventually was allowed to sit up.

Then very late into my stay I could get out of bed and walk around. After being on a high hospital bed for so long I felt like a tiny little leprechaun walking along the floor.

I was able to leave the hospital after a month, only coming back to visit a friend who I had made and who was there for some time after me.

" Isn't that the kid who kicked you?" I was walking through the park after school and looked up and recognised the boy who had indeed put me in hospital "Aren't you going to do anything?" By that I knew the person I was with meant go and "duff" him up. Without any encouragement from me he walked over to him and I followed without really thinking and then my old assailant suddenly realised who I was and that he was slowly being cornered in the park. My friend looked at me as if to say go on hit him. But I could not see the point and let him run off with a very strange look from my companion.

I failed my eleven-plus and went to a secondary school where all the other failures went. The successful pupils went to a grammar school. I do not think there were any such establishments as comprehensive schools at the time

÷ ÷

Arthur Smith, comedian, writer and broadcaster wrote, "The first chapter of most biographies is nearly always worth ignoring. Our hero went to school and got into scrapes? Big deal" I agree. However this book is not an autobiography and not about heroes. The following needs to be mentioned early on or you might miss something later on.

÷ ÷

Years passed by without any other real problems apart from the occasional kidney infection resolved by drug treatment.

The hospital kept an eye on me and I was seen usually after a bout of bleeding. While examining me one doctor asked when I had last gone to the toilet. I told him I could not remember. With that he stopped, backed away from the bed, sighed, took his glasses off and berated me for being obstructive and that he was only there to help. I explained that I simply could not remember. He would not accept this so I just made up a time, which he appeared to accept thinking I had been withholding all along. What I hoped to achieve by doing that is beyond me, but anyway then and only then did the examination continue.

Bleeding was becoming so common that I used to doublethink when I went to the toilet and had asked myself what colour it was supposed to be. I got worried about the possibility of being caught during a bleeding episode (that's not in the swearing sense of the word) and so did the shy male thing and got into the habit of peeing in one of the cubicles. I was already embarrassed by occasionally being teased for having unusually red lips and was accused on several occasions of wearing lipstick. I have since wondered whether that was a side effect of the kidney condition.

My family moved up to the North of England and the school had an unusual set up in terms of how they taught science subjects. They did not teach chemistry at all and just before the start of the CSE/ O level two-year course the boys were expected to do physics (budding scientists you see) and the girls were expected to do biology (nurses you see). In my previous school we did all three so consequently they were ahead of me and so any chance of catching up and doing well in the sciences as lost.

I left home for college and a few months later, just before x-mas I fell ill with glandular fever, my folks came to pick me up because I was unable to cope in the student residents on my own during the holidays. My tongue was so swollen that when I spoke I had to use my hands to put it back in my mouth, which I did not do very often because no one could really understand what I was attempting to say. I was soon hospitalised as I was not drinking enough and there was a real concern that the resulting dehydration might damage my kidneys.

At the hospital I became aware of the growing seriousness of my already vulnerable kidney condition and the marked concern about my high blood pressure.

" Very unusual for someone of his age to have such high blood pressure".

It was said in such a way that it sounded to me like I was somehow to blame. I heard this at the bottom of my bed, not directed at me or relayed on later but just two doctors talking to each other. It was not even a case of a poor beside manner. They had not even got that far: it was a poor bed end manner. The conversation was about my health but did not include me. It taught me two things: do not let it happen again: interject and secondly watch the silent eye contact doctors were having with each other: I thought it meant something was seriously up or they were not sure what to do.

I was not totally ignored during the conversation they would break off from the conversation and turn to me and ask something like if I had moved my bowels today and I would receive a quick summary of what they would be doing before they left my bedside. (What is the collective noun for doctors? a diagnostic of doctors?)

I was to discover I had polycystic kidneys*. This is where you have slowly growing cysts on each kidney but as they grow the functional part of the kidney is lost. It is a hereditary condition. An American web site (see back of book for the address) dedicated to this condition states that it is "the most common genetic, life threatening disease affecting an estimated 12.5 million people world wide...In fact, PKD [Polycystic Kidney Disease] affects more people than cystic fibrosis, muscular dystrophy, haemophilia, Down Syndrome and sickle cell anaemia combined". My computer has no problem with these medical conditions and as I look above my present typing the only word with a squiggly red line underneath it is – and I am about to introduce a third one – polycystic*. When I click on it it tells me I must mean "polycentric". I inherited it from my Mum but at this time she had few problems and only discovered herself that she had passed the condition on to me. Although it had been diagnosed after the school attack. I was unaware of its serious significance until my hospital stay with glandular fever. Previously relatives on my Mums side from a generation or so ago had died prematurely but no one knew why but it now emerged that their deaths may have been due to this condition. It has been suggested that in previous centuries people have died of this condition but they have been diagnosed as suffering

---

*Aren't footnotes irritating? You have to leave the part of the page you are reading to read the minor little point and then find your place again. Why do they do it? Either it is important, in which case put it in the main text or if not put it at the back of the book. What I cannot stand is............

from Bright's Disease. This still interests sufferer's grandchildren today as I discovered recently on the internet. "My Grandmother died of Bright's Disease. In the 1800's and early 1900 many kidney disorders /infections were grouped under this name"

Like the kick in the playground a car crash was another unfortunate incident that accelerated the kidney deterioration process. I was in the back seat behind the driver coming back from a party and the car skidded on some ice, crashed into a railway bridge and I smashed into the back of his seat. We all had to get out quickly as we thought the car might topple over on to the railway track below.

My two friends in the front went through the windscreen but they were able to get out of the car but this time using a more traditional point of exit. I had a dead leg and couldn't get out very fast. Eventually, once I was reminded about the precarious position of the car, I hobbled across the road and immediately lay down. Then the ambulance arrived. The two friends who went through the windscreen had been looking over me to ask what was wrong and enquiring why was I not standing up. The blood from their facial cuts went all over me when the ambulance man asked me where I was bleeding from. I explained the blood was not mine.

When I got to hospital my problem turned out to be internal bleeding as I soon discovered when I went to the loo. I told the doctors about my kidney condition but as it was not fresh blood I was discharged and told to contact my GP. The next day my GP came to visit and I was sent back into hospital.

I phoned my family to tell them about the accident and that my kidneys were injured. This was very distressing for my Mum. She felt guilty (ping) as she knew only too well that I had inherited the problem off her. And in turn this made it more difficult for me as I felt guilty (pong) that I had

*There you are. Only kidding but I bet you're completely lost now aren't you?

inadvertently upset her. In future - as I surely knew there was going to be a future in this – I knew that I should mainly speak to Dad and he could gauge how much to reveal.

My bleeding did not stop and so I had an investigative operation, which involved a tube being inserted down the centre of my penis, a procedure known as a "cystoscopy", to see, with the aid of a small camera, where I was bleeding from: whether it was one or both kidneys.

As a general anaesthetic was needed I wasn't able to eat or drink anything for 24 hours beforehand. ("Nil by mouth") This is to prevent suffocation if you were to vomit while unconscious.

I was offered my last meal until 24 hours later: kidneys in gravy! In those days hospitals did not provide a choice of meal.

Usually I was very polite but on this occasion I muttered something under my breath and decided to go without. A nurse over heard me and said, "Michael. I have never heard you swear before." Kidneys in gravy! And that was on the same day when a man in the same ward had a part of his kidney removed.

When you fall asleep and wake up you know you have been unconscious. You just do not know exactly how long for until you look at the clock. However when you come round after a general anathestic you have no sense of time passing. It is strange but it is as if it is just a moment later and you do not appreciate that many hours may have gone by.

When I came round from my general operation I was not hungry but very thirsty. I made a few request for water but the nurses were very busy and I was promised one later. I waited for the next nurse to pass by but from the speed she was walking knew she had something far more important to do. Eventually I decided to go to the tap at the corridor sink and drink straight from it. Then I heard a nurse loudly proclaim: "Michael. What do you think you are doing in your bare feet drinking straight from the tap." I tried to explain and was met with " Well why didn't you ask?" I was getting told off ....not for the last time in a kidney ward.

It was discovered that I was bleeding from both kidneys. I stayed in hospital for longer to see if it would stop. This time I was not restricted to my bed and having to lie flat for weeks.

One problem people will never experience unless they become a hospital inpatient is the feeling that sometimes your body does not fully belong to you. For example, medics arriving at your bedside without notice and immediately wanting to examine you. However the situation becomes even worse if you are a healthy male and it's first thing in the morning when you body seems to a have a mind of it's own.

The sound of several pairs of footsteps slowly moving around at the other end of the ward alerts you to their impending arrival.

Amy Turtle, Ena Ogden, Margaret Thatcher......,

May be this morning they will not need to examine me. Touch wood. No such look.

".......and over hear is a young male. He has polycystic kidneys......"

The sluice room, the contents of the sluice room, muddy boots, vomit, cow sheds, the contents of the cow sheds.....

"Morning Michael. I wonder if you would mind if one or two of these young doctors could examine your kidneys." (short discussion with a now jam packed bottom of the bed). Yes certainly she can go first"

She! DOG TURD, COWPATS, CARSICKNESS; blamanche. No, not blamanche. Tree bark. Hedge trimmers. No, not hedge trimmers, helicopters engines......"

One of the last duties of the night shift nursing staff was to wake the patients up at 6.30 am, which annoyed me, as it was so pointless. There purely for the administrative convenience of the hospital. It was a real palaver. It involved readjusting the top of your bed by pulling out the backrest and repositioning the many pillows. All this extra junk at the top of the bed made it near impossible to go back to sleep once the nurse departed. I soon realised it was pointless to argue so when they finished and retreated back to their staff room I re positioned the pillows, pushed back the back rest and went back to sleep. It was a silly rule:

waking patients at 6.30 am ready for breakfast at 8.30.am to assist with the shift switch.

During this hospital stay one late evening I heard a nurse say to another patient " wake up, time to take your sleeping pills" What? Well there is justification for this: it ensures a good night sleep for those who nap through out the day and consequently cannot sleep properly at night but it did not half sound stupid to me.

"Fire! Fire! Michael there's a fire" I looked up from my bed during a quiet afternoon at the ward and saw one of the nurses with a big grin on her face. Apparently I was seen as calm, on the surface at least, and several times one or two of the nurses would tease me in this way to try and get some reaction from me.

In the bed next to me was a very ill old man. So much so it was difficult to even get an acknowledgement let alone a conversation out of him to help the day pass by. One morning when I woke up and looked across. He was gone. All his belongings had also been removed .His bed was made up ready, presumably, for the next patient. The cleaner was there making the final touches. It took me some time to realise he must have died in the night because nothing was said and you were just left to speculate.

On talking to the cleaner I discovered the real local dialect. Several months of hanging around mostly middle-class students and lectures and I hadn't yet acquainted myself with the local accent. I had to go to hospital to discover it.

Recalling this reminds me of the story that apparently emanated from Bolivia. A bed in an intensive care unit had a very poor record in survival rates. The doctors were suspicious and concerned as patients in that bed were not the most serious yet they died so they set up a camera on the bed 24 hours day. The reason quickly became apparent. When the night cleaner took her vacuum cleaner near the bed she carried the plug to the wall and pulled out the socket for the essential life support system, put her plug in, cleaned around for five minutes and then replaced the original plug.

While convalescing I was in the TV room watching a hospital drama and believe it or not this episode was based on the story of someone with renal failure. I was the only one in the room and another patient turned up but as soon as he realised what the subject was, walked out while making comments suggesting there was something wrong with me. There was: I had kidney problems. As he was leaving I said he could turn it over if he wanted.

I must have been in a minority but I wanted to learn as much as I could even from crass TV hospital programme. Some people tend to want to know as little as possible. While some patients do not ask or are afraid to ask, I was one who was always asking questions.

I nurse came into the room as she needed to take my observations ("obs.") Normally they are pulse, temperature and blood pressure. After taking my pulse she commented that I would never die from a heart attack, which I took to mean I had a slow and strong pulse.

One of the younger patients was a man with an unusual problem: he could not ejaculate. There was a blockage. Although it may have reduced the laundry costs it prevented him and his wife from starting a family. He told me the day before the operation that when he was about to be shaved a male nurse auxiliary arrived with a cutthroat razor. If that was not bad enough just before he began the shaving, he took out his glass case and when my ward mate looked up noticed the extent of the magnification on the lenses, held his breath while the auxiliary held the future prospects of his family in his hand.

The bleeding would not stop and so it was decided that I should be discharged. I went to convalesce at my parent's home. When I returned my Christmas holiday housing benefit had been stopped because I had not signed on thus I had rent arrears, which complicated matters, as I was one of joint tenants. After several letters explaining my position I was given my housing benefit back.

I continued to bleed for a few more weeks but eventually it stopped. Some months later I was invited to the hospital for an experimental operation. It was to see if they could stop the kidney function deterioration by bursting some of the larger cysts. This entailed lying on my back and an X-ray being taken. When this happened all the doctors and nurses would hide behind a screen in the corner of the x ray room. I got a bit worried. If this is their regular place what's the radiation doing to me? I wanted to ask if I could join them! Of course the occasional radiation is not going to harm me but the medical staff needed to protect themselves because they are near the radiation most weeks. When they located the sites of the larger cysts I was able to watch live on the "TV" monitor as they put this six-inch needle into my back and I could see fluid been drained out of the cysts and trickle down my back. Unfortunately the experiment didn't work and very slowly the deterioration expected of polycystic kidneys continued. There continues to be no treatment for polycystic kidneys.

***

I switched courses and had to do summer jobs to pay for the first year of a law degree because the local authority wouldn't let me have a second first year grant, which was fair enough. I then did several holiday jobs and term time bar work. I knew I was fortunate in the sense that temporary jobs were just that. I was able to think in terms of a career, unlike the people I was to work with who did not have the opportunity to hold such a high and mighty goal but were just pleased to have a job. I found it strangely consoling in that if I were to become a solicitor (Class A :professionals) I would at least have known what it was like doing manual work and taking the usual step of school to college to solicitors practice. So I spent a bit of time at Class E (unemployed and student) as well as Class D (manual). Thankfully this archaic system has since been changed but I do not know how accurate the new categorisation is. However the odd labouring jobs I had gave me in an insight into how people are treated which got me reconsidering what I would eventually do with my law degree if I got it.

The Closed Shop

"Will you join the union?"
"Sure"
"Ok you start on Monday. You know how to get to the paper mill"
"Yeah"

I did not but as the paper mill was reputed to be a mile long I am sure I 'd find it. When I arrived at work they were shocked to find I was not in the union

" But I am willing to join. I did not realise I had to go off and join in time for Monday. I just assumed I could join now."

"Oh no lad. You 'll have to go into town and join now. Have you got transport".

"I 've got a push bike".

"OK. Off you go. Join and then come back a soon as possible".

I discovered it was a "closed shop". The term I heard about all the time in the media in their quest to knock the unions. I was now about to join one.

The job title was " fitters' mate" which I thought would require a few years apprenticeship but it did not. The mills were closed for several weeks in the summer for the entire machinery to be fully serviced.

The job was pretty straightforward: I followed the fitter around all day like a little lost puppy, ready to jump up to him when asked and hand him a tool with the excitement of someone bored out of his tiny little mind. He checked and repaired the machines and I was his gofer. The only snag was he clocked off at 4.30pm each day and I clocked off at 6pm but the rules were that I could not work without the fitter and equally I could not be seen to be lounging around so for one and half hours at the end of each day I had to look busy which was very difficult. It was Ok to do nothing looking at your fitter working but you could not do nothing not looking at your fitter working. I would just walk around with a big spanner in my hand pretending to be on an errand.

The Tar Sprayer

I found another job, which meant getting up at about 4.30 a m every morning (who said students were lazy) and cycling down to the docks. Once while cycling along the side of the harbour in the early morning twilight I did not see a chain between two concrete pillars and a second later I was lying on my back, my bike several feet away. I got up, picked up my vacuum flask, shook it realising it was smashed and thought what am I up for this early doing this job. The job itself entailed standing on the back of a tar-spraying lorry for the resurfacing of roads, the responsibility of the local council. Unfortunately the council in question was miles up the motorway hence the early start.

The first run of the road was easy: we just had all the vents on and sprayed the road with the gravel lorry slowly driving backwards just behind with its load tilted up. So far so good. Then it got a bit tricky, because when you did the second run of the same stretch not all the taps were needed as you crouched and looked under the back of the sprayer you increased and decreased the amount of taps needed, depending on how wide the road was at any given point.

When the tar sprayer driver beeped his horn to indicate he was about to stop, the gravel truck driver should follow suit. Once when he did not I became aware of the risk and I dived off the lorry on to the pavement and with newly cut elbows looked up and saw the gravel truck crash in to the lorry where I had been standing a few seconds before.

One time the tar sprayer was bombing along at 8 miles per hour I lost my bobble hat and it fell off the back of the tar lorry only for me to look back at the next bend in the road and see my nice Steve Hillage type bobble hat become part of the new resurfaced road.

The tar lorry-driver I had the privilege to work with always showed a bit of irritation every time I called his lorry a van. He was very proud of his van, sorry lorry, and at every opportunity he told people where he had sprayed. I used to hear it time and time again: "yes I sprayed in Bristol, Glasgow, Devon, Gloucestershire, Turkey, Somerset." We all used to take the mickey out of him: "yes I've eaten lots of different sandwiches containing corned beef, cheese, ham, beef, turkey." He hated students and used to relish attempting to humiliate me in front of his pals particularly about the fact that I hadn't had a proper job and was still studying at my age. We were eventually laid off unfairly because the company kept on others who started work after us. They probably knew we would not be with them for years to come but the fact remains we were treated poorly. I think its called unfair dismissal.

The Industrial Press Operator

I had to attend a portocabin to fill out an application form for a job in a warehouse. I was left to fill in the form with another bloke when our potential new boss left the portocabin and as I was filling it out I looked up and this man in his fifties just stared at the sheet and then looked pleadingly at me. I realised he couldn't write and I suggested I would fill it out for him. He jumped at the offer. As I passed it back to him our potential new boss returned and looked at me and said, "haven't you filled out that form yet?"

The job was totally piecework. There was no basic wage you got a half penny for every piece of metal you processed and I had no idea how much I would earn at the end of the week. I did know however it would be tax-free, being a student it was worth the risk. The job mainly involved putting a flat round disc into a press, closing the safety cage, pressing the foot pedal so that the press would crush the disc into a cup, the shape needed for part of a piece of scaffolding but I did not know the first thing about folding scaff.

I would arrive at my post at 7.30 am. Even before I started I thought: not another day putting the flat piece of metal in the press, closing the cage with my right hand, putting my foot down to activate the press, pick up the next round flat disc, and start all over again. This was piecework. At eye-level I saw "000001" and then I did a plate and I saw "000002" I couldn't take it. I found a long piece of industrial cloth and wrapped it around the counter to hide it from view. After a few days I was told that if I did not speed up I would be "asked to leave". They needed at least 5,000 a day. I had only done 4,000 but nobody told me. The next day I asked the forklift driver to move the flat discs container nearer to me and place the empty one directly behind me. This speeded up my production, as I was able to get to the next disc quicker and able to throw the finished product over my shoulder. Initially I was bad at throwing accurately because I would hear the disc miss its container and bounce along the factory floor but eventually got the hang of it consoling myself with the fact that the missed ones could be put in the container during the tea break. Once I quickly looked behind and noticed an older member of the work force just watching me and I heard him shout across the warehouse "Hey Bert come and have a look at this"

What didn't help was I had effectively over shot. 4000 was a minimum, 5000 was seen as good. I reached 6000 and had now inadvertently set a new rate for my working "colleagues". When I say colleagues I use the term very loosely: they hated me. I was a student, which was bad enough in itself; I did not pay income tax on my earnings and I had now set an increased daily rate. They no doubt thought I was a goody goody two shoes. But if I hadn't sped up I would have been booted out.

I had made myself very unpopular. The other workers began throwing things at me when my back was turned when I worked on the press. Folded up industrial gloves bounced off the back of my head on numerous occasions. For a few days I was temporarily moved to another job because they had a sufficient store of these cups and after a tea break when I went to use the fixed drill stand it just fell apart having been tampered with.

There was also fun to be had during the breaks, especially the mid-afternoon and mid morning breaks. Once I was just about to sit-down and a steaming tea bag was thrown on my chair. Another time I put my hand in my pocket and someone dropped some thin sheet-metal that can cut you quite easily if you are not careful.

When I eventually explained I had to leave and go back to college I was asked to stay. I then told them about the incidents and I was told I should have reported it. It would have made it worse. I would have been totally ostracized. My strategy was to get them to realise I was not what they thought I was but I ran out of time.

***

In the first year of the degree we did tort (civil wrongs like negligence, nuisance, defamations etc); administration law; contract law and the history of law where we were still in the twelfth century by Easter and, judging by the gown the lecturer wore he thought we were still in the eighteenth.

If you said "R v Smith" as it was worded he would go nuts and shout, "It is not a football match " Apparently you are supposed to say "Crown Against Smith"

Often in the middle of a lecture theatre containing about a hundred students he would stop and complain that no one was taking any notes. Then in unison everyone would look around like meerkats thinking "oh it's not just me then but I am not going to write down all that rubbish about Henry the bloody Second or whatever his number is."

During the exam at the end of the first year we were honoured with his appearance as one of the invigilators when for this special occasion he would not only wear the gown but the mortarboard. When he slowly walked up the little lanes separating the rows of students we all had to be ready as his cape whooshed past, as we all had to grab hold of our spare pen or pencil case to stop them being knocked off the desk by the floating cape.

The first year had the biggest percentage of failures, which was about a third (well that's a fraction but you know what I mean). This, I guess, was due to not being able to think the way the law wanted you to or being away from home with a student grant and not taking the course very seriously throughout the year.

In the second year we did crime, equity and trusts, land law and two subject options. During the summer break we lost the land law lecturer, as he was killed in a driving accident. He appeared to have been a character as the year before he entered the first land lecture in a three piece suit with a severe black brief case, walked up to the lecture stanchion, opened up his brief case and took out a large piece of turf, slammed it down on the table in front of him and said "This is land".

The two options I chose were employment law and accounts, they would be part of the solicitor's final course so I would hopefully be making life easier for myself in the future.

However the popular options were company law and conveyancing (money, money, money) and this resulted in some of the small tutorial rooms being full to capacity yet other subjects were half empty.

Well at the start of one of these tutorials there was a shortage of chairs and the latecomers had to go next door to pinch one.

"He who comes to equity must come with a chair".
(That is a really good joke if you were a law student)

The accountancy lecturer had just been in the national press for having built a nuclear fallout shelter in his back garden. Hold on for just a mo. This guy had built this fallout shelter for his family and was willing to advertise the fact! He clearly had not thought it through. I am sure, however he had all his food tins down there. But did it ever cross his mind if there was a four minute warning everyone would come round kill him and his family and take it over. "Get out. This is my property. I'll call the local constabulary". Oh will you now? There 's a four-minute warning and we are now into our last minute .I doubt if there are any police officers in their warm canteen checking their expenses willing to respond to his call, assuming there was a staffed phone line in the first place. I imagine that when people purchase their place in the fallout shelters, on the day – the last day – as they show their passes to get in it might not go so swimmingly. There will be other people trying to get in who have not got a valid pass. "Well I have not got a pass but I am a friend of Malcolm. Oh go on let me in. Tell you what you can have my house."

He always used to give prolonged analogies during his lecturers referring to aspects of accountancy. Maybe to keep us - and himself - awake. One day it was about thinking ahead. Today's analogy was about when he was cementing his front drive ("Hey everyone: I know where there might be another fall out shelter: in his front garden!") and his wife brings him out a nice cup of tea and he puts his shovel in the bucket of cement and has a nice chat with his wife (" Oxygen? No we will not need that. We will only be down there for a few hours") when he went back to the bucket, had a sip of my tea and horror!
" No sugar!" I said and I should not have done. The anecdote was taking ages. Get on with it!!

I distinctly remember the first employment law tutorial. The lecturer, strangely, in my opinion, went around the group asking each of us in turn what s/he thought about trade unions. What has our opinion got to do with anything? I was to be asked last as he started at the other end of the table. Everyone was negative and I heard stuff like " they're so irresponsible": "they are on strike at the drop of a hat", "nothing but trouble". "They have far too much power...do you know one day at my uncle's factory they put the head of the Manager on a spike and walked around the town centre demanding special chocolate biscuits for their tea breaks. I ask you". Or was it the Assistant Manager?

Then it was my turn. I disagreed with everyone and said something to the effect that trade unions have no power and that is why they strike.

I think that particular lecturer should have kept his nose out of each student's political opinions and concentrated on his own contract of employment as he took up a post as head of another law department leaving us students without a lecturer and the Poly had to find someone who was not a specialist employment lecturer..

Another year without a grant so I had earn more money for the next academic year. During the summer holidays I got a few temporary jobs.

The warehouse night shift

This involved filling and emptying containers of books and gifts etc. We had a supervisor who also didn't take kindly to students especially when we suggested alternative ways of working which would have made the job easier and quicker. Then the fool pulled down a series of boxes from the front of the large container intending to make it easier but some of them landed on me and gave me a black eye.

This backfired on us later as we found out that when his boss asked him how we were doing he just slagged us off and we were both sacked. Days later I phoned to speak to the boss and on being told when he was next in, I cycled to the warehouse to point out the true situation: that we were hard working and his supervisor was lying. When I got there

I was informed he was too busy to speak to me and I felt an idiot making futile journey but could not just ignore the injustice of the sackings.

The old barrel rejuvenator

The next job involved tarting up old used oil barrels. A classic clocking on clocking off conveyor belt system existed with stop/start sirens throughout the factory. We were barely human. It started off as an empty oil barrel, dented and smashed in. You had a particular job depending on where you were positioned at the conveyor belt. My station involved taking all the tops off and if the top was stiff all you could do was lift it out to stop barrels accumulating and put it back on the belt when you tried again to take the top off during a slack period. If you were unlucky you had three or four in a row all with stiff tops. Chaos ensued, as you had to put all these barrels around you on the shop floor. Sometimes barrels would turn up with skull and crossbow stickers. It was seen as macho not to wear the mask that you were given but after a while I thought it was stupid not to wear it because you could not avoid inhaling the fumes when you managed to open a barrel. You had a 15-minute mid-morning and mid-afternoon breaks and if you went back to your position and the conveyor belt had already started, the person ahead of you went crazy as he would be presented with a barrel with the top still on.

A friend was working there with me and as he did not have any money for lunch we had to rush to a bank in the fifteen-minute midmorning break. So when the siren went we rushed to his car. I queued at a bank, constantly looking at my watch deciding when I had to give up and go back. We got the money, did a Starsky and Hutch drive back and when the engine stopped we heard the siren and with a simultaneous high pitched squeak, both ran back to our stations and I spent the first minute pulling barrels off the conveyor belt to unblock it and working twice as hard to get an opportunity to put the barrels back on the belt. He is now a senior partner in a firm of solicitors so if anyone will be borrowing money next time it will be me.

Building site labourer

I found yet another temporary job on a building site. I helped put the scaffolding up around a house in order to be able to build a new roof and render the outside walls. Early on I put tiles in a bucket and hoisted them up to the roof with a rope and pulley, then I made the cement in yes a cement mixer and each morning the 4 year old daughter of next-door watched me as if I was painting the Mona Lisa. She asked me what I was doing and I explained I was "feeding the monster, and each morning he had porridge for breakfast".

During the day when she escaped from her house her mum would come out, grab her and take her in. At the end of the day I had to clean the cement mixer out and threw in a large breezeblock to help scrape the cement from the inside. On being asked what I was doing by my young apprentice I explained the monster had now had his evening meal and was finishing off with cheese and biscuits (I only work with middle class cement mixers)

When the building was complete we were told that there was no work and all that was left was for us was to clean up the site and continue to be paid at the same hourly rate.. This was not really thought through. If they had said, as soon as you clean it up I 'll pay your £100 but he didn't. We were being laid off and so we took our time. It was pointless rushing.

**

During term time I was employed as a part time bar worker. I was asked to pour the contents of the drip trays into the standing pint of beer, which I promised to do but never did. After a few months the landlord explained that since I had been in charge of the bar net profits were down 5%. I was very proud of myself.

**

I went on a sponsored hitchhike to Paris during the charity student rag week. After carrying a metal framed rucksack on my back for several hours however my kidneys started to bleed again so I had to carry it a different way which would also relieve the resulting aching kidneys that also developed that weekend. One of the charities that the money was going to was the renal unit that I was getting rather familiar with. My kidney function was being regularly checked at that very same hospital.

During my check ups I had several requests by doctors to help them rather than always them helping me. Once I was party to a series of tests on a new drug. I agreed but at my last session another doctor from another part of the hospital was there asking me if would like to partake in yet another series. This was even before I had time to roll my shirtsleeves back down and button them up. I thought this was a bit quick and rather pushy so I said no. I thought they were taking me for granted.

I was once asked to attend a hospital medical lecture and have each medical student, no doubt queuing up in turn, able to have a good feel of my enlarged kidneys. I turned this down as I felt I was getting close to becoming part of a freak show and possibly only there to liven up this particular doctors lecture that week.

But I am sure other patients would have loved all the attention. For me it would have been a long embarrassing session and no doubt I would be there in my underclothes or hospital gown being prodded by people of my own age, possibly thinking poor bastard he must be the same age as me. However I did allow single medical students to exam me after my doctor had checked me over in that game of "What's wrong with this one then?"

I always felt guilty saying no but I had so many requests and I thought I had done my bit and I thought I was going through enough as it was.

Each check up involved the examinations of blood and urine. Samples were taken. Did you know a urine test is the only test you have to pass before you can even take it? When the blood was taken I would press my fingernail into my skin on the other side of my thumb nail to distract from the pain about to begin elsewhere which was important in case I jumped when the needle went in. Some of the staff were better at it than others. The results indicated my kidney function was slowly deteriorating and it was affecting my blood pressure, I was now anaemic so blood pressure and iron tablets were prescribed to be taken daily and indefinitely.

While waiting in a greengrocer-cum–off-license with some friends on the way to a party four loud skinheads came in and started to shout and behave rather unruly. I was at the counter and one of them tapped me on the shoulder and said something. I turned around I said "sorry?" and he said, "Are you trying to be funny?" It is moments like that that you know you have walked into a situation when some one is trying to pick an argument to provoke a fight. I tried to be as pleasant and amenable as possible and then four of them attacked me. Two hitting me on the head with their bike helmets and the other two kicking me in the legs. Initially I was not defending myself as I was stupidly trying to fathom out why they were beating me up. Also at that time I often would keep my elbows near my sides as an extra precaution against being accidentally knocked in that area. When ever I went into a room, whether it was bar or lecture room, if there was ever a choice I would instinctively go for the seat with a back or one with most back protection such as those chairs that had sides as well. Sometimes you can become totally helpless. A few months earlier a friend of mine had crept up behind me and simultaneously grabbed either side of my waist and squeezed. It was just a jocular gesture but turned out to be very painful to me because of its location. He did not immediately release his hold so I spontaneously turned around and thumped him. It seemed quicker than having to explain the situation and make a request that he remove his hands. I was not prepared to point at some library "silence" sign, put one finger to my lips and then thump him. I immediately apologised profusely and tried to explain. He sort of understood and then I nervously awaited my next few visits to the toilet to see if my kidneys were about to bleed again.

Oh where was I? Oh yes I remember: getting beaten up. When I gathered my senses I started to fend them off, remembering to stay standing whatever happened because once on the floor – or "decked" as I understand is the common parlance in the ruffian community - they could easily kick me in the kidney region which would mean I would probably be on dialysis earlier than even the doctors had expected. Eventually one of the shop assistants said "right lads that's enough" " which I found particularly odd. It was not as if we were all rehearsing for a play. It was four against one. At what stage is it no longer acceptable to have such a one sided contest? Anyway I was pleased as punch that I hadn't been in my kidney region and had managed to stay on my feet. I then walked out of the shop and from a distance I could see my friends walking back towards the shop asking me what I had been doing. They had been waiting for me and were totally oblivious to the friendly little ruck. I had an odd story to relay.

Still standing up and still up for the party we went to it. Once there one friend was trying to get me – of all people - to have a drinking contest. His choice of weapon was some home made brandy wine that he had just found a bottle of. I was first to down the first glass, which was going to be my last, and he said, " double or quits " so we agreed to a second round. Still contemplating the earlier incident that evening, I realized that I was one of those few young men who was only too aware of his non-invincibility, his very extreme vulnerability. So in a fit of pique tipped my next glass on the carpet and held the empty glass to my chin while he was still gulping his down. He, still blessed with the vanity of youth and full health then, realizing he had lost again said "double or quits" again. I placed the contents of my glass in the same place and the sticky pool on the carpet got bigger. Other friends looked on not knowing how it was all going to end. After failing another four or five times to beat me as the stakes were raising my drinking companion was a bit worse for wear and a bit surprised I had beaten him every time. It ended up not being a contest of double or quits but for him, one of double or squits. He got is own back as he ended up sleeping on my floor in my sleeping bag.

"Dear Michael, Your recent renal results show a marked deterioration in your kidney function and I think the time has come for you to have a fistula fitted. Please will you come to the unit tomorrow afternoon? Yours sincerely."

That was near enough the content of the letter I got from one of the young hospital doctors so I went to law library in the morning with the intention of leaving my books there, popping up to the hospital to have this fistula thing fitted and then returning to my books that evening.

When I arrived at a hospital after listening to what the doctors had in mind I realised I would be in hospital for several days which was not mentioned in the letter so I had to go back to the library and collect my bag, dump them at my flat and head on back to the hospital.

I politely pointed out to the doctor who had written the letter that it was not clear that I had to stay over. She said it was obvious. By that she meant if you know about fistulas it was obvious you could not have such an operation and go home the same day. I realised it was counter productive continuing the discussion. I was in her hands for the next few days and should not be antagonising anyone but concentrating on discovering what the operation entailed.

It took some explaining to the nurse who was given the task of settling me in to the ward that I did not own any pyjamas. All those patterns and hardly anyone sees them and then only for a very short while. The little chest pocket always used to amuse me. What is so important that cannot be left on the side of the bed?

As it turned out this fistula fiasco required an operation on my arm, which involved the artery, in the middle of arm, being linked to the vein just below the surface. This is necessary to allow blood to flow out of your body as otherwise you would not be able to dialyse. This process involves your blood being "cleaned" outside your body and then being returned. The operation involved me stretching out my left arm, which was hidden behind a board to prevent me seeing the operation taking place. A nurse stood by me to make sure I was OK and that the local anaesthetic was working. There was no real pain but I could feel what was going on.

During one moment I felt my artery being tugged. I felt the sensation all the way to the top of my upper arm.

Back at the ward I would initially have my obs taken every 15 minutes. An extra ob was directed at my heavily bandaged arm. It was being checked for a stronger pulse, a throbbing sensation, which indicated that arterial blood from the artery, was flowing into the vein. The fistula needs to grow before it can be used. Over the next few weeks the vein will grow to many times its usual size ready for dialysis needles to be inserted. During that hospital stay my blood pressure prescription was increased to keep it under control.

A friend incredibly offered to give me one of his kidneys. I did not take it very seriously at first until he mentioned that he had been to the renal unit and spoken to the doctors. He told me that they were not very encouraging which is the correct response to take because the onus had to come from him. Anyway he was not a relative and the chances of him being compatible were very unlikely. Sadly he has since died which in itself is ironical for two reasons: he was a perfectly healthy young man and is no longer with us while I still am and by the time his body was found it was not possible to donate his kidneys or any of his other organs to someone who could have benefited from them.

The third year of my degree involved Jurisprudence (the theory of law); Family law; Evidence; Criminology and a dissertation (just a project really) of your choice.

I now was told because my kidney function was worsening that would have to go on to a low protein diet of 65 grams per day and I had to drink two litres of fluid every day. This is not so easy when you are not thirsty and having to do it every day is a chore. However it was essential to flush out all toxic substances that otherwise would be left inside me. The reduced protein and increased flushing out would reduce some of the feelings of sickness and tiredness.

My daily protein diet meant that I could have two ounces of meat at each of my two daily meals. There were also vegetable protein units. For example one slice of bread was a vegetable unit, which weighed about three grams. I was allowed to replace a meat unit with an egg, an ounce of cheese or one and half ounces of fish. I was given a pair of scales and had to weigh everything I ate from then on. It was now not just fish that needed scales to survive. Staying a vegetarian was going to be very difficult.

I got to know the owner of an Indian restaurant as I regularly used to go there. Once I advised him on some legal problems he had. I was still only on a low protein diet and so remained able to eat out and have vegetarian dishes. I had maintained my vegetarian diet as I had followed a theory after reading a small booklet. It suggested that meat produced more sulphur toxins and so if I reduced that, by remaining a vegetarian, you never know, I might delay the day, which by now was only a question of time, when I would go on to dialysis. I mentioned this to my Dad; he relayed it on to my Mum's renal consultant at another hospital. He thought that there might even be something in it. My Mum's kidneys were still holding on and she was not restricted to any diet but taking medication to try and hold back the process. Anyway I digress. The restaurateur promised me a meal on the house when my exams were over for helping him with his legal problem.

Down my regular nightclub I was walking through one of the many corridors and one bloke took my pint of water, tipped the contents on the floor and while handing back the empty glass said "When you come down here you drink proper drinks" and his mates looked on smirking. I walked away but after about three steps I stopped and decided to turn around and confront him even though he was bigger and taller than me - although I am 6 foot 2 - and twice as broad and thought what the hell. Wow I might end up in hospital, not necessarily the ward I had in mind.

"Do you know why I am drinking pints of water?" I enquired. No reply. So I explained and his attitude changed. On future occasions when I walked along his favourite corridor where he "hung out" he would acknowledge me and I managed to walk passed him and his cronies and turn the next corner with my pint of water still intact.

I was still studying at the student union building and they had recently installed a drinking machine where you could get cold drinking water without putting money in the slot for the cold drinks where the coin gave you a cup and some powder. Once while I was helping my self, as I had drank too many cups of coffee that day, one of the porters saw me and said:" I see getting something for nothing eh?" I replied, "Well it's only water " He was non too plussed and I could tell he thought I was behaving like a thief.

This extra fluid exasperated another noticeable symptom: swollen ankles at the end of the day. It is called oedema and is a direct result of a disfunctioning kidney.

At bars I used to ask for a pint of water because although I still drank beer, after a pint or so I would be setting my self up for a bad hangover especially if I tried to drink two litres a day! This was usually handed over reluctantly and very occasionally I was charged or refused it then, after an explanation I would get my pint but even more reluctantly.

The fistula was slowly growing. Sometimes whilst reading a broadsheet newspaper, the side of the paper would touch the fistula and you would hear a strange russelling sound until I readjusted how I was holding the paper. Sleeping already difficult became even more so because if I slept with my head on or near my left arm I would hear a very loud throbbing seashell ocean sound so I had to sleep with my arm well away from my head.

Sometimes it got a bit embarrassing when someone would try and get my attention, say in a loud party /disco and inadvertently touch my arm and immediately pull away thinking I had just given them an electric shock. So then I would have to explain everything and then s/he would get his/her friends to come over and touch my arm astounded at the effect.

"Have you been eating garlic?" When someone asks you this, especially if it is at a groovy disco you cannot very well say "No. My breath smells." You really have to lie and say "yes". Years later I learnt that this is one of the other common symptoms of renal failure. So now people can say to someone who has halitosis. "Are you in the latter throws of final stage renal failure ...or have you been eating garlic?"

****

CHAPTER TWO: THE FINAL COUNTDOWN

The symptoms of renal failure are non descript: a general feeling of tiredness all the time; shortness of breath, pale skin, irritability, loss of appetite, lack of libido, nausea, vomiting, itchy skin, poor concentration, leg cramps, restless legs, swollen hands or ankles, poor sleeping, headaches, puffiness around the eyes, regular metallic taste in the mouth, changes in frequency passing water and increased thirst. The first six are the direct result of anaemia generally.

If you had one or two of these you would not think :I've got renal failure. Most people from time to time will have some of them but not continually nearly all at the same time. I was suffering from chronic - slow, long term- as opposed to acute - or quick - renal failure; a slow deterioration over years. There is no treatment. All the doctors can do is reduce the symptoms and possibly slowdown the process. You take tablets to control your blood pressure. The diet limits your protein intake so as to reduce the toxins in the body that the kidneys cannot get rid of. So you have to drink a lot and cut down on salt – sodium - as it will increase your blood pressure.

I had been told to drink India tonic water because it contained quinine and, although also helpful for malaria, reduced the night cramps that would wake me up. I eventually worked out that if I got out of bed, crouched down and put my body weight on my toes, this would stretch the twisted muscles easing the cramps temporarily. I also understood that the more regular sudden jumps you experienced while falling asleep, as if you had actually fallen off something, could relate to oncoming renal failure.

I was also getting nightmares. According to my flat mate I used to scream during them but I did not recall a thing when I awoke.

I was also getting a bad skin rash, psoriasis which according to the alternative medics was the body trying to rid itself of the toxins through a different route. Well we will take that with a pinch of ....salt. Well you can: I 'd better decline.

I was increasingly having more problems, aches and pains. Before one of my regular check ups I was not feeling too bright. In a sense I was glad the appointment had come at that time, as I needed reassuring as to whether or not the day had finally arrived. I walked the few miles to the hospital. Once all the tests were taken, the two doctors looked at each other without talking and I knew things were getting worse. My blood pressure was very high. I was told I was going to be admitted to hospital. I waited outside the consulting room and two porters turned up with a wheel chair. I told them I could walk but they insisted and I knew it was no use arguing so I got in and I was pushed through the hospital. I was annoyed and embarrassed that I had to use a wheel chair. I had just walked miles to get there without any problems. Maybe I was refusing to admit how ill I really was or acting like an injured, cornered animal, not allowing anyone near me who was only trying to help or, as I liked to think, I did not want to see myself as an institutionalised hospital patient because then I might give up fighting and give in to being a long term patient which I knew was around the corner.

The hospital exit was around the corner of the next corridor where an ambulance was waiting to take me to another hospital. The two porters had difficulty lifting me. I asked if they wanted me to get up and on myself. They said no but after another 30 seconds of faffing about I exclaimed that this was ridiculous, got out of the chair and hopped on the ambulance. The porters thanked me. I knew they could not invite me to hop on, or for me to be allowed to walk down the corridor because if anything happened the hospital would possibly be liable for negligence. Me hopping on myself incurred no liability. I think this obsession with hospital authorities covering their back can get a bit extreme sometimes.

Maybe they should get me to sign a consent form but they will probably have to hand me the pen at the last moment in case I stab my eye out with it.

By now my kidneys weighed about eight pounds each - they should weigh about 2 pounds - and therefore my stomach was extended. I looked like I had a beer gut and some people teased me on it. Other comments were about my "suntan" but it was my skin changing to a muddy colour.

As the symptoms are non descript you generally feel run down and tired and lethargic or to use a Bill Bryson quote, suffer from "a severe disinclination to boogie". The best analogy I can come up with is that it is like having the drained and tired feelings of constant flu but without the cold, sniffling, coughing and sneezing but because it is all the time you do not know you have it. I had been like this for a year or so but had not appreciated it because it only very slowly catches up with you.

Consequently you are seen as unfit and a hypochondriac. If I had had a gaping wound I would have got more sympathy. Obviously my close friends and of course my relatives who were in another part of the country were pretty concerned. I am sure some people thought that with my longish hair, my weight and odd coloured, unhealthy skin complexion, that I was a "smack head", that I was taking heroin. In fact one of the consultants told me he had to go to a prison cell in the middle of the night to help release one of his patients as he was arrested for suspicion of being "on drugs". The police had mistaken the similar appearance. After checking his arms for needle marks and finding his fistula he had some explaining to do but even so that is no reason to arrest someone.

If someone said "How are you?" or "How's it going?" I took it as an actual question and gave them an update on my renal failure latest news. Unfortunately on many occasions, looking back, I misread the remark and they were just greetings like "awright" and that seemed to alienate some fellow students and no doubt I was down as a whinger ("Stop going on about your bloody kidneys") and possibly someone to stay clear of.

Walking along one of the Poly corridors I would occasionally spot someone on crutches brought about by a motorbike or skiing accident. They were having the fire door opened by about three or four fellow students. I felt resentful that these, what I called the weekend disabled, were being helped and I was not and even accused of being a hypochondriac as nothing was as visible as a plaster of paris or wooden sticks. Admittedly no one could assist. It was not as if I could borrow someone's kidney for a day. It was worse when I was in a corridor with a student on crutches and I had to hold the door open for them.

A bigger cynic then I once said "you'll find sympathy in the dictionary between shit and syphilis". I did not want sympathy I just wanted a bit of empathy. I only found that in the dictionary between eczema and enema.

I was a regular with the resident Poly campus GP. During one meeting (it would be incorrect to call it a consultation as he could not do anything and most of the prescribing was done by the hospital unit but I still needed to see him) he pulled out a letter that was dated the day I was born and I read the sentence that mentioned even then as a few hours old baby that my kidneys were noticeably enlarged or as I recall the word that was used, palpable but baby fat and my general growth hid it for many years until they enlarged further. My Dad told me that I spent the first few days in an incubator because I was premature and needed a blood change because the blood of the mother was interacting with that of the baby's.

During my many periods of waiting to see him I got so familiar with the waiting room that if anyone had removed all the health information posters I could have put them all up in exactly the same place. I could spot a new one very easily. I 'd also always check the plants because as Erma Bombeck said" Never go to a doctor whose office plants have died" in the same way you should not trust an electrician with no eye brows. Who 's Erma Bombeck I hear you cry. Well she was an American humour columnist who died in 1996. She had Polycystic Kidneys. We are everywhere.

While waiting in line at the back of a small queue to see the receptionist at the front I heard: "I was given these tablets for my cold three days ago but they do not work. Is there anything else the doctor could give me"

It found it quite incredible how people think doctors have a drug for everything. One poster in the waiting room stood out, as it was new. It was trying to relieve these naïve people of this perverse misconception that you must leave the doctors surgery with a prescription. Dr Phil Hammond, now also a campaigning comic for better health care and a broadcaster tells in one of his shows how his previous boss had plans to put up a sign in his GP waiting room stating: "If you have the flu .." and then a very rude word. Such was the amount of time wasters at his surgery. Most people who say they have the flu are wrong anyway. They may have a cold, sore throat and sneeze occasionally, poor things, but unless they ache all over and hardly have the energy to get to a surgery they probably have not got flu. There is a poster often found on walls in hospitals saying as follows: "Antibiotics don't work on colds or most coughs and sore throats "

Along with these regular visits to the GP during the run up to my finals I had my hospital check ups. I was also told that at that time only about 7% of my kidneys were working. That's not 14 % but 7% in total. About a month before my law degree finals began I asked how long they thought my kidneys were expected to last before their complete collapse, at which point dialysis would commence. The hospital doctor said, "I would say about a month." So my kidneys would collapse at about the time of my finals.

It was getting really difficult revising or, for some parts of the course, should I say, simply vising. It all seemed so pointless. In a few months time I could be on a kidney machine possibly for the rest of my life. I doubt if I could use the degree assuming I passed it. I would often go to the law library sit down open the books and just stare at them, not being able to concentrate, rereading the same sentence over and over again as I was not taking anything in. This was especially difficult with the apparent need in law to have long sentences that can last far too long, often found in archaically written legal documents such as contract clauses and Acts of Parliament. The only way I could make head or tail of it was to play "find the verb." It can be difficult at the best of times. You have a go.

> "If and whenever the said rent hereby reserved or any part thereof shall be in arrears for twenty one days after any of the said days hereinbefore appointed for payment thereof (whether the same shall have been formally demanded or not) or if there shall be any breach non-performance or non-observance of all or

any of the covenants agreements and conditions herein contained and on the part of the Lessees to be performed or observed then and in any of the said cases it shall be lawful for the Lessor to re-enter into and upon any part of the demised premises in the name of the whole and thenceforth peaceably to hold and enjoy the same as if these presents had not been made without prejudice to any right of action or other remedy of the Lessor in respect of any antecedent breach of any of the covenants by the Lessees hereinbefore contained."

Hello. Hello. You can wake up now. When I read something like this for the first time I would usually lose the thread, and then after a few more punctuation free lines, I would slowly lose the will to live. I had to find the crux of the sentence and work backwards. For instance, in this example, at line eight after cutting through the word and phrase jungle you are met with "shall be lawful for the Lessor to re-enter". Right then you'll be evicted if .. and then I would start again.

In law they're so many double negatives that you have to do a double take on what the sentence actually means. For instance, "You will not be a qualifying person unless: ..."

Who cares that there are 109 exceptions to the law on hearsay.

So what that there are different conditions to successfully apply for an ouster as opposed to a non-molestation injunction.

Who gives a damn about the rules on competent and compellable witnesses?

Who gives a fiddler's fart that you have to be employed full time for at least 6 months before you can claim unfair dismissal. In fact not even the government or any one since. Over the following years it went up to one year then two, than back down to one. So you can be unfairly dismissed even if you have worked for less than a year unless one of the few narrow exceptions applies. However the full time condition has been removed.

I used to revise at the student union building, one of the reasons being that if I attempted to study at my flat I would soon find things to do. The fridge needed defrosting. I really have to do it now. Must clean the carpet and so have to go out to the shops to just buy that one particular brand of carpet cleaner. All false strategies to avoid the inevitable. I was in no physical state to do non-essential duties anyway. I would rest my weary little head and even smaller brain on my lower arms on the desk top for a ten minute doze and wake up and find two hours had gone by.

The student union building had a restaurant on the top floor. One day the meal included four fish fingers as a serving together with the usual dollops of different types of vegetables. By now I had given up the battle to remain a vegetarian as it was becoming too difficult with my low protein diet. Four fish fingers to me meant two meat units (three fish fingers) plus some thing extra. I was still trying to stick rigidly to the diet as I was trying to avoid the increased tiredness and nauseous that would ensue by the extra toxins in my body which my massive fluid intake could not help get rid of and therefore I would end up revising even less.

"Just three fish fingers please"
"It is the same price as four. You might as well have four"
"No it 's OK I just want three thanks"
"You might as well have four. I cannot charge you less: I 'll have to charge you for four even if you have three".
"That's OK. I don't mind"
"I tell you what. I 'll give your four. You look as if you could do with feeding up if you do not mind me telling you ". (Gee thanks) "Go on have four. It will be good for you"
"LOOK! I do not want your fucking fourth fish finger!!" I yearned to say but ending up saying:
"OK"

By then I had given up trying to explain my diet so I took my unwanted full plate away and then had to eat my way around the unwanted fish finger determined not to breach my diet because I knew if I did it once it would be a slippery slope to breaching it again and again.

I was discussing matters with the head of the law department. He pointed out that I did not have to take the exams. I could still get my degree, which would be based on my course work. It was something called an "aegrotat" degree. This was not an honours but an ordinary degree and so the mark I would get in my dissertation, or thesis, which I had been plugging away at during the year could not be included as they were only supposed to be undertaken for the honours degree. Right at the beginning of the year I had a problem with this. The title was found to be unacceptable by the external examiners because one word in it, decriminalisation, was not English but an Americanism. (Hurrah. It is now because my PC has not gone and just underlined it in red and I am using the UK not the USA language software.)

I refused to back down and eventually they relented. The purpose of my project was to extend on the idea contained in a legal article I had read where it was suggested that because there was a big a gulf between civil and criminal law, that a "third way" could be introduced. This was to dissuade people from partaking in certain activities but not to criminalize them. At the moment someone can sue you in the civil court and get an enforceable judgment against you. The state can prosecute you in the criminal courts and on conviction you can be sentenced. But what if you breached, what was termed a contravention. For example, the so-called "victimless crimes" such as drug taking and prostitution.

Deciding whether to just jettison all the work I had put into it was a difficult decision to make. Like many things when you are under pressure whether it be a death in the family or a divorce arrangement you have to make a big decision in very trying times. I obviously wanted an honours degree. An ordinary degree very rarely counts for much and I was already going to be disadvantaged when applying for a future job due to my medical history that I am about to create for myself. Also the work I put in to my dissertation would count for nothing and I got a B for it. There were no A s and Bs were rare. I had to make a decision soon. The Poly was trying to help but was restricted by the degree authority rules. It was like TV quiz pressure.

"Our first contestant is Michael O'Sullivan. Hello Michael. How are you feeling?"
"Well actu…"

"Well nice to hear that. Are you nervous Michael? Don't be nervous Michael "

"Without further ado let's begin. Do you know the rules? They are very simple? If you want you can take home the aegrotat degree tonight. That's safe. You can keep that. And you'll have no exams to take. But if you want you can gamble and go for an honours degree. This will mean you can use your thesis towards your final degree which will all be a waste of time if you take home the aegrotat degree But if you take your exams and fail then I am afraid Michael you will go home empty handed with nothing. Is that clear Michael?"

"Sort of"

"Well before you make your decision I' d like you to tell us a little bit about your project"

"Er dissertation "

"Oh yes sorry, dissertation. So what was it about?"

"A commentary on the decriminalisation of certain crimes"

"Oh that's sounds interesting. You must be very clever"

."No, just copied chunks from obscure legal periodicals and linking long paragraphs with a few of my own sentences like everyone else"

"Ok then times catching up with us. Start the clock."

"Tick tock, tick tock"

"So have you made your decision?

"Tick tock, tick tock"

"Er yes"

"Tick tock, tick tock"

"Well what's it to be Michael: the aegrotat degree or the honours degree assuming you do not flunk your forthcoming exams. Have to hurry you"

"Tick tock, tick tock"

"I'll go for the honours degree"

"Well I am sure you have made the right decision"

"Thank you Michael for playing "Big decisions you'd rather not make at the moment!"

If I fail then it will be "...and let's see what you would have won"

A few weeks before the finals began I was sitting at my friend's desk up in the library waiting for him to return, and I looked down at his notes and thought they were strangely familiar. Although I was doing a law degree and he was taking a social science degree I realised that they were identical notes to my non-law option entitled "criminology". He was doing a half-module entitled "deviance". (Well the law department had to call it something legal sounding didn't they?) When he got back I asked him who his lecturer was and found out it was the same as mine. I then asked him when his exam was. It was four days before mine, which would be the last exam of my law degree finals. I then had an idea and went to the library issue desk and got out the past papers for the last few years of both exams and discovered the first ten questions were identical! The Social Scientists like the lawyers had to answer four questions but they had twenty questions to choose from while we had ten.

Looking back it's probably that this social science lecturer did not appreciate that left wing socialists studying for a social science degree occasionally mix socially with those awful right wing reactionary law students. There was an element of truth because I remember a discussion outside a lecturer theatre with about six other law students about capital punishment and I was the only one against it. However there were others in the year who would have sided with me but no doubt we were a minority. Anyway with this gem of a discovery I decided to put revision on this subject on the back burner. By now I had effectively stopped intensive revision and decided to revise when I was able to and just attend the exams and hope for the best.

My kidneys were trying terribly hard to prove that doctor right, as a day or so before the first exam I started to get severe headaches. The blood pressure tablets were not keeping it under control. My GP discovered it had risen and my dose was increased. I took the exams with these headaches but my GP suggested I visit him just before each one so that we would have a record to help if I flunked them.

My friend's Deviance exam was in the middle of my week of exams so I took time out from staring at my law textbooks and waited outside his exam room for it to finish. I felt like some dope head waiting for his drug dealer. In fact

I was beginning to look a drug addict with my pasty, ghost like appearance and unhealthy looking skin with a tired, drawn look and increasingly visible fistula. My skin had changed to a muddier colour brought about by the anaemia and the very low renal function. So much so that once or twice someone would comment on my recently acquired sun tan.

My social scientist friend came out of the room, gave me the paper and I went back to stare at a different page of my lecture notes. I picked out four questions and they all came up, as planned, in the exam a few days later.

My degree and exams were over. I just had to wait and see if I passed or failed and possibly regret not accepting the aegrotat degree.

I had nothing much to do after the exams were over. It was a massive anticlimax. I could not go anywhere or plan anything. I had to stay in town and go to my hospital check ups and wait. I was effectively marooned. While other students could go on holiday or to their hometown or even start jobs or further careers, I had to wait for the fateful day, the mother of all check ups that was to result in being told my time was up. When you learn about your need to start dialysis it is daunting, not only because you are artificially kept alive but also not knowing when and if a possible transplant might present it self.

I tried to carry on as best I could which was to join an employment agency and I was given a job at a NHS laundry. Ironic or what? I had to cycle miles each morning because of the inadequate bus service and only lasted three days .I was knackered before I even started the days work which was surprisingly hard: pulling soaking wet clothes out of industrial washers, untangling them as they moved along a conveyor "bath" and putting them in large industrial dryers. One morning while on route and already late I phoned the agency explaining I was not going in. They told me not to bother coming into their office again. I explained my health problem and they said we might be able to consider you again for less strenuous work such as an office type job if you get a doctor's letter, which I did but was never offered another job.

I therefore realised I was too unfit to do manual work but although the doctors could not do anything to delay the inevitable I made a few feeble attempts to try and put off the fateful day. I had several appointments with a homeopathy doctor who was also a qualified and practising GP. His appointments cost £5 a consultancy, which I had a few of. That's appointments as well as fivers.

I even saw an Acupuncturist who charged much more but only had one appointment. It involved lying on his couch with loads of tiny needles in all parts of me. In fact the only part that was a needle free zone was where my kidneys were. I lay there for ages after he left the room and for a moment I thought it might have been early closing and he had forgotten about me.

I did not expect a cure but I could not do nothing and wasting a bit of money seemed worth it at the time, as I could not very well spend it on much else. What could I do with the money? A slap up meal? A holiday? New clothes? I suppose I could buy a nice new pair of pyjamas. No, my mind was elsewhere.

During one very long walk, which I tended to do a lot, I went a bit too far. After a while I got an ache in my side and I could tell that walking was agitating my enlarged kidneys. I decide to rest and sat down against a tree in a small park waiting for the pain to subside so I could walk back. But when I decided to get up and walk back I could not move. The stop had meant it was now even more painful than ever to start walking again. At one stage I thought of calling someone over but then thought better of it. What chance of anyone willing to help. For a start I did not show any clear visible physical problems Eventually I went for it and once I got walking again the pain diminished. When I got home and lay on the bed I then realised I was in the same predicament again. I could not move.

I decided to phone the ward to see if they could explain why this was happening and the nurse who answered, who knew me, said they would send an ambulance to bring me in.

For me this looked like the turning point: although part of me was relieved that once in hospital I would not have to move and I would be fed, it also meant I could no longer look after myself. As it turned out a few days in hospital resulted in me being able to walk without pain and

I was discharged but the kidney function continued to get worse.

I was now about to be introduced to a far stricter diet. Far worse than the low protein one. Potassium restrictions. Salt (sodium) restrictions. Phosphorus Restrictions. A low protein diet was easily manageable compared to these. Not only had you to think hard before deciding whether you could eat anything that was put in front of you but the consequences of breaching it could be fatal.

You have to stay off the salty food as it increases your already high blood pressure. You have to stay off high potassium food because otherwise you may have a cardiac arrest.

You therefore had to know your onions and not have them raw or fried. I was not going to be buttering many parsnips as there was a total ban on artichokes, broccoli, brussel sprouts, pumpkins, squash, fresh tomatoes, tomato juice, paste and puree, vegetable juice, baked beans, pinto beans, mushrooms, peppers, spinach, turnips, sweet potatoes, and all pulses such as chickpeas, Soya beans, fried beans and lentils etc.

Nowadays there are so many theme names for cafes and restaurants such as an Eatery, a Fryery and a Carvery. (They are so new the spell checker on my computer has had to be over ridden so I can type this bit.) Well if anyone was mad enough to set up a cafe for renal patients it would have to be called a Boilery.

All the vegetables that you could have had to be boiled well and the water they were cooked in discarded. Anywhere else potatoes would be on this "do not touch" list but I guess reluctantly dieticians allowed it due to the English traditional diet but they needed to be boiled for forty minutes. That's the potatoes: not the English or the dieticians. Of the permissible vegetables you were only allowed about two cups each day.

On the fruit front the diet was not a bowl of cherries nor a bunch of bananas; grapefruits, oranges, grapes, apricots, avocado, cantaloupe, honeydew, kiwi, mangoes, nectarines, papaya, fresh pears, fresh peaches, pineapples, rhubarb, watermelon, figs, greengages, prunes, (where are you when I need you) and all dried fruits (eg apricots, currants, dates, prunes, peaches, raisins and sultanas)

Similarly you had to stay away from orange juice, prune juice, pineapple juice, grapefruit juice and tomato juice. Of the allowed fruits you were allowed three cups, for example, a medium size apple could count as a half-cup or a fruit unit.

It was no good hunting down an obscure fruit or vegetable not on the list and assume it was OK .It probably was not. You could not expect every type known to be listed, just the most common. Not on my list were Lima beans, Swiss chard, succotash, cantaloupe or papaya. They are all high in potassium and dangerous. Any such list has to be treated as a non-exhaustive list. Now if you eat anything from the total ban, like say a couple of grapes, it would not be fatal but equivalent to something worthwhile eating such as a whole apple

A pie in the shop is pie in the sky because you have no idea what is in it - how much potassium or salt - which is a problem with nearly all pre-packaged or precooked meals

You have to avoid nearly all canned foods pickled vegetables, ready-made meals, smoked or processed meat, fish and poultry and bacon, ham, sausages, cold cuts, hot dogs, hamburgers, corned beef, anchovies and sardines etc.

Are you getting the picture? I have not finished yet.

You can't even put your faith in cheeses because of the salt and of course the protein restriction. You are to avoid chocolate and milk products. Milk. Once your first meal. Now a risky food to consider. You could consume it with a bowl of cereal – the right kind, not full of dried fruit or high bran type –and with your limited amount of tea each day but it was not only a "meat" protein unit, but also high in potassium. Nature does indeed move in mysterious "whey's".

You need to avoid all biscuits etc with nuts and chocolate, the same goes for any desserts, custard, yoghurt and other puddings.

Coffee is not your cup of tea or hot chocolate or similar drink products.

The diet was a balancing act between having too much protein, salt and potassium and malnutrition. You still had to get your modicum of fresh fruit and vegetables each day. So what will the fashionable renal failure patient be eating this season? Well I 'll take you shopping later.

I bumped into the Indian restaurateur and he asked me when I was going to take up his offer of a free meal he had kindly promised due to the legal help I had given him. It was extremely difficult to explain I could not eat it. I felt he did not understand and was never totally convinced of my explanation.

I got two letters in the post one day. One letter was clearly from the hospital as it was just after my previous check up. I did not open that one first as the other was from the Poly. My exam results. I passed and got a 2.2 honours degree. The head of the law department had hand written "Well done" but I did not know if he had written that on all of them or just on mine.

The hospital letter said something like "Dear Michael, Your kidney function has reached a level where you will need to start dialysing. Please can you come into the unit tomorrow afternoon"

I phoned my parents to tell them the exciting news .As far as the exam result was concerned I said it was a bit like a bald man winning a brand new hairdryer.

CLICK..................................... . WKQ: 2+2+0=4

CHAPTER THREE: DIALYSIS DAYS

Many people have no idea what dialysis entails. Some think you are connected to the machine 24 hours a day hoping for a transplant to release you from being chained to the machine. This situation conjures up images of the old fashioned iron lung that polio victims were connected to. Others think you go into a big box type thing, probably with your head sticking out of the top like you see in those steam bath machines in the old American films and some how things happen inside that do the job that a kidney should do. Then you come out feeling like you're new born and you can get back to your original normal life until, that is, the next time you have to go back on. You can eat and drink what you like as long as you get back for your next appointment with the machine. By this time you will be crawling to the machine on your hands and knees for your next session, feeling ill and desperate to get back on the machine.

It is however nothing like that at all.

In a 2001 broadcast of a BBC Radio Four programme entitled "Doing what comes naturally", Dr Jonathan Miller said: "....few of us fully understand the importance of the kidney and why it is so difficult to do without it and why does life come to a standstill if we cannot produce urine. It is because the kidney is one of the most important mechanisms maintaining the physiological stability of our internal environment without which the cells, which we are composed of, would be unable to survive or thrive. Hugh de Wardener, a kidney specialist, has devoted his life to the analysis and treatment of the "apparently humble kidney."

Hugh de Wardener: "The kidney is really to keep you in balance. You eat salt and water. You only need a certain amount so all the excess goes out through the kidneys. There a cataract of stuff which filtered through in a drop that comes out and the in between is controlled by nerves, hormones, substances, concentrations which tell the tubules, the tubes what to do. So really the kidneys are servants of …" "…. the consistency of the internal environment". Dr Miller finishes off the sentence in this radio program after they exchanged French phrases meaning the same thing but meant nothing to me. It really annoys me when people start using French expressions not appreciating that we are not all au fait with them.

I thought of an analogy to try and explain the position you are in when you suffer from renal failure. Imagine your body is not a temple but a boring sink. Bear with me on this one. The plughole is your kidney function. When you eat or drink it is a bit like someone turning the tap on. If you have good functioning kidneys - or an unblocked plughole - you are OK. However much you gorge your self the sink will never ever appear to fill up. It will flow out virtually as soon as the water arrives.

If you have acute renal failure someone suddenly puts the plug in. This means that whenever you drink or eat - turn the tap on – the sink begins to fill and it will eventually over flow and disaster: a wet kitchen lino!

If you have chronic renal failure the flow is hindered. The sink is not about to overflow but begins to fill up. Not yet anyway. So to slow the process down your intake – tap flow - is restricted. The sink takes longer to empty and something looks wrong, as the water is no longer gushing straight out. Eventually the sink gets totally blocked and you had better do something before you have to get the kitchen mop out again.

A kidney machine will try and keep the mop cupboard firmly closed. What it does – still on the stupid analogy – is it acts as a pump every so often it is activated to lower the dangerously creeping level of the sink where the plug is effectively sealed and the tap trickle cannot be reduced any further.

At first the nurses put you on the machine, insert the two needles in your fistula arm where the vein is now massive and very visible. The needles are wider than the ones you have for taking blood or are used in hospitals for injecting medicines. Your blood leaves your body to be "washed" by going through the kidney machine containing the artificial kidney and back in by way of the other needle. Very long bloodlines can be seen entering and leaving your body. Your blood goes in and out of your body many times during the allocated hours you are attached to the machine.

Dialysis fluid and water are pumped into the machine. Meanwhile so is your blood. They pass each other only separated by a membrane which is full of tiny holes that are so small blood cells can not pass through but the toxins can. The toxins will be drawn to the dialysis fluid because nature will want to level out the density of the two liquids: the less dense fluid and the very dense blood fluid heaped with toxins. This process is called diffusion.

The dialysis fluid contains bicarbonate and calcium, supplements your body needs that your kidney and diet can no longer provide to try and avoid bone disease. This is also diffusion but going the other way.

I recall reading somewhere that in the very early years of dialysising fluid that the patients began to suffer from dementia until it was discovered the cause of it was the aluminium in the fluid, which was getting into the brain. In October 2001 there was a scare in Spain, Croatia and the USA over what was discovered to be contaminated dialysate where patients were dying due to air bubbles forming in their blood during a dialysis session. Baxter International Inc eventually accepted liability and compensated the relatives.

The most basic role of the machine is to get rid of excess water. This is ultrafiltration. Also known as "u" .. "f" .. ing. Sounding like the beginning of a censored comment by the patient when bloodlines are accidentally stood on or someone trips over them possibly resulting in your needles being pulled out and your blood going everywhere but where you want it, back into your body.

However dialysising also gets rid of the good stuff so that is why you have to take vitamin tablets and calcium capsules. There is no point taking them just before or during your session on the machine, as they will simply be dialysised straight out of your body.

The first few session begin to get rid of the back load of toxins in your blood. You are then supposed to feel much better than you have been for ages. It is ironically known as "the honeymoon period". I did not appreciate any miraculous change. I did not achieve a feeling of well-being; just not as ill. No doubt other patients have different symptoms reducing experiences once the backlog is removed. I am not sure if the NHS leaves it as late as possible because of budget restrictions or that, given the choice, patients would rather put off the day for as long as possible regardless of the extra accumulating symptoms

The symptoms while on or shortly after coming off can include: vomiting, cramps, fatigue, irritation, itching, fainting, temporary loss of vision, chest pain. The first four were my favourite.

Haemodialysis is seen as the more aggressive form of dialysis compared to the other type known as peritoneal dialysis (PD). PD takes place inside the peritoneal cavity but I guess you are non the wiser. This cavity is inside the abdomen and contains liquid but has the capacity to expand the quantity of liquid. Bags of special fluid are drained in and out. It is a gentler form of dialysis for those who are unable to cope with haemodialysis. Dialysis outside the body, haemo (blood) is the most common form. For the average patient the advantages outweigh the disadvantages.

The renal transplant unit was at one end of the hospital grounds and the dialysis unit was at the other. Since the hospital was built this branch of medicine, transplantation, had developed considerably. Now there was lack of space and money was needed to build a new building that could incorporate both units. This eventually happened in the mid 1990's.

I started haemodialysis in the renal unit. You gradually increase your hours depending on your blood results. Once you are well enough you have your sessions at the dialysis unit where the mode of transport was something resembling a milk float but where you could be wheeled on to. This was the unit where you are trained for eventual dialysis at home.

Soon I was given a regular schedule. It was five hours on the machine three days a week, Monday, Wednesday and Saturday. The fistula vein grows even more with use and it gets easier to put the needles in which by now you are encouraged to do yourself. After a few weeks I was being very gradually trained up to be able to manage the whole process myself: setting up the machine, taking your obs; weighing yourself; injecting the locals and the heparin starter dose. Heparin is a drug extracted from pigs that prevents your blood from clotting. Without it dialysis would not be easy.

Only then do you insert the needles and start the session. Then simply wait five hours or whatever time you have to do, being careful that you do not knock your needles out when you sleep or doze possibly forgetting that you are on the machine. I used to be very nervous about the occasional air pocket in the lines. I knew a lengthy one could be fatal if it passed through your heart. Nurses always reassured me that they had to be very long and not be just an inch long, which was what I would usually have to contend with. I never got to know what was a serious length.

An hour before you are due to "come off" you would turn off the heparin so your blood resumes its clotting capability for when you take the needles out.

Then it's time to clean up the machine and tidy the cubicle for the next patient, washing the artificial kidney, which can be reused about ten times before it is too clogged to be of any further use. The five hours are only part of it when taking into account all your duties you have either side of each session. It may be for even longer when there are delays or you weigh more than your normal weight usually due to drinking too much. The machine does the work your failing kidney tried to do so now you have to reduce your fluid intake. You no longer need to continually flush your kidneys out by drinking large quantities as the machine is now doing the equivalent task.

Three times a week an ambulance would take me home and pick me up for the next session. On one occasion I left my usual calling card and threw up all over the inside of the driver's nice clean ambulance just as he pulled up outside my home.

" Blooourrrr"

" Sorry about that mate."

"Oh that's alright. Bye"

"Bye. Cheers. Probably see you day after next at 7.30 in the morning"

On my free days I had the luxury of waking up when I felt like it. The neighbours' curtain usage was on overtime as they were very interested why an ambulance was always picking me up.

My flat mate had also completed his degree and he had left town I was on my own in the flat and the landlord wanted me out so he could re-let it and no doubt charge more. I was in no mood to search for a new flat mate or contest possession proceedings. I had to look around for somewhere else to live. I found a room in a shared house that was a few miles nearer to the hospital, which I thought would be an advantage.

I had been told that if I was to have any chance of a transplant my kidneys would need to be removed. The intention was to do it within the next few weeks. I was told to come in to hospital as an in-patient rather than just for the next session. I had no time to unpack or even meet all the people in the house.

My previous operations had all been mainly investigative or explorative if you exclude the fistula fitting: some requiring a local and some a general anaesthetic. This was to be my first real operation or major operation that would include an element of risk. I was told that a very small percentage of patients die on the operating table but you can play so many games with statistics. For instance older people are more likely to be at risk so immediately that average figure was misleading in my situation.

I have always enjoyed the stories of people who misunderstand the concept of statistics. There is the story of the sailor who stuck his head through the hole made by one of the enemy's canons thinking that statistically it was now very unlikely that the next one would hit that part of the ship again. Or the person who always took a bomb on board a plane he was travelling on because statistically the chances of there being two bombs on the same plane were astronomical. The same distorted logic still happens today. For instance some lottery ticket buyers where shown on a TV documentary recording numbers that came up assuming the numbers that haven't come up for a while are bund to appear soon.

I would console myself with the fact that I would never know if I had not survived the operation. I would only know if I did. A certain percentage of the population die in hospital but a lesser percentage die in delicatessens so maybe I should have a word with the surgeon and see if he would be kind enough to do the operation there, just this once.

There is no turning back when they take out both kidneys; it's transplant or machine. I used to ponder if you can stay alive after both kidneys were removed. I had not heard of it before. There is always a part of you thinking maybe my kidneys are just having a bad year, renal horribilis, they might recover, and maybe I should leave them in. What if it is possible they may improve. If I have them taken out that's it. I will be totally dependant on the machine.

I phoned my family and told them what the doctors had decided to do and they seemed a bit shocked, as it was not something we ever had in mind. Yes remove them when there is a transplant but surely not before.

I arrived at the hospital with my stuff for what was expected to be a two-week stay. We all had our own NHS private room due to the extra problems kidney patients have: the continual threat of cross infection by half of us being immune suppressed and the other half being run down from being dialysis patients. You will not be too surprised to learn that my room had a bed and the usual bedside cabinet. It also had a urine bottle (after tomorrow who knows when I'll next be using that, probably for throwing up into when the vomit container call out does not get the immediate response you hope for); the usual resuscitation stuff and a radio system installed in the wall that hardly ever worked and when it did it was only hospital radio so you couldn't even try and forget where you were whilst listening to the radio.

"Hello to Bert who just had an operation today. Hope it all went well Bert. Get well soon says Jeff, Mark and all the lads. See you down the local very soon."

"Well, Alison your mum and dad say get well soon and keep on taking the tablets and you will be out and about and fit as a fiddle again in no time at all "

" And a special get well for Melanie from all your family and friends. Hope you are recovering well and hope to see you soon back to your all tricks /right as rain/back working in your garden/fully recovered in the not too distant future."

"And a special hello to Michael O'Sullivan at the moment recovery from an operation. Get well soon now Michael. Now a song for you. Hope you like it. The punk band The Jam : "Going Underground""

Just a few examples that I would hear interspersed with the standard joke about the nurses and the hospital food (try dialysis hospital food Mr DJ, which for me was ironically more varied than I could cobble together myself).

The night before the operation the surgeon came to see me and told me that my kidneys would be removed from the front and spoke about the machine keeping me "alive, in the meantime, so we can hopefully find you a successful transplant." It was a breath of fresh air when he said that. The straightforward language, the bluntness in contrast with the cagey speak I was usually met with. It encouraged me to ask more direct questions. I wanted to ask: will it hurt? Should I give up thinking about fathering children? Can I have my favourite teddy with me for when I come round?

I was told my operation (medical term: bilateral nephrectomy) was the next morning and as such I could not have anything to eat or drink 24 hours before. ("nil by mouth"). All my body hair had to be shaved (" knees to nipples" as it was tactfully put) and there was the usual parade ground inspection by a nurse to check you had not missed a bit.

I then got into my white, very revealing theatre gown, which was open down the back and hardly worth the effort in attempting to tie the few little cotton strips available to prevent, if you're lucky, revealing your bottom to the world.

That well-known organisation, the Hospital Infection Society published a report in April 2002 recommending further research into this standard pre operative practise. Need embarrassed and traumatised patients have to wear the ridiculous gown and the hat: have removed all rings and jewellery that are nowhere near where all the activity will be taking place. The Patients Association, at the time of writing, is trying to get the government to finance this research and answer that perennial question: should you have to take your underwear off for a knee operation?

I took my "pre med": a tablet to calm you down in preparation for the operation, which is supposed to make you sleepy and, if you are lucky, sleep. I was then handed a consent form to sign, I did not bother to read it. At this stage what could you actually do if you were unhappy with paragraph four? You're as nervous as hell, you are hopefully feeling drowsy, you are in no mood to read a newspaper headline let alone two pages of small print.

When you go to the operation theatre you are faced with hospital staff in white gowns and masks. It is as if you're back in a pram when bodiless heads are looking down at you. Looking past them you see others. It is as if you are back stage at a Klu Klux Klan rally although some blue (or was it green) uniforms are about. At each stoppage along the route to "theatre" my wrist bracelet was checked to make sure they were not taking two healthy kidneys out of another patient. A white substance in a syringe was put into my arm as someone says "a little prick" which did not help. Then another stranger puts a funny contraction over my face and says "breathe deeply". Flash back to a young boy when your mum sticks a hanky in your face and says "blow" such is the total vulnerability you are placed in. Then I am asked to count to backwards from ten. Ten, nine, eight, seven ..... zzz....zzzz.

When I came round I was in some pain. I was told I could not have any painkillers for the time being because my blood pressure had dropped and if I took any drugs I was likely to have a cardiac arrest. I had to wait for my body to adjust to the lack of kidneys. The pain was, how should I put it, as if someone had got a knife and cut the front of my lower stomach from one side to the other and then sowed it back up again. It gave me a small glimpse into what it would have been like being injured in battle during the middle ages, lying there and having to put up with it. They, of course, did not know about modern medical assistance. I could not even rely on the magic sponge that professional football players have access to. My pain was obviously not as bad as the pain as seen on these professional football players when they are badly tackled but unlike them I did not make a sudden miraculous recovery as soon as I got a free kick or penalty or the other player got yellow carded but I did have a vague recollection of wearing an oxygen mask.

It was not so much the pain level itself, although that was bad enough, but the continual pain from which there was no respite, not knowing when you could get some pain relief and how long it was going to last.

I appreciated the quandary the medical team were in. They obviously wanted to ease the pain for me but could not risk it. Every fifteen minutes my blood pressure would be taken to see if it had gone up so I could safely take painkillers. It did not do so for several hours. Every quarter of an hour my blood pressure was taken again. I would look pleadingly at the nurse to see any flicker of a smile to indicate it had risen so that she could go and get a doctor to prescribe something. Sometimes a particularly considerate nurse would take my blood pressure even more frequently to see if there was any sign of improvement.

Eventfully it showed some sign of moving up but it was a very long and painful wait for it to recover sufficiently so I could get some pain relief. During this time I was asked if there was anything I wanted and apparently I was later to learn I had said something like "a revolver and one bullet" so I must have been aware and not in complete agony but now looking back it was as if it was someone else who had gone through those long drawn out hours.

The first few days I was restricted to my bed and had bed baths. The first real baths were a bit painful when easing yourself in and out, feeling like you were about ninety-five years old. My scar was covered with waterproof adhesive as soon as the last stitch was made at the end of the operation. When it eventfully came off just before the stitches were to be removed it was not much fun due to all the new hair growth underneath.

I wanted to see my kidneys. Apparently this was very unusual request. I did not want to give them one last kicking for old time sake but this time with me no longer attached. No. I was just curious as to what they looked like. Eventually, after a few gentle reminders I gave up asking because I soon realised I was wasting my time and after a few days who knows where they had got to but if there was a local pie shop with a very good deal ....

"Body disequilibria" is apparently what it's called: when, without any kidneys you return to the kidney machine and your body gets even more confused than normal. Dialysis was now worse then before. Now I would get headaches after being "plugged in" and it lasted the full session. It is a type of headache I would associate with migraine: all embracing, nothing could take your mind off it. Lying down in a dark room and waiting for it to go away seemed the only course of action. I created my own dark room by pulling the blankets over my head but this was problematic with the commotion in the unit; worrying that if I moved my arm I would dislodge my needles and then have to come out of my little hideaway and readjust them. I could not take any painkillers because as soon they got into my blood stream the dialysing would clear them out. Nurses were very sympathetic and I would occasionally hear a voice "How's the headache Michael". "Sorry but I cannot give you anything until you come off." "One hour to go Michael. If you still have it then we can give you something"

I took the painkillers when I "came off" but this disequilibrium took hold in another form: the shock of coming off the machine.
When I returned to my bed I was retching for several hours (bloooourrgh... "Oh painkillers. Leaving already? Don't go. I was hoping I could introduce you to my bloodstream"). I initially retched continually, gulping like a hippo to get my breath and then at about five second regular intervals for an hour or so when it gradually reduced in frequency. By then I had not only nothing to bring up, not even bile, but I was sore internally from the activity and lets not forget the small matter of the operation scar that I was trying to hold with one hand as it was noticeably more painful each time I retched.

I was not even able to talk to the nurses in complete sentences without being interrupted by my little, uncontrolled physiological need.

"Michael you have not completed your menu cards for the next few days "

"Well...blouuuur....could you read out the choices ......blooourr"

"So for tomorrow's dinner you want fish fingers and boiled cabbage and for dessert?"

"Blouuur........"

"Sorry?"

"Bloouuur............"

"Blamange ? No Michael you know you cannot have blamange you know it is not for dialysis patients. It is high in potassium and is a meat unit due to all the milk"

"No ....bluuuurrhh"

"Blueberry pie but that 's got fruit in it. Very high in potassium. You're being silly now"

I am a bit but you get the picture. On one occasion a nurse actually asked such questions during this time. It was the strangest period, while I was concentrating on taking my next breath between my retching, once in the distance I could hear from down the corridor an argument with someone who was insisting on seeing a patient but was being refused. I thought I had recognised the voice but could not place it. Then there was more retching and when it subsided for a while I would continue to try and recognise the mystery voice.

Anyway I am not trying to suggest that the nurses were oblivious to my condition or did not care. Far from it. In fact I remember one saying "Your poor thing. What are they doing to you over there? Surely there is something that can be done" At the time I was in mid fake discharge mode and was unable to say any thing even though I wanted to acknowledge his concern.

The next day after the session the headache reduced but by the time it had gone completely the next dialysis session was due and it was to all begin all over again. I got worried. Will this go away or will I have it until I get a transplant. I was assured it would.

Slowly but surely my sore body adjusted but it had at least one less duty to perform. Now there was no chance of getting rid of any fluid naturally; if you have no kidneys you cannot produce urine so you cannot pee. A few weeks earlier I was being asked to drink two litres of fluid a day. This was drastically reduced when the machine took over but now the machine could perform the duty and anything I now drank had nowhere to go. It was trapped in my system, in my blood supply. Any extra weight found on me by the weigh-ins just before each session could not mean anything other than that I had drunk too much which meant more time on the machine to get rid of it. I was told that a possible risk of over drinking could result in a brain haemorrhage. But since then I have checked and cannot find anything to substantiate this claim. The first stage is oedema in the ankles. Then if you drink even more you are likely to get water on the lungs (pulmonary oedema) likely to cause breathing difficulties.

Once I had had a breakfast cereal and early morning tea any more fluid beyond a pint for the rest of the day was a possible risk. Fluid obviously includes milk in cereal or custard if you managed to program your diet to allowing such consumption. If you sweat or cried you lost fluid so you could replenish any lost fluid. Tips to manage thirst included sucking ice cubes; a glass of ice cubes was equivalent to a glass of water; using mouthwash and sucking a sour boiled sweet

Over the next few days I was beginning to notice problems with thinking straight when nurses or visitors spoke to me. After a few words of my reply I completely lost my train of thought. I forgot what I was trying to say and there were long silences when people were waiting for me to finish a simple sentence. The operation had initially affected my body. Now it was affecting my mind. I began to develop an ache in my fistula arm that came and went. I couldn't sleep at night because of it.

My mental state appeared to worry the doctors more than the earlier physical symptoms did after the bilateral nephrectomy as I was to discover when I spotted the silent eye contact between them at the bottom of the bed during the ward round. (A concern of doctors?) I knew something was up but not sure what. I often thought I was going mad but I recalled the saying that if you think you are going mad then you couldn't be. I was told they would get a psychiatrist to visit me. "Nothing to worry about but we just need to find out what the matter is."

After a brief introductory chat the psychiatrist said he was going to ask me a few simple questions and I was not to be worried if I could not answer them correctly. He took his wristwatch off and pointed at the strap and asked me what it was called. I searched for the word in my confused mind but I could not remember it. He pointed at one of the hands and asked what it was called. After a brief panicky search through my mind I realised I did not know. He got off his chair and came up close to me to show that he was pointing at the winder and asked me what it was called. I did not know! I was getting exasperated that I could not find the words and concerned what the significance was for the impending diagnosis. After about five or six questions in which I could only answer about one he told me there was nothing to worry about. I was just in shock after having my kidneys removed and it is likely to be temporary and I should be OK soon

He then continued to explore my mental state and commented on the fact that losing my kidneys and having renal failure at such a young age must be traumatic and how did I cope. I answered something to the effect that I braced myself for the worse so that if it happened I would be prepared and if it did not then it could only be good news. He said that was very unhealthy. So I waited for him to tell me what I should do. He continued the conversation but did not make any suggestions. So there I was not really expecting help and when he began showing concern I was enthusiastically awaiting some tips but they never came. More fool me. I was crestfallen. I thought he was about to give me some helpful advice. Should have seen it coming really.

Years later I read into this and my " unhealthy" attitude. I read that perpetually anxious people have their own form of bullet proofing which consists of setting expectations low, preparing for the worst possible outcome and planning how to prevent it from happening. It is termed "defensive pessimism" by Julie K Norem, a psychologist and professor at Wellesley College, Massachusetts. She says, "

This focuses them on things they can do, and away from the anxiety. An awful lot of people do learn how to do it for themselves in a concrete way." Barbar S.Held, also a psychologist and professor but this time based at Bowdoin College, in Maine argues that the "tyranny of the positive attitude" should end because it may well back fire and make the person feel even worse. I discovered this from the American Psychological Association. Their web site is at the back of the book.

Suddenly I re-emerged. From where I do not know. I was on a bed and attached to some machine and I felt I had just landed from **another planet,** a parallel universe. I was aware of my surroundings but no clue as to how I got there. There was a lot of commotion around me: of the people working in the room and another person to my right on the adjacent machine. When I tried to speak I realised I could not and panic gripped me as I thought I had gone mad and I was trapped in my body and it would now be impossible to communicate with anyone else ever again. I thought I might be trapped in my own little world bubble forever. You sometimes hear of nurses saying, usually on TV, "it's very sad he can understand everything you are saying but cannot communicate" or "I am afraid he is totally unaware so don't be alarmed if he shows no indication of recognising you". I am not sure what's worse. I was the former but everyone else might think I was the latter. (Dramatic I know but that's how I felt at the time.) Then the patient in the adjacent bed asked me a question I suddenly snapped out of it. (I'll name that universe in one) and answered her. Then all the nurses in the room looked at me and one said "Michael you're speaking again. We have not heard anything from you for the last three days!"

I was so relieved I wept, which set off all the nurses. I then started to panic thinking that this was only temporary and I would slip back into my desolate, lonely private bubble, demanded a pen, paper and started to write down the names of anyone I knew so that they could come and help me if I was to slip back inside it again. I eventually calmed down asking questions of the previous three days. The nurses explained I had effectively become mute. To this day I cannot remember a thing about that period. It must have been due, once again; to the shock to my body having it's enlarged kidneys removed. After all at about eighteen pounds it was like giving birth to twins or even triplets.

Loss of memory is often seen as amusing by the non-afflicted. It is not. There appears to be this image that the rest of your mind is working perfectly but one small aspect remembering who you are and your history is wiped clean. But your mind, in my case, was in total disarray. Earlier I could not find the words I was looking for. As if someone had mysteriously removed that particular word from the folder containing that type of word, which was held within a folder in a cabinet drawer in my little brain. I felt as if the entire contents of everything in each folder in every single drawer had been tipped onto the floor in the room where all the cabinets are held. I would then in my mind be rushing around picking up a single piece of paper, trying to make sense of it and see if it could help.

I returned to my room and began staring at the patterns on the curtains in my room, seeing strange faces and being amazed at how strange it was to be lying on a metal legged structure with soft foam material on top which was placed in the centre of the room. It was as if I had never before laid on a bed in my life. I then began reminiscing about my school holidays.

***

As a schoolboy I used to work on my uncle's farm in North Wales. He used to run it with his sister, my auntie. It had not taken up all the modern techniques because milking by hand and dry stonewalling was still practised. The hens were free range. I used to collect the eggs twice a day hunting in all the ingenious places they were laid.

I would accompany my uncle up the mountain to check on the sheep occasionally helping him and the sheep dogs bring a few sheep or sometimes the whole flock, down to the farmhouse. At first I was in the lower ranks of his employ: merely a trainee sheepdog but eventually was able to order the dogs around in Welsh myself. The neighbouring farmer ordered his sheepdogs just by a series of whistles. Once I hid behind a tree, copied him and watched as total chaos ensued on the mountainside. The sheep dogs where getting confused with the contradictory instructions and the farmer was getting more and more annoyed with them as he was unable to hear me.

Some of my uncle's sheep dogs would take a fancy to smashing and gulping down the raw egg they came across. They soon stopped after receiving a free gift: an egg that had had its natural contents removed by use of a syringe and replaced by mustard carefully ensuring the shell was not broken apart from a tiny hole. Cruel you may say but it stopped them.

One particular farmer in the next valley was sceptical of his neighbour's supposed new electric fence. He wanted to see it in action. He picked up his faithful sheep dog, stuck his nose on the fence – that's the dogs not his. Now that is cruel – but as he was standing in a puddle he got the electric shock and the dog did not feel a thing as the shock went through the dog's body.

A few valleys north of the farm is the supposed grave of a legendary dog. The translated inscription reads:

"GELERT'S GRAVE

IN THE 13TH CENTURY LLYWELYN PRINCE OF NORTH WALES HAD A PALACE AT BEDDGELERT. ONE DAY HE WENT HUNTING WITHOUT GELERT THE FAITHFUL HOUND WHO WAS UNACCOUNTABLY ABSENT. ON LLEWELYN'S RETURN, THE TRUANT STAINED AND SMEARED WITH BLOOD JOYFULLY SPRANG TO MEET HIS MASTER. THE PRINCE ALARMED HASTENED TO FIND HIS SON AND SAW THE INFANT'S COT EMPTY. THE BEDCLOTHES AND FLOOR COVERED IN BLOOD THE FRANTIC FATHER PLUNGENED HIS SWORD INTO THE HOUND'S SIDE THINKING IT HAD KILLED HIS HEIR. THE DOGS DYING YELL

WAS ANSWERED BY A CHILD'S CRY. LLEWELYN
SEARCHED AND DISCOVERED HIS BOY
UNHARMED BUT NEAR BY LAY THE BODY OF A
MIGHTY WOLF WHICH GELERT HAD SLAIN. THE
PRINCE FILLED WITH REMORSE IS SAID NEVER TO
HAVE SMILED AGAIN. HE BURIED GELERT HERE.
THE SPOT IS CALLED

BEDDGELERT"

This legend is now a tourist spot and easy to search for
on the internet.

While I was at school my parents used to deliver me to
the farm during the Easter and summer holidays. In the
summer I was usually in the open fields, involved in all
stages of the hay harvest. It began with the cutting of the
grass and a few days later the turning of the top - dry but
no longer green - grass. While my uncle used the grass
cutter, then the hay turner, I was spreading out the cut
grass to get it to dry out fully especially in parts of the field
the tractor missed or could not get to. He nicknamed me
"Michael the Pykle", the name for the pitchfork.

Next, the tumbler was pulled around the fields by the
tractor, which turned up all the hay to really puff it up and
dry it out. Finally the bailer arrived on the scene together
with local farm labourers taking the bails to the haylofts. By
now I was the "Townie"

In the later years I got to drive the tractor and
sometimes even the bailer! Most of the hay fields were in the
valley but there was one field above the road. One day I got
a bit cocky. I drove in top gear while using the hay turner on
part of the field with a steep incline and one of the tractor
wheels came off the ground. In my panic I thought the hay
turner was over balancing because it was in the "up"
position so I lifted the lever to what I thought would bring it
down but it was already down and by moving the lever I had
moved it up which was all it took to guarantee that the
tractor would turn over. On realising this I decided to jump
off. However as I landed I looked up and the hay turner was
coming down on me. I lifted my knees up in a pathetic
attempt to protect my self but miraculously, the engine was
still running and the turner started to press down on me

when the wheels of the tractor hit the ground, the tractor moved on scraping off me.

During the school easter holidays there would at times still be a complete snow blanket over the North Welsh hills. I would take sheep cake around the fields. I also emptied out the barns of multi-layered cowpats and gave the cattle their cattle cake. I was amazed at how they could put their tongue in each nostril but obviously not at the same time.

After observing my uncle inject a few ewes with something I was sent on an errand to inject one miserable looking ewe with what looking back must have been a foot and mouth inoculation. She was about a mile or so from the farmhouse. I nervously walked to an old house ruin where she was last seen, with syringe in hand. When I got there I filled the syringe ensuring no air remained within before I was to inject. On previous occasions I had been an assistant to other farm animals having jabs just in to the muscle. For instance calves would be given a jab where you would rhythmically tap them on their hind with one hand and then, in time, inject the needle held in your other hand and the calf would not feel a thing. Nor did you, unless you forgot to remove your other hand in time. I had to inject this ewe into the vein. It meant withdrawing some of her blood into the needle to check on a good flow and then injecting the drug. Who would have thought years later I would be injecting myself several times a week with the local anaesthetic and the heparin, not to mention the dialysis needles.

Easter was also lambing time and one of my regular duties was to roam the 365 acre hill farm twice a day looking for any lambing problems. There are certain high marks on the hills where you could walk to and peer down, sometimes using binoculars, looking down to avoid having to walk those extra miles. You would have to look out for newly born lambs or ewes with problems. I was looking out for the two-headed monster: not an uncommon problem during lambing. Once in a while the lamb was trapped inside the mother and although the head was visible it was at this stage that the natural birth was in need of a helping hand. This involved releasing the front little hoof from inside the mother. First I had to catch the mother, put her on her side, pull out the lamb, and clear all the afterbirth from its mouth to get it bleating and stand back. As if you had just lit the touch paper on bonfire night waiting to see if anything would spark off. Occasionally the mother ewe would be so exasperated - if they have that mental capacity - at having been in such a predicament for what could be many hours that she would simply walk away and disown the lamb. In these cases I had to carry the lamb down to the farmhouse. Often when I had retreated there would be a happy ending, the mother would begin to lick all the afterbirth off and I knew the lamb would be all right on the mountain and would not end up on my back.

One time I had caught a ewe in this predicament, released her new born and while I was helping it to breathe for the first time, mumsy decided to make a break for it. She ran across this mountain brook that had a deep pool when just then her second lamb was born ..... straight into the pool and started to drown.("LAMBSY WAMBSY:BORN:8.15 AM.DIED 8.I5AM") I looked around this very bleak Welsh hilltop for a telephone kiosk so I could change into my Super Shepherd outfit but there wasn't one, more to the point there wasn't time. I quickly rushed into the brook, pulled out the lamb, put her/him with her brother/sister and crossed the brook to find mum ("You've got a beautiful baby boy ...or er girl er or two . er. You've got twins"). I eventfully found her, chased her back over the other side of the brook to the newborn twins. Luckily she took to them and I did not have to carry both of them down to the farmhouse on my back.

When a farmer has to take a lamb in it can also be due to the mother dying at birth. Once I saw a fully conscious ewe being eaten alive by crows, I could see inside her rib cage with its beating heart. At the top of a mountain in a situation like that all you can do is slit its throat to end the misery and concentrate on saving the lamb.

The orphan lambs were initially left by my auntie's kitchen fire where they were given cows milk from a bottle. The strategy is to try and pair these lambs with ewes that have lost theirs. The ewe will shun the orphan lamb unless you deceive her by skinning the dead newly born lamb and get the orphan to wear it as a winter coat. They did not have a choice. On coming out of the changing room, I never heard once any of them say: "Well I am not sure. I think I want to try the first one on again." I winced shortly after they were put together for the first time because as soon as the starving lamb went for a teat the ewe would head but her and send her flying against the side of one of the hay bails which were the material to build the enforced family home in one of the barns. The ewe is eventually convinced that the lamb is hers after she gets fed up with head butting it a few times and having been stuck together for so many days. Then the dead lambs coat is removed and once my uncle is happy with the new family relationship you stick them out in the field again until humans decide they want to eat them.

*

Why did I now recall my life as a schoolboy "on the farm". Maybe it was simply the freedom, the outdoors, the countryside and the healthiness compared with me now stuck in hospital. It could even be me subconsciously recalling the time I was looking after other beings as opposed to now, solely dependant on others. But I doubt it. It could be that it was a place I recall from my earliest memories that I can still and do visit. A link from early years to now. I definitely got a good basic grounding on the ferociousness of nature.

***

It was during the night that being in my own little private room was the worst. It was due to the long never ending periods of quietness, elongated by the reduced night staff, few distractions compared with the many people moving through the ward during the day: cleaners, doctors, visitors and nurses. It was only an occasional visit by a nurse to do my obs. One night I pressed the buzzer as I was desperate to speak to someone. I was in a terrible state and blubbering. Although the balance of my mind had returned I was now unable to cope with the realisation of what was in store for me once I was eventually discharged. The ward member of staff who answered my buzzer sat with me for an hour or more.

I was still not yet ready to be discharged. I got into a routine at the hospital as I had still not stabilised. For instance my blood pressure was still all over the place.

As I slowly recovered the ward routine took hold. In the morning my "obs" were taken, the last duty of the night shift nurses and then a hour or so later breakfast arrived brought by the day shift nurses. Gone were the days when the night shifts last duty was waking you up, sitting you up, pulling up the front of the bed structure and rearranging the pillows so you could not go back to sleep.

My drugs would arrive in their familiar tiny eggcup like container. Once that and breakfast in bed was over I had to be prepared for the doctors visit – the ward round which meant a bath beforehand. While out of my room it would be cleaned up and my bed made. I do not mean the carpenters came in and measured me up for one but I wish they had done so as all the beds were too short for me. After my bath I sat in the chair waiting for them to finish while saying, "I would not bother, as soon as I get back in I am going to pull up all your fancy work." I am six foot two and if I did not destroy their skilful work I would be hanging out of the top of the bed like a baby kangaroo in it's mother's pouch.

Then the wait for the doctors round around the whole ward, together with full entourage. This image is often associated with James Robertson Justice in that 60's film characterisation but in reality junior doctors are in my experience not treated like that. Most of the time it was fine but occasionally I got a bit peeved. Everyone talking about me or rather my body. I would occasionally be asked a question like have you moved your bowels today. Often I would interject and say sorry to interrupt but this is my body. Slowly I got more involved in the discussions. (what about a gathering of doctors?)

Then it was elevenses and the attempt to catch the paper delivery person, making sure you don't end up having to buy a paper you would not normally under any circumstances take a first glance at. Usually it was already too late as the previous wards had left you with little choice. In the later few weeks of my long stay I often walked to the other end of the hospital ground to buy a proper newspaper.

Obs again then menu cards would arrive where you would pick your dialysis choice for the next few days and then wait around for lunchtime. New faces. a nurse shift changed. More drugs. After lunch a few hours wait before possible visitors, afternoon tea, dinner, supper with new faces again another nurse shift. More obs in the middle of the night obs then the next day

But do not forget that was every other day. On alternate days I was dialysing, coming off dialysis at mid afternoon and brought back to my room.

One day I was lying on my bed attempting to read what was on that clipboard always found at the bottom of all hospital beds. I was trying to understand all the squiggly lines and funny numbers when I heard "You shouldn't be reading that Michael". A nurse had just arrived.

"Why not?"

"They're for the doctors. Not for you"

"But I am entitled to know what's happening. It is my body"

"Well you should not"

Once this particular nurse had left I ignored her instructions and continued to fathom out my systolic and diastolic blood pressure figures, why they moved up and down from one day to the next. My temperature and pulse appeared to stay the same but blood pressure appeared to be a problem and I think the main reason I was not being discharged. I really wanted to learn more about my medical condition. The doctors were too busy and I sensed I was asking more questions than the average patient.

Now don't get me wrong I am not about to relate incidents to knock the ward, the hospital or the NHS generally. Far from it. This hospital has kept me alive and does so at each dialysis session and will continue to do so. I do feel, however, it is important to relay these incidents on so other patients stop being so passive in their treatments.

"What's that one?"

"It's a new drug that the doctor prescribed you today"

"Well she did not tell me she was going to. What's it for?"

"Just take it Michael. She prescribed it just now. It is for you".

"Sorry I am not taking it until I know what it is".

Thankfully we did not get involved in the "it will make you better" scenario. The nurse left not too pleased and to be fair the doctor came back when she was free, explained why she was prescribing it and I was happy and took the drug. She was probably too busy to get into the habit of explaining everything she decided upon or rush back to me if she made a decision once she had seen me.

Another occasion, another nurse.

"No the dose is wrong"

"What do you mean"

"I am not on that dose"

"Come on Michael just take the drug. Don't be awkward"

"I am not being awkward. Look you go and check. If I am wrong
I 'll apologise. If you're wrong you can apologise"

Nurse leaves room not too pleased. Returns. Hands me eggcup with dose corrected and leaves.

I tended to stay in my room, the nurses saw it as unhealthy and at meal times suggested that I should join all the other mobile patients in the day room to eat my meals. They craftily stopped bringing my meals to my room and reported it was waiting for me on the table in the dayroom. All it had to offer were jigsaws. The majority tended to be of Lady Di and Prince Charles, which did not actually aid my delicate stomach. The photo, which the jigsaws were most frequently based on, were so familiar as they were plastered everywhere since their engagement and wedding that you could do the jigsaw without the photograph.

During one bedside chat with a nurse she was encouragingly trying to cheer me up and said:

"...and another thing: now you haven't got a spleen when you get a transplant in the future it is more likely to take"

"No spleen. What do you mean no spleen?"

"Oh hasn't anyone told you. When they took your kidneys out they also took out your spleen. Very common in your type of situation."

"Well fine but why didn't anyone tell me. What does the spleen do?" I asked urgently

She said something like "The spleen is a secondary source of white cell manufacturer so the body has less ammunition to attack a future transplant."

"While we are on the subject is there anything else I should know. Did they take out my left lung?" was my sarcastic retort.

I was more surprised than annoyed at this news. I was not even aware what the spleen did but I did sadly realise then that whatever it does I will never be able to vent one ever again. I was sure no one told me. I am all ears when I am told news about my medical condition. It is feasible, I suppose that after the op someone said that it was a success, if such a word can be used in this situation, but I must have missed it, as I was otherwise engaged. "Your great aunt has just sent you a £5 postal order and we also took out your spleen". If I was told I was possibly not in the right condition to pay attention.

In the process of writing this book I had another go at finding out what a spleen actually does. I will now quote from the Daily Telegraph's "The Family Encyclopaedia of Medicine & Health (a quid in a book club introductory offer if you must know),"The spleen is an important organ of the body" (Oh shit!) "Its main function is to act as a filter for the blood and to make antibodies..... very few ill effects seem to result from its removal.." (phew!) But hang on. You just said it was an important organ. It cannot be that important if there are very few consequences. " The appendix and your tonsils are an important part of your body. Do not leave hospital without them" It continues: "..., although it is possible to see changes in peripheral blood, such as the presence of Howell-Jolly bodies." But nothing in this book about what they are.

What about Bailliere's Nurses Dictionary? The spleen "manufactures lymphocytes and breaks down red blood corpuscles." That's cleared that up then. "Lymphocyte - a white blood cell formed in the lymphoid tissue. Lymphocytes produce immune bodies to overcome infection." "Corpuscle – a small protoplasmic body or cell, as of blood or connection tissue." "Protoplasm- the essential chemical compound of which cells are made."

This is a good example of why it is very risky looking through medical books especially those not intended for the general public. GPs, especially must curse the internet when patients come into their surgery with pages from obscure web sites. After all if you are not very careful you could easily die of a misprint.

I had a splenectomy. How many more ectomies am I going to have before my mortal coilectomny?

Most of the nurses I got on with really well. It was only occasionally I had a bit of friction. Another sister came in to see me because I had apparently been "rude to one of her nurses". I must have said something that was not pleasant but I didn't shout, raise my voice or swear. I am sure sometimes I may have been a bit blunt but to come in like that after one incident was a bit much. This young nurse may have been hurt but maybe I should have been told look I know you must be going through a bad time but could you be a bit more careful what you say. This nurse probably went home to her own bed and never even mentions the incident ever again. A senior nurse tells me off. I would have been in that small room, between dialysis sessions for about 5 weeks by then about to go crazy all over again.

There were occasions when there was a shortage of nurses even after you take into account the agency nurses that are brought on to the ward when it is particularly under staffed. You have to remember in such a ward you cannot have nurses with cold and flu like symptoms ready to pass it onto the patients.

Because the ward could clearly do with more members of staff I would suppress my desire to ask questions? When one or two of the doctors took out a pen and paper and draw diagrams as to what was happening I would lap it up but not always understanding it. I sometimes felt guilty that I may have been over doing it and expected one day they may get their own back and I would hear a commotion outside my room when in would be trolleyed an overhead projector and the lights would come on. "Right settle down everybody. Nurse Jenkins. Lights. Right tomorrow at fourteen hundred hours we will be entering the patient here with the hope of getting to a destination here. Any questions? Yes you at the back. No you. Yes. No not you. To your left. No. The person lying in the bed. Sorry? Is he? Oh I see. Yes Patient Michael."

One Sunday afternoon my parents were visiting me and a person walked in, acknowledged me, and picked up the sacred clipboard. He was wearing a jumper that clearly wasn't a recent xmas prezzie. He asked me a few question and then left. My Dad wondered who he was. I explained he was the surgeon. "My God. I thought he was the gardener." I thought that was great: he had popped into the unit during his day off to check on his patients, which was commendable, to possible return to his garden. Who knows? Who simply cares? But a good illustration of the end of pomposity such as wearing of the bow tie, which incidentally I understand was worn in preference to the tie as it would not get in the way when leaning over the patient during the examination.

*

Although I was very grateful for the contact from my friends and relatives I really had a problem with the get well card. I have just had both my kidneys removed. How on earth am I going to get well? Most people get ill, see the doctor, get better. There is this assumption firstly that doctors can fix you up with a wonder drug or if not time is the great healer and you will get better naturally. Long ago I realised doctors could not do anything for my polycystic kidneys. They could not give a drug to me or operate on them to make them better.

A friend phoned and then he asked me if he could borrow my bike which I thought was a little undiplomatic. I did not know how long before I could ride it again. It reminded me of the film on WW1 "All quiet on the Western Front." Someone asked this soldier who had just had both his legs amputated if he could have his new boots. A few weeks later my friend phoned to report that the bike had been stolen.

One of the many concerns patients have about being in hospital is the increased likelihood of constipation, usually due to the drugs you take particularly for general anaesthetics (surgeons do not want to see moving intestines once working inside you) and possibly the sedentary lifestyle. Why else do doctors regularly ask how regular you are? Years later a friend of mine was going into hospital for an operation and asked me for tips, being a bit of an old timer on the subject, as to what she should do to reduce this problem. All I could do is suggest fruit and fruit juices. A luxury I did not have on account of low fluid and low potassium diets. It is a real problem. Often found amusing by the non-afflicted.

Like all kidney patients my haemoglobin (iron count) was low, possible half of what it should be. I was prescribed iron tablets every day. But they bung you up. I was told that only about 5% can be absorbed into your system so 95% is not, consequently it leaves you, turns your motions completely black and in turn your already low mood. I thought the discomfort compared with slight increased iron count did not make it worthwhile. I did something I had never done before and have never done since: I stopped taking them as prescribed but instead I took them only on alternate days. I vowed I would compensate by being extra vigilant in not losing blood going on and off dialysis, which can so easily happen. You do this by always ensuring all the blood gets back into you at the end, not leave anything in the lines, making sure your needle does not slip out and send arterial blood spurting out of your arm like a garden hose. I thought I could maintain my haemoglobin that way rather than take these stupid tablets and get further bunged up into the bargain.

Well I got caught. The sister confronted me with a tiny black round tablet showing it to me between her thumb and forefinger. I had carelessly forgotten to discard it and left it on my bedside table. While most people my age were out enjoying the summer months, possible partaking in the pursuit of "recreational drugs" on the beach, at parties, in their flats, here I am in hospital getting "busted" for not taking drugs!

My secret rebellious decision was too late. I was not moving my bowels enough .I was given suppositories. Great. It was like a horse race where the familiar starting call is at the end. We will call it the Queen Victoria Suppository Handicap.

"They're all squeezed into the paddock.... Waiting for the starters gun ..... a bit of a delay .. the tension is mounting...and the blankets are thrown aside and he's up.... no he's not.... he's got his toes trapped in one of his sheets ..... he's escaped and he's up.... he 's out of bed ... slippers..... he's found his slippers ....the other slipper....he cannot find the other slipper....... . he's out in the open corridor....... coming up to the final hurdle....... the toilet ....someone else is in there ...... he's sprinting down the main corridor and he is heading for a very tight finish .. he is in the toilet .....toilet seat is down......pyjamas bottoms.... string..........in a knot ...... and they're off."

I had to rush out of my room, standing by the nearest ward toilet were three or four nurses chatting and when they saw me one said, "here he comes". Not very nice. They're not always angels you know. I began to wonder if they had a bet on in their little syndicate guessing the time when the patient would come flying out of their room with that uncomfortable urgency on their face.

So many patients have from time to time this difficulty. It is something most people do not want to talk about so it goes unnoticed. We need national demonstrations, people in the street with placards such as: "WE 'RE GOING POTTY!"; "WORKING BOTTOMS FOR ALL."; "DOWN WITH TOILET SEATS!"; "SUPPOSITORIES- YOU KNOW WHERE YOU CAN STICK THEM" and "FREE THE CHOCOLATE HOSTAGE". I would of course insist that the money was ring fenced.

Just after elevenses one day I saw a divine sight: my biggest fear: a bloke with an oddly arranged collar: a vicar. He was coming this way. I prayed he wasn't going to ask me to. As it turned out he didn't impose his beliefs on me, automatically assuming I had, or should have them. I was a devout atheist. We had a nice chat but I could not talk about my condition to him. What would he know? How could he help? What could he say that would change anything?

I was brought up a Roman Catholic and soon realised you cannot seriously inherit a belief. I began looking out for the spare thunderbolts and after a few years of having no religious beliefs and no burn marks I realised I was going to survive. To make things a little awkward for me I learnt that some of my relatives were praying for me.

But hear this guy. An American stand up comedian on stage in front of an American (an American) audience.

"When it comes to bullshit, big-time, major league bullshit, you have to stand in awe of the all-time champion of false promises and exaggerated claims, religion. No contest. No contest. Religion. Religion easily has the greatest bullshit story ever told. Think about it. Religion has actually convinced people that there's an invisible man living in the sky who watches everything you do, every minute of every day. And the invisible man has a special list of ten things he does not want you to do. And if you do any of these ten things, he has a special place, full of fire and smoke and burning and torture and anguish, where he will send you to live and suffer and burn and choke and scream and cry forever and ever 'til the end of time! But He loves you." (George Carlin. Watch out for the thunderbolts George)

When I realised that I was going to have renal failure the standard reaction is "why me" and "what have I done to deserve this."

I cannot understand religion but appreciate many find solace within it. I have often noticed situations where some people appear to turn to religion through weakness or despair: never through happiness or strength. Renal failure was simply a condition, a hereditary condition or a genetic disorder that my mum had inherited from her parents. For me, there was no point looking to anyone for help. You cannot complain of the physiological make up you inherited anymore than you can complain that water is too wet or not wet enough.

Grapes as a gift for a hospital patient are an old cliché. One day a friend brought in a bunch of grapes plus a load of pornographic magazines. This fails on so many levels. Where do you begin? I could not touch the grapes: massive potassium content and the porn magazines! I had to get him to take both straight back out when he left. If the nurses ever found out my life could be hell. In a sense I find it cute when you get hospital visitors that, not having been hospitalised, have this notion that you are not really ill but confined to bed and waiting to be discharged. So many people leave hospital able to put the stay completely behind them as a slight inconvenience now totally cured.

A nurse mentioned to me in passing one morning that an elderly patient along the corridor in the ward had asked her to ask me if I could get her some cannabis. A certain ambivalence initially came over me. Why would people think I was a prime candidate to possibly know this sort of information? Is it because I was a student and they all smoke pot don't they. Or that I appeared street wise or so untogether that I must be on something other than the prescribed varieties of drugs. Anyway I did not know or want to know who it was but had to explain that I could not help. It was a kind of request I bet many kidney patients consider, bearing in mind they cannot drink, or drink enough to get inebriated but smoking dope may allow a bit of escapism from their present plight.

I am afraid I initially kept the degree ceremony quiet from my parents but when I realised they really wanted to go I relented. Several friends on the course refused point blank to go but you are not doing it for your self but for your parents. I was let out from hospital for the afternoon .I still had a saline drip tap in the upper part of my hand due to a drug course I was on at the time. I tried as best I could to cover it up and no one spotted it.

Dad and me were more concerned about Mum. Although her kidney function was satisfactory she was constantly getting kidney infections, which is something I hardly ever got in the later years (and for the time being it was going to be pretty difficult to get.) At the ceremony she complained of feeling very hot which usually was associated with her having another kidney infection and she was worried that she might faint.

It was weird being out of the hospital and seeing all the familiar faces and young people who were not nurses or doctors for the first time in about six weeks. My degree seemed like it ended years ago now. Some had just returned from a summer holiday abroad. Some had already enrolled and started at the Poly again for the one-year postgraduate Solicitor's Final Course. I asked around about what the course was like, one lecturer very diplomatically warned me about how this course would be nothing like the degree and very intensive. Every other day I would be popping off for dialysis sessions. This and my other soundings confirmed what I believed: that it was going to be very difficult to get through the course let alone pass the exams.

The head of the law department came up to my dad after the ceremony and said "your son has got more spunk in his little finger than I have in the whole of my body". So that's where it's all been hiding.

At the ceremony each of the exciting and proud new graduates were called up in turn to take their parchment which was really a blank piece of rolled up paper tied up with red ribbon that you did not even take home afterwards. I was told by several of my friends that I got the biggest applause when I walked up to receive mine. I did not notice as I was concentrating too much on making sure I did not fall flat on my face and rip out the needle for the drip awaiting me back at the ward.

We were all given an opportunity to have our photograph taken which I suppose is the most important thing of the day: keeping a record for posterity. I was asked by the photographer if I wanted four different photos or just the one. Assuming the latter would be cheaper if we bought four I went for it. I latter learnt that was not the case. So with nearly two months in hospital within a matter of minutes of a temporary discharge I managed to get myself ripped off. I felt a complete prat: with the piece of black cardboard on my head and half a batman's outfit. At least everyone looked equally stupid.

My parents drove me back to the ward, travelled back to their home and I went back into the normal ward routine and prepared myself for dialysis the next day after experiencing the strange, fleeting glimpse of the outside world.

One of my friends was encouraged by the nurses to take me for a car journey to further the process of getting me ready for my eventual discharge which was looming as my blood pressure had begun to settle but it did not go according to plan. "Stomachchurn Countryside Tours – get out and about! Feel that uncomfortable feeling, then get ready for that unsettling feeling as you go over each pot hole, round each sharp bend in the country lanes and then, when the feeling becomes more intense, ask the driver to stop, open the front passenger door and for a short moment wonder at the colourful pretty, genetically perfect wild flowers on the road verge and throw up all over them"

****

CHAPTER FOUR: HEY LOOK NO KIDNEYS!

I was eventually discharged from hospital and got back to my new room in the shared house. I had to unpack. I moved there only a few days before my operation but two months later I could begin to live there and meet all my housemates. I must have become the mystery person who moved in and cleared off. They probably thought I had died in hospital. I also had to start the Law Society Finals course several weeks late and catch-up on all the lectures I'd missed.

My first real task was to get to the Poly and collect my grant cheque for the autumn term. I ventured to an unknown corner of the Poly site for the first time, the administration block and was told that because of my delay in picking it up they had sent it back to the local education authority. I had no money, I had to borrow a fiver off one of the law lecturers that day to be able to eat as I had stupidly assumed I would get my grant cheque to the bank and be allowed to draw out cash. By the time I realised that this was unlikely the bank had closed. I was not even able to ask for an overdraft facility.

It slowly dawned on me that with this new problem, the lost time, the continual catching up necessary after every dialysis session and my general health, I might have to leave the course. These problems may have been surmountable while doing a degree but not on this intensive postgraduate course. On the other hand I would not have the distraction of partying and socialising. I was sceptical from the start about getting through the course but was persuaded to have a go. However I could possibly take it the following year, you never know, I may get lucky and have had a transplant.

I ended up signing on and getting into a routine of going into hospital first thing in the morning for my three days. My dialysis sessions were initially for three five hours, I was picked up from home by an ambulance or other hospital owned vehicle and occasionally by an expensive private taxi during a shortage of such vehicles. Usually an ambulance would pick me up, I would get a breakfast at the start of my shift, stay on the machine for five hours and then an ambulance would drop me off at my home. Sometimes I'd have to wait an hour or so for one to become available.

At the unit at the same time there was a young girl of about sixteen who dreaded the needles. It was dramatic for the whole unit. It would take two or three nurses to persuade her to allow them to put the needles in so that she could start her session. Her screaming and fighting was distressing for all concerned and some days were worse than others. The nurses tried hard to make her life less upsetting. Once she was thrilled to be phoned up by a Saturday national TV children's programme and on her birthday she arrived to banners emblazoned upon the unit's walls and hanging from the ceiling wishing her a "Happy Birthday!".

Occasionally I was asked if I would mind if nurses, learning the ropes, could put my needles in. They said I had "good veins". The word good when describing any part of my body was enough for me to say yes. I would always agree, not only so that I could do something useful, but to avoid a non-expert putting this young girl's needles in. They could train on me as I had my thumb and fingernail on standby if they really made a mess of it.

I was also on dialysis on my birthday and was hoping no one would notice. This was tricky with so many pieces of paper around with my date of birth on. If anyone discovered it was I'm afraid I would have said something downbeat like "big deal the earth's gone round the sun again." I am not usually a miserably bugger but the one thing that riles me is enforced cheerfulness.

A few months later I was moved onto the late evening/ night shift for eight hours twice a week on Tuesdays and Thursdays. I would make my own way in for about 6.00 pm which meant you had to get there well in advance. As time went on I went in earlier and earlier to start early so I could finish early, a practice other patients had tried but eventually the nurses dissuaded us.

When I arrived I would look around eagerly to see which bay I was in because not all had televisions (black and white in those days.)
This was quickly discovered by looking on each of the beds, all covered with the usual accoutrements, for my name knowing that was where I was to spend the next ten hours, hopefully with a working telly. A faulty one, which would constantly play up, was in a sense worse than none as you could not easily resign your self to not having one and would be trying to get the nurses to get it to work.

Once on the machine you could have your meal, if taken in the first hour of an eight hours shift you could breach your strict diet. It was not that beneficial health wise because a lot of the goodness would be dialysised straight out but it gave you an escape from the strict diet twice a week. I would be given the option of tomato or mushroom soup from a can. Some patients would bring in all the goodies they could never have apart from those two hours each week, which I noticed were usually crisps or chocolate. I did not bother because I saw it as teasing yourself. You might as well accept the diet and take the goodies the hospital gave you at meal time rather than work yourself up into a frenzy by purchasing things in advance to bring in and eat in that first hour whether you wanted it or not. It was a bit like removing a prisoner from his/her cell and putting him/her in a field for ten minutes, allowed to run around like a sprightly young foal only to be stuck back indoors just by the time you fully remembered what you are missing.

Throughout the session your fistula arm remained outstretched, otherwise the blood flow would be restricted if you bent your elbow and then the alarm would go off. This occasionally happened if you moved then one of the needles in your arm twisted and was up against the inside wall of your veins or worse the needle came out and you had your very own blood fountain, particularly impressive because you had arterial blood flow, nearly hitting the ceiling. It never happened to me but I have seen the results of it happening to others.

In those days there were no zappers with each TV set, you had to ask a passing nurse to switch channels. As time went on I got more adventurous and a bit naughty. I would slowly get up, wait to see if I was not about to go hypo (faint due to low blood pressure), if not rearrange my leads, carefully watching my needles so that they would not move inside my fistula and set off the alarm. If they did I would feel like an escaping Colditz inmate but unable to put my hands up once the nurses arrived to see what was up. If I managed to avoid that I would then edge over to the TV located on a high shelf and try to hit the channel change button. This would usually work fine but sometimes I could not reach. I would occasionally coax a nurse to pass me a window pole so I could change channels from a lying position. A sort of cave man zapper.

I had a copy of the Scrabble board game. I persuaded the patient in the next dialysis bay to play if I could arrange it. The problem was getting us either side of a table. A nurse said she would help us manoeuvre out into the centre of the unit by moving our machines and leads. It felt like bribing a friendly prison warden.

The game was set up. I went first and placed my word. My fellow patient then moved. At first I could not work out what his word was. Oh no I have not just gone and challenged a bloody intellectual. What was it? Latin is not allowed in the rules, surely not. Then realised he was placing the letters of the word backwards up the board. No!

He does not know how to play! After all the effort and bribes to get this far I could not very well ask the nurse to move me back and had to go through the charade of playing when all I would be doing would be teaching, therefore not much fun.

After each evening session I had the choice of sleeping over or going home. I preferred to cycle home and sleep in my own bed rather than sleep at the hospital and getting up at 7.00 am so that the day dialysis patient could get stuck into some top-notch dialysising.

I was now dialysing myself from beginning to end: set the machine up (about 40 minutes), weigh myself, take my blood pressure, record all, open up new, well packaged, disposable lines and needles, inject the heparin, the anti clotting agent and, beforehand, the local anaesthetic for the dialysing needles if you were a big softy like me. You are advised to use different entry sites to help enlarge the fistula, which results in several small scabs, so when inserting the needle there is less pain whenever endings are killed off. Then you do not even bother with the local. Then you either sit on the chair or lay on the bed for the next eight hours, or more if you were above your normal weight due to drinking too much since your last session.

As an inpatient I would get many visitors. However as a dialysising out patient attending practically every other day, visits fell dramatically away. I often hinted that someone during, say, a boring Tuesday night might want to come to the hospital and have a game of chess ..or ten but very rarely was the offer taken up. One excuse was the dislike of hospitals, especially the smell. Well join the club. I will never forget those who did visit, especially if I did not know them very well, but will try and forget those who I know better who never did.

One nurse had an unfortunate idiosyncrasy when talking about some patients. I once asked her where one particular patient was who I spoke to from time to time. I had not seen her for sometime and I thought she had got a transplant or began home dialysis. The nurse started giggling and her colleague explained to me that the patient had died and also tried to explain her colleague's strange response when reacting to stressful news.
A Guardian newspaper article:

"When the news cameras have left and a close-up of the kidney machine has been edited for the recent topical news story the patients have to continue with their long session on that dialysis machine. And the general public move on to considering another sympathetic story about people that can no longer take their health for granted. These patients dwell and dream on the fact that they may be on that machine for many years to come.

I came across a four-month project by a photographer named Gina Glover considering how the patients and staff at a dialysis unit coped. She came away clearly educated about the atmosphere within the unit and said such things as "the people in this situation are almost universally brave, courageous, patient, and, in contemplating their individual features, enjoying the philosophical" as far as the staff were concerned she mentioned: "stamina, patience, sense of humour, and understanding of each patient" and pointed out that with all the slagging off that the NHS gets she sees the staffs efficiency and dedication.. She did mention however that when she came to one patient she told her to bog off which I can fully understand"

Coming off and cleaning up afterwards is not straightforward. You do not take the needles out fold your arm and five seconds later put a nice little plaster on, get up and walk out saying: "See you next Tuesday" You're completely drained. In fact you always feel worse afterwards than you did before, the opposite of what other people imagine. You now have to take the last needle out only after the last few red cells of your precious blood go back into you with the extra saline, take the needle out and hold it there for several minutes or put a big clamp on, make sure you do not knock it while you continue with your chores still feeling a bit strange and sometimes light headed as a result of the session. The blood takes much longer to clot because of the heparin that enables your blood to go in and out of body for hours. This is why it is turned off an hour before you come off the machine.

Then you have to take the artificial kidney into a back room and flush it through continually for about 40 minutes, as I recall. Meanwhile you go back to tidy up your cubicle, throwing away all the lines as they are only used once

Then and only then can you go home or go to sleep in your cubicle drawing the screens listening to the evenings session slowly ending as you dose off.

" Michael. It's time to get up. We need your dialysis bay for the day patients. They will be arriving soon and we need to get it all ready" I would then cycle home; luckily most of it was down hill, which was about three miles. And I would usually get in between 1.30 and 2.30 am and be able to listen to the 3am BBC World Service.

Cycling was my usual mode of transport. It was mostly up hill. I would have to force myself to cycle to the next lamppost and then award myself with being allowed to get off and push the bike up the rest of the hill. Once getting off the bike, I had to get my breath back, look down at the bike pretending there was something wrong with it because of the indignity of passers by thinking what an unfit young bloke I was.

One time I had to go through a picket line NUPE (National Union of Public Employees), as they then were, now part of UNISON. I cycled in and was ready to explain why I had to go through thinking about what an interesting conversation I was about to have and they just let me in.

I would occasionally walk to the unit, passing people coming back from work, I distinctly remember one occasion when a family had not drawn their curtains, the lights were on and they all had their meals on their laps as they all watched the telly. They were so engrossed they were not even looking at what they were eating, apart from that millisecond when it was time for the next fork stab. I remember thinking how they had no idea that some of us could not eat what they had on their plate as it could possibly kill us.

One day I was late for my dialysis and had to get a taxi, which I couldn't really afford. I told the driver I needed to go to the hospital and he said "nothing serious I hope." I told him the reason for my journey and you'll never guess what he said, "I 'd rather be dead than be on a kidney machine".

I think it is called a sepulchral silence: that atmosphere inside a church. He probably thought it was the most philosophical thing he had said all day. Apart from "where to mate?" I just stared ahead at the dashboard. I am not usually stumped for an answer in a situation like that but that comment did stop me in my tracks. Part of me wanted to do my usually "I think you'll find your brain already is mate" and get out but I just sat there and said nothing thinking how insensitive he was. To give him the benefit of the doubt he was just ignorant of my plight and was trying to make a conversation. I was not upset: I had long passed that stage. Why is it though, that when you want to feel and be sick you can't be? I could then have accidentally turned away from the window and after the slight mishap say, "I 'd rather be signing on than be a taxi driver and have a passenger throw up all over my lap"

As I got out of his taxi on arrival at the hospital I avoided his gaze in case I saw pity within it and was thinking of giving him a tip - do not consider any volunteering for the Samaritans. ("You wouldn't guess who I had in the back of my taxi yesterday: this ill looking young bloke. Amazing. He was on a kidney machine and wanted to stay alive"). That's the last time I will be using Troglodyte Taxis. I suppose the name gave it away a little.

So what is the fashionable dialysis patient consuming this season?

****

"Excuse me my good fellow but by chance on my mid day perambulation in this fair city I smelt the consequence of your produce where upon I could not help but notice above this fine culinary establishment your sign. Are you able to furnish me post haste with some fish and chips?"

"Are you awright mate?"

"I am fine."

"Good for a moment I thought there was something wrong with you."

"No. May I request that you boil the potatoes that you intend to use for this feast in twice the amount of water usually required for the said root vegetable, then to guarantee you will then pour the resulting liquid away and thereby make the chips with what remains."

"You want some chips?"

"Yes kind sir. Yesterday I had a refreshing and invigorating 8 hour dialysis session but before embarking on my weekly purchases and so replenish my bare larder I require some nourishment."

"Sorry mate I do not know what you are on about. Do you want some chips or what?"

"Yes sir."

"Right. Small or large?"

"Small sir if they could comply with my earlier instructions thus eradicating the high potassium content thereof."

"Sorry mate we do not do potassium chips, just normal."

"That my good sir is my problem. I cannot consume chips as advised by my physician without first following the instructions I have hitherto expressed."

"Look mate let's get this straight: are you asking me to waste 40 minutes boiling your poxy small portion of chips before I fry 'em?"

"Yes sir"

"No sorry too busy and anyway they 'd be nothing left but mush."

"That is where your skill is required."

"No, sorry. Chips, small portion, fried in normal way. Take it or leave it."

"What about the fish."

"Yeah what about it."

"Well could you be so kind as to sell me three ounces of fish."

"LOOK. Are you taking the piss or what? We don't sell fish by the frigging ounce. Now what do you want cod or plaice."

"Either but only 3 ounces."

"Look I'll give you a bunch of fives soon. Sod your three ounces and your ultra boiled chips. Now get lost and do not come back."

"Good day sir."

****

During one car journey we were looking for food in the middle of the countryside but all we found open was a fish and chip shop. I had to sit there as the rest of the hungry car occupants stuffed their face re-offering me chips time and time again not fathoming out why I couldn't eat them even though I had tried to explain many times.

Put that down. You are coming shopping with me .You can carry the basket. Right.   Let's see what the fashionable kidney patient is eating this season.

Frozen section. Grab the milk and that double cream not the single cream the double. Now ignore all the cheese apart from the Caerphilly as it is low sodium cottage cheese. Yoghurt no. Deserts no because no idea of potassium contents on ingredient list on outside

Pork chops. A pack of two will supply several exciting meals. 2oz per meal.

Fresh fruit. Apples (not that many. Can only realistically have one a day). Put the bananas back. Are you trying to kill me?

Vegetables. Carrots, cauliflower and cabbage. Potatoes. Yes but the preparation involved is hardly worth the effort.

Bread. yes but make sure does not contain anything extra like dried fruit.

Rice as long as none of those instant types or those with sauces or seasoning

Eggs. Hey let's be sparing with this one.

Spreads. You can forget about savouries like marmite, Bovril but sweet jams are OK.

Biscuits. As long as no chocolate or dried fruit bits in it. Only one packet as it will count towards my vegetable units.
Non-salted crackers OK

Sweets. Boiled ones fine, but no fruit gums or liquorice

Drinks. Diluted squash, barley cup is fine but do not forget I can hardly drink. No ban on alcohol like lager but for half pint a day is hardly worth it. But never ever strong ale, stout or cider.

Cereals. Basic ones are OK but nothing with extras or high bran contents or muesli.

Tinned food. No tinned vegetables or corned beef. Fruit .a possibility depending on the fruit. Get the tinned pears and fruit salad ones.

Jars/bottles of sauces. Big no no.

If you do not get it right you can end up with the threat of malnutrition. The tendency for depressed people is to eat more as a comforter. I ended up not eating much and even eating under my diet until I was told that could be worse than going over as your body would break down itself and large quantities of potassium would get into my bloodstream.

I heard of a potassium suicide. An elderly man had given up. He could not take the dialysis machine anymore. He went home and consumed large quantities of coffee and chocolate.

It was possible to bake your own bread with flour devoid of protein, so you could eat as much as you liked but I couldn't see the point because over a period of time on such a diet your stomach shrank. I didn't want to encourage it to crave food by eating a lot of food one day and not the next. It was after all bulk food to fill you up. "Dialysis bread: with nowt ever in."

Quite often people simply didn't believe that I had no kidneys. A typical exchange would go like this:

"Would you like a drink?"
"No I cannot drink any more thanks."
"Then have a soft drink"
"Well I cannot drink anything. You see I do not have any kidneys and can only drink very little each day"
"No kidneys. What do you mean you have not got any kidneys"
"Just that. I had both removed. I am on a kidney machine. I had to have them removed, as they were too large. Otherwise I could never be considered for a transplant in the future"
"Gosh. But I did not know you could survive without kidneys .I have heard you can survive with one."
"Yes that is true. People live with one kidney without any problems"
"How can you live with no kidneys"
"Well you go on a kidney machine"
"But you cannot have no kidneys. How do you pee"
"You don't"
"Come on. So how do get rid of the urine"
"You don't make urine"

"So where does all the fluid go"
" It 's taken off while you are on the machine that's why I can't have very much to drink .If I did I could have a brain haemorrhage."
"Your not winding me up are you?"
"No"

If I got really infuriated I'd get them to feel my pounding fistula. Then they could not believe there was anything in there but blood flow.

I even had one of these typical conversations with a qualified nurse whom I had met socially. You will be relieved to learn that she was not a renal nurse or working at the same hospital. She just refused to believe me. She understood the need for a fistula but not the absence of kidneys. I felt her looking at me thinking I was a sad bullshiter. Then she walked away.

Once when I was confronted with another non-believer I turned to my friend for back up and said: "If we added up the number of kidneys we have between us how many would that be", he said "three." The non-believer huffed and walked away. I then asked my friend how many kidneys he had and tried yet again to explain to him I had a deficiency in the kidney department to the tune of two. He knew I was on a kidney machine but had not yet grasped the fact that I had no kidneys.

I went to meet some friends in a pub and just sat with them and after about 20 minutes the landlady came to the table and began to empty and clean the ashtrays and said to me,

"I noticed you been here for some time and you still haven't bought a drink. Can you now get a drink or I will have to ask you to leave."

I took a deep breath and said, "I cannot drink anymore today. You see I have no kidneys" and she said,

"Yeah and my name is Napoleon. Now get out".

So I left her pub leaving her to complete her plans for her advance on Moscow, once she had finished cleaning the ashtrays. I was hoping that the people I were with would show some solidarity but they probably weren't sure whether I was telling the truth themselves so I walked back home.

Walking around on level ground was OK. It was the hills that did me in. It was worse if there were people around, as you did not want to draw attention to yourself. I would need several rests walking up a steep hill. If it was a busy street you could stop and pretend you were looking in a shop window until you realised you were staring at a window full of women's under garments. You would also be breathing heavily and would now really be drawing attention to yourself so the only option was to plod on until you found an acceptable shop window to feign interest in.

On one of my many aimless walks into town I decided to treat myself. Most people do not think twice about popping into a café for a break or a breather if they are in town. They'll buy a drink, possible even a nice piece of cake without much thought. They are probably not in the least bit thirsty or hungry but cannot very well use the café as a resting place without buying something. If you are a dialysis patient, however, it is not as simple as that. Whatever you are about to drink or eat, assuming you find something you can eat on the menu, becomes part of your daily diet. You always have to bear in mind that anything you have now means there is less left for the remainder of the day.

Anyway I went into a cafe and decided to buy something to "eat out", which would mean someone else would have to cook for me. It would not be much but apart from dialysis food at the hospital you have to cook everything yourself. Otherwise you were never able to control what was in the ingredients, such as potassium contents. I studied the menu and deduced that my choice would be egg on toast. I took a seat by the window to watch people walking past in the street out side. Behind me I could hear snippets of the queries from the newly arriving customers. "Do you do olives with your piece of pizza? Oh you don't. Oh in that case I'll have something else then. Now what shall I have?"

When my snack arrived with my small cup of tea brought to my table by the woman who ran the café she said apologetically "sorry I broke the egg so I gave you a second one", glancing at me for a possible thank you but from the look on her face I may not have portrayed the expected look of appreciation back and may have grunted something as a substitute.

I then spent the next 15 minutes or so trying to enjoy the novelty while all the time the second egg stared up at me with its wide innocent yellow eye. Of course I could have eaten it but two eggs (with my diet!) come on! It would have meant reducing my meal meat units that evening or going over my diet limit that day which was a habit I was trying to avoid so I left it on the plate. The cafe owner returned to collect my plate and giving me a quick derisory look as she spotted the non-empty plate, while I finished off my now cold tea and left, not bothering to try and explain.

I had by now, given up trying to explain. It was something no one would immediately accept without me having to go through a full explanation not knowing at the end if they were convinced. So many people making instant judgements because they did not care to stop and consider that I may be telling the truth. Immediate knee jerk responses. I wonder if Gelert would have agreed with me.

I remember two occasions when I needed or thought I needed to go to the loo for a pee. But this was illogical. So convinced was I that I went and nothing happened which my brain was trying to tell me al along but my body was giving a contrary view. Once I realised I was wasting my time I could not get rid of the feeling. In fact the futile attempt had made it worse and it took a long time trying a few mind diversion techniques to slowly take my mind off the urge and rid the feeling away.

Getting support was always a tricky one: I did not want to tell my family and upset my mum and I had learnt not to fish for it with people I knew as they or I could not win. they did not know what to say and what was usually said would ether be something which would indicate lack of understanding of the situation (is you other kidney working OK then?) or a lack of interest or an allegation of moaning. The best place you would have thought would be the unit which indeed it was but once there you would look around at all the other patients and realise they were in far worse situation and it felt totally out of order to raise the matter.

**

Rather than just sign on I looked for voluntary work with a legal slant which might help me in the future. I may as well use the limited amount of legal knowledge I had and see if I could or would want to use it in the real world away which is a far cry from the academic one I had so far only experienced. I spent some time volunteering at the local law centre, which occasionally involved going off to the university to do research, as their library was more extensive.

During the day I would sleep a lot. Walking into town left me feeling slightly alienated. I would notice groups of people in pubs sitting with their pints at the tables where the empty glasses still remained; the restaurants where during the summer you could see people tucking into such things as a T-bone steak which was probably about a week of my meat protein units not to mention the potassium heavy duty vegetables sharing the same plate. Then you would pass some youngster giggling at her holiday snaps in the street, too excited to wait until she got home to look at them.

That reminds me. I must tell you of one holiday abroad story I heard about. A woman was about to ski, had just got all her gear on and was caught short, which is one problem I did not get anymore. She decided to go behind one of the sheds. Unfortunately a gust of wind sent her out from behind her cover and as she was still on her skis she traversed down the slopes, picking up speed follow, follow, follow, followed by a yellow..... That is something I 'll have to forget about: skiing, being abroad and getting caught short. The next time I 'll be caught short will mean I have had a kidney transplant.

Having no kidneys and being on dialysis when your food is limited and your fluid intake is practically reduced to nil obviously reduces your social life. On the occasions I would take up an offer and on this one I went to the local summer festival only to discover that my friends had already been drinking before they pick me up. In fact when I was in the front seat and the driver was those in the car down a long hill I noticed that only that he was drinking a half bottle but on some occasions he would lift it up to his mouth and pulled a few mouthfuls but unfortunately because he was so out of it -- which I was to discover their name -- it sometimes was more than a few mouthfuls. On one occasion I had to take over the steering because while he was all been down the alcohol the car was appearing off the road. I was in no position to do anything but try and survive the journey to the festival site. However on a more humourous note the driver's attempt to get across the suspension Bridge was so hilarious to me that I cried so much that after the event I realised I must have been entitled to at least a quarter pint of water.

To get across the bridge you lead in the 20p coin but the driver didn't have one that I had just one. I had to call in my hand ready to pass over to him when he live opposite the slot machine just in front of the barrier. He managed to drive adjacent to it but unfortunately he was too far away to take the coin open the windows stretches at the heart and find the slot. He therefore had to reverse and coming near. There was however a queue behind in hand the card beats began and all of them had to reverse because he had to reverse. He brought in along the coin slot; I carefully handed to him the only 20p coin in the car. He took it he leant out of the window; he dropped it. He then opened the door to retrieve it is now too near the coin slot machine and he couldn't open the doors of visionary him to get outside sending down to the floor and search for the coin. This meant he had to reverse. Again. And again the card beats start off again this time far more aggressively.

Meanwhile all this shunting back and forward and dancing around the coin machine resulted in another friend who was also drunk being sick account of the passenger back seat window directly behind me. At this point I was glad I didn't have to go through the trauma of overindulgence in alcohol considering I can't even overindulging water.

Eventually the coin was spotted. He walked back to the car got in drove gingerly up to the coin slot machine and very carefully what the coin in the slot and the barrier shot up and he had to quickly readjusts to the continuation of the journey and travel on to the festival site.

As I mentioned earlier I was not in a state to even help him because I was helping helpless with laughter but I lost so much fluid I thought I was entitled to a nice drink of water when we got there.

Ding dong merrily on dialysis. It's Christmas time. I do not like this festive season at the best of times and nor do many others. Take George Bernard Shaw for example:

"It really is an atrocious institution, this Christmas. We must be gluttonous because it is Christmas. We must be drunken because it is Christmas .We must be insincerely generous; we must buy things that nobody wants and give them to people we don't like, all because it is Christmas – that is because the mass of the population, including the all-powerful, middle-class tradesman, depends on a week of licence and brigandage, waste and intemperance, to clear off its outstanding liabilities at the end of the year"

Not sure if I follow the last bit, even after looking up the words   brigandage (plunder) and intemperance (overindulgence). Many people round about this time of year go in to debt or increase their existing indebtedness. I particularly feel sorry for impoverished pensioners who sometimes starve themselves to be able to buy a gift for each of their grandchildren while keeping their financial problems quiet from their own children because they feel embarrassment by their poverty.

During this period many hospital patients are sent home for a few days and that of course does not relate just to kidney patients. Although not an in-patient I was given the option to dialyse in the hospital in my family's town for a week or so. In previous months my folks made provisional enquiries as to whether I could move up to their home and dialyse there indefinitely as I would then not living on my own. My parents were discouraged in pursuing this enquiry as there are only a fixed amount of hospital dialysis places and with the resulting administrative chaos, I could lose my place on the dialysis programme which would be a bit of problem. However a few sessions away would not cause any confusion, as everyone was aware when my next session was scheduled for in the New Year. I was not sure if living with my parents would help anyone. My Mum would be reminded every day of what I was going through. Also I may have gone down hill if people began to look after me. I felt having to fend for myself kept me going.

The sad thing is I was looking forward to it. I would get away from my student/hospital town which I had not left for over a year or more, I would see my family, live in a warm house, and this is the really sad bit, see how another kidney unit worked and meet other patients, doctors and nurses as my social life was not actually that full.

They were pretty tough up there: they did not use "locals" before inserting the large dialysis needles. Luckily for me I had by this time accumulated a nice range of hardened scabs on my arm. Something a heroin addict would envy. There were many sites available as all the nerve endings were dead it did not hurt too much when inserting the needles without a local.

You were allowed a reprieve from the strict diet during x-mas. I guess this was a decision reluctantly made by the doctors as people were bound to be unable to resist the temptation of brussel sprouts, mince pies, Christmas pudding, all very high in potassium. There was a catch: to be allowed this concession you had to drink this gritty drink, resonium, because the powdery substance tendered not to dissolve properly in water. It also was part of your fluid intake for the day. It seemed pointless having to take something nasty just to be able to have something pleasant later on.

This medicine, resonium, taken several times would apparently "push" the potassium out of your blood stream into your tissue until your next session. I for one could not see the point. I would rather not take it. It was just like the first hour on the machine or the offer of dialysis bread. You might as well accept it; you cannot have these foods. No point. Just forget about it. Accept your lot. You do not need to be reminded of what you cannot eat.

The relative visiting and the largely attended festive meals made sure you did not. "Is that all you're having?", "Christmas cake?", "Nuts?" "Mince pie?", "Grapes?".

"Chocolate? Go on a few want kill you (don't bank on it mate ...I mean auntie)

I returned to my usual unit in the New Year and thankfully they were expecting me, as there was a place for me at my next designated session.

It was a cold winter that year. Snow blankets took sometime to melt. For a week or so the water pressure was low due to burst pipes and the supply was intermittent. So much so that the neighbourhood around the hospital had no supplies for certain times in the day as the hospital took priority. Not only were we very expensive patients but we were now also taking the local tax payers regular water supply. This water crisis sent the regular dialysis sessions into chaos. Not all the machines in the unit could work at the same time due to the reduced water pressure. Only about half were in use. This meant it was three sessions every 24hours as opposed to the usual two. There were lots of unfamiliar faces particularly those patients that had to be called in as they would usually dialyse at home. They had insufficient reliable water pressure in their town to get the machine to work. You would consequently turn up for your regular session and wait hours for a machine to become free. I got curious about what would happen if there was a power cut. What would happen to us?. I was reassured that the hospital had its own generator, which would automatically kick in if there was a power cut. I was told this had already happened recently but it worked so well you did not really notice.

It has to be mentioned that many people on dialysis are able to hold down a full time job and many of these jobs are very physical such as labouring. I suppose I could have claimed a sickness or disability benefit rather than sign on as just someone unemployed but I did not want to institutionalise myself. During the period when the sessions were in confusion due to frozen water pipes I was late signing on.

At the DHSS, as it then was I got to the front of the queue to sign on and was asked why I was late. When I explained that I had been on a kidney machine I heard a chuckle behind me and only realised its significance when the DSS officer attitude changed and her lips thinned. Then I realised they were sniggering at my explanation and the official thought I was being sarcastic to her. She then asked me to sign below the note she had just written on my file, which said something like: "Was late because he said he was on a kidney machine." I signed somewhat saddened that everyone around me thought I was lying. When I had finished signing I turned around to leave taking the opportunity to glance at the people in the queue and was met with two smiling young males, one who had his thumb up saying "nice one mate, nice one". I was getting used to people disbelieving about the lack of kidneys but not believing I was even a dialysis patient was a first.

Cycling back from the unit early one winter morning I came across a car stuck in the snow being pushed by three blokes. " 'scuse me mate you couldn't help us here for a mo. Need help getting this car moving." I wanted to say no but what could I say that would be believed "sorry mate, weakling, just come off a kidney machine. No energy. Totally knackered." I am sure I would not get an understanding response, probably a sarcastic dig as I cycled off at about two miles per hour to my bed. So I got off my pushbike and went to help push the car. I am sure I did not help much. I may have even hindered. Had they looked to their side they would have noticed that their new mate kept on disappearing. I was usually to be found hanging on to the bumper being dragged along making the job even more difficult for my healthier young male colleagues. Eventually their car started to work again and I had to go in search of my bike in the bleak rural white landscape. Ignoring my psychiatrist's advice, I walked along the desolate street expecting to find my relatively new bike pinched but to my surprise the loyal thing was still there, exactly where I had left it on its side munching its bail of hay without a care in the world.

Years before when I had my school boy paper round I recollect cycling home in weather very similar to this when I skidded on some ice at a roundabout, fell off the bike and knocked myself out. I remember coming round, not knowing were I was, not being able to get up apart for a second when I would have to lay down again as if to go back to sleep. On one of these attempted head raises I saw a milk float approaching. When the two occupants got to me they picked me up put me back on my bike and just pushed me off. I was now in double shock: first the concussion and secondly the realisation I was being placed in jeopardy by being sent on a journey where I had not really got my senses back. Somehow I cycled all the way home, put the bike in the garage and went to lie down. I then woke some time later thinking I had missed my paper round and dreamt it all. It was only when I inspected my damaged bike that the reality truly stuck me and was amazed at not having been run over.

I could easily sleep eighteen hours a day especially if I over did it on the protein. In the winter it was even more tempting to crawl into bed because the only heater was a one bar electric fire. To be able to get up in the morning, I had set up the electrics so that I could turn it on from my bed before releasing myself into the cold room. While in bed I heard a noise from inside the wall and wondered what it was. Then it dawned on me: a chimney. I jumped out of bed and tapped the wall in the general area of what looked like a fireplace and I quickly fathomed out it was only covered by hardboard and wallpaper. So I went to work in dismantling it - bugger what the landlord may think. It was freezing. I found a fireplace set into the wall.

Before planning a big fire I crumpled up some newspapers and set fire to them ready to put them out if the chimney was blocked which it did not appear to be. To be doubly sure I went out into the street, looked up the house and saw evidence of smoke .I then set to work searching the neighbourhood for skips and to my delight noticed some council workers up trees with chain saws. I was able to scavenge some chunky logs.

I enjoyed making my own real fire and would spend many hours staring into the red and yellow glow thinking very deeply. Maybe too deeply but it was a wonderful escape and warm.

The rest of the house caught on and the house caught fire. I was in a local pub presumably nursing a coke or if I was really going for it, a half pint of lager that had to last me the whole of the time I remained there. It was on one of those very rare occasions when I had not yet had my full quota for the day. Then one of my housemates ran in to report that the house was on fire and the fire brigade had just arrived. It transpired that the person sitting next to me had left his fire blazing away without a fire guard using wood that would splinter and jump out of the fire which is exactly what happened. One piece jumped out landing between the wall and his bed. Luckily only his room was burnt out. The housemates had to team up to clear and redecorate his room so that the landlord would not find out. No doubt he would have banned all real fires and bricked up all the fireplaces.

The remnants of the fire were thrown out of his window to the cemented front garden. Passers by would stop asking inane questions like, "what happened here then?" My riposte would be: "Well we had a house warming party and it got a bit out of hand" but I thought better of it as they might know the landlord and grass us up so I repressed my sardonic lip.

Another reason I did not want to worry the landlord was in case the hospital authorities decided to investigate the possibility of installing a kidney machine in my room and send a day nurse to be with me whilst I dialysed. I could be creating a bottleneck in the unit as it was always meant to be a temporary arrangement.

Others would remain at the unit because of the difficulties in dialysising at home such as the partner not being able to cope. Once you were trained and so able to put your self on and off the machine you were usually expected to get a machine fitted at home but you needed a partner or reliable relative or friend willing to be with you through out the sessions as many things could occur most notably the lowering of blood pressure, thus going hypo and fainting. Also you needed to either be a homeowner or be given permission from your landlord to allow the alterations. I failed on all counts. The instalment cost would be about £1,000.00 (at the time) and would include plumbing it into the main water supply.

I was concerned that the landlord may think he could be legally obliged to have this installed with the resulting plumbing and try and get me to move out. Anyway I did not fancy evenings in by my real fire with a hot cocoa- OK skip the hot cocoa- browsing through that new style magazine "Home and Dialysis Room". "It is that heparin moment when you know, once again, you will soon have to leave the best decorated room in the house."

The main reason the hospital was content that I remain dialysising at the unit was that there was a possibility of a kidney being donated from one of my relatives.

Throughout this period there was interest by some of my relatives to donate a kidney, which was very kind of them. I did not really show much appreciation at the time of what they were willing to do. I guess I was emotionally neutered .It was eventually down to my sister and my Dad. The doctors were very wary of allowing women of childbearing age to lose a kidney especially when sometimes after the birth both of a mother's kidneys can collapse. A few sessions or weeks or months on a kidney machine, taking the pressure off the kidney somehow allow them to recuperative. Other times they do not and they have to wait like others for a suitable transplant. This happened to one of the patients whom I often spoke to during our dialysis sessions.

My Dad therefore became a contender. Initially I tried to put him off. Another patient in the same unit who was much younger than me had refused point blank to allow his father to donate a kidney how ever much his father convinced him he wanted to donate. I did not take that hard line and felt guilty being so selfish. My Dad had never been in hospital in his life (like father not like son) he had just started his own business and being away for the operation and the inevitable period of convalescing meant he would have had to plan the timing very carefully. The main issue of course was he - or was I - compatible? The first tests showed it was not going to be a perfect match but it could be a match of sorts.

The first hurdle was confirming that we had the same blood type but it was the tissue matching that needed careful investigation. In very simple terms tissue matching can be seen as comparing six heads. If it was a 6-6 match you had just met your identical twin. This would be the only real perfect match where you did not even have to take any drugs to keep your body's immune system at bay. If it were a 1-6 or 2-6 the kidney would immediately reject if the operation took place. If it was a 5-6 it was, to all intents and purposes a "perfect" match. I do not know where my Dad came in on all this but probably something in between.

The test was to see how my body reacted to my dad's blood. When people have a blood transfusion, if it is the same group your body can still react to it, recognising it as foreign but not resulting in any damage or symptoms and still be a good blood donation. If my body reacted in anyway to my Dad's blood the transplant would be off because it was then bound to react to the kidney and attack it as soon as it was implanted even with the use of the anti rejection drugs. This was made very clear very early on.

I was only to find out the whole truth of what next happened years later and had I not written this book I would probably never have known. Dad showed my doctors an article from the Lancet, a medical journal, about how American doctors who, well before such a transplant, regularly got the donor to give blood transfusions to the recipient. This was an extra precaution to be sure the transplant would not reject. My doctors agreed to go with it but made it clear to my Dad that if there were any negative results the operation would be off. He accepted that and they went ahead. I would receive the blood during several of my sessions on the machine. He would get up at 5.30am on the days he would travel down to my unit to give blood in the many months before the planned operation. It was also decided that my sister would no longer be considered any further for the transplant.

Also his kidneys themselves had to be checked. Firstly for function, also checking his blood vessels near his kidneys were fine, checking they were not strangely wired up, which can happen. Some people can live a totally healthy life without ever realising they are differently plumbed urologically. Some later in life are found to have even three kidneys, which is not a big problem. The doctors also had to decide which of the kidneys to take out.

A few weeks before the final decision whether the operation could go ahead I was walking in the city centre with my Dad who was about to cross the road and had not noticed a bus heading straight for him and so – as you do- I pulled him back and with mock indignation he accused me of thinking of more than just safeguarding him from injury and more concerned with the valuable cargo he had on board.

CHAPTER FIVE:
No Longer Half Welsh, Half Irish

We were all set. The operation – or should that be operations -were going to go ahead. But when? Would it be successful? My Dad had to sort out all his business affairs and plan for the few weeks afterwards. He would clearly have to convalesce because the body of the donor in a transplant operation will be in more shock than the recipient who was going to gain from it.

The night before the big day I went to visit him in his ward, which was at the other end of the hospital. We were looked after by completely different set of doctors so there was never any conflict of interest between my Dad's health and my own.

CLICK...WKQ: 2+1+1=3

Coming round was not as traumatic as the bilateral nephectomy. The nurses, some of whom I know very well by now told me they always knew I was OK as soon as they heard intensive swearing coming from my bed. There is nothing much wrong with a complaining noisy patient. The quiet ones are usually the cause for concern, especially when they have not regained consciousness by the expected time. Apparently farting is also a good sign because it means your system is moving again after all the anaesthesing drugs. (I must remember this excuse next time I am in my next law lecture.)

Back at the ward I was moved to my own special room in the transplant unit where the process of " reverse barrier nursing" was to begin. It was the quantity of urine produced that was the most important indicator of all. Having said that you still had to check it was removing the toxins from your body and not accept it just on face value. I was on a saline drip, not allowed to drink normally at first. The fluid amount was monitored so they could tell how much goes in and comes out, an indicator of kidney function. The transplanted kidney is not put where naturally placed kidneys reside but at the front in the abdomen just above the groin.

When I came around I was extremely thirsty but was not allowed any food or drink. I was allowed ice cubes to suck for my very dry mouth. It also had the advantage for the nurse attending to me that I would shut up and stop moaning about the pain and discomfort.

Barrier nursing is used where a patient has a contagious condition and segregated from the rest of the ward or hospital. It usually brings forward images of people returning from a tropical climate with a condition that if not contained could spread very quickly. Only official visitors such as doctors and nurses can enter your room, then only with masks to protect themselves from the patient.

However reverse barrier nursing is where you, the immunosuppressed patient is protected from everyone else because you could pick up any virus on offer with dangerous consequences. I was to be in this strange world for a week. No visitors, no books or magazines, anything from the outside for the next seven days. No get-well cards although nurses would read them out. I became aware of their relevance, possibly for the first time in my life. I just lay there with my pain-killing drug drip (luxury); a catheter exuding a strange yellow fluid I had not seen for ages; the extra non-intrusive catheter for draining off my wound and all the heart monitor connections on my chest.

The ward was in the middle of leafy grounds but if my room could have been transported along side a high street pavement, passers-by could look in and wonder, "why is everyone in there making so much fuss about that bloke in the bed and his bag of urine." They would not see many smiles just mine, as all the others would be wearing masks but could see, like me, just smiling eyes. And with all those happy eyes things were looking up.

Visitors could come to the entrance to my room and sometimes they came up to the outside window. My dad could visit me but I could not visit him. A nurse from the dialysis unit came to the window just after she began her shift to see how I was.

One day I thought, hey I should have been on my eight-hour dialysis session yesterday and I didn't go. I didn't have to go. Maybe this kidney transplant think might work as it is working so far.

On the third day I was taken to the X-ray department, a nice trip out for me, to check the kidney and see how it looked. This appeared a bit risky considering all the potential viruses hanging about the hospital corridors but the x-ray was essential. The hospital, I guess, could not afford a massively expensive x-ray machine for that unit. It was presumably a calculated risk as long as I spent as little time as possible away from my germ free room.

On my way back to my room I noticed a young girl in the other reverse barrier nursing room who apparently had also just had a transplant. This was confirmed by the nurses. Her darkened skin colour was due to her very low iron count. It was caused because of her parent's recent conversion to the Jehovah Witness religion. An apparent doorstep conversion no less. The parents had refused any blood transfusions throughout her period of renal failure. Haemoglobin counts for healthy males are about 13 and for women theirs can sometimes be slightly less than that. At this time while I was on dialysis mine was about 7. This poor girl's was 5.

This religion forbade blood transfusion because it says in the bible something equivalent to "thou shalt not take another mans blood. Verily" I would have thought that meant do not stab him and take his blood. It would hardly say, "oh and by the way when thou discovereth blood transfusion that also is included" and "thou shalt not have a kidney transplant". What did they think was in the kidney? Ribena?

From my little knowledge of the law I did not understand why the hospital authorities could not apply to the High Court to make her a Ward of Court. Maybe her life was not in danger. I felt annoyed for her and like a frustrated Jehovah's Bystander. I understand that during these operations extra measures need to be taken to collect any blood that is lost during the operation so that it could be recycled back into the body. (Definitely not a practise that any pub landlord should do with any spilt beer!). But what would have happened if there was a problem during the operation and extra blood was urgently needed? Religion. Eh?

I have since done a bit of research into this religion. Genesis 9: 3-6 "Everything that lives and moves will be food for you.......But you must not eat meat that has it's life blood still in it." That is one of the biblical references they quote to explain their belief. OK chaps, if you are going to take the bible literarily let's not pick and choose. Hope no one worked on their web site seven days a week. Exodus 31.16 "Whoever does any work on the Sabbath day must be put to death"

If a member of the fellowship got ready for an illicit rendezvous one night and borrowed their sisters expensive scarf because it was a bit nippy be warned: Deuteronomy 22.5: "A women must not wear men's clothing, nor a man wear woman's clothing, for the Lord your God detests anyone who does this." Deuteronomy 22.9: "Do not wear clothes of wool and linen woven together". Deuteronomy 22.22: If a man is found sleeping with another man's wife, both the man who slept with her and the women must die"

And if someone nicks some grapes and then does not pay an old debt don't forget to let them off. Deuteronomy 23.24 "If you enter your neighbours vineyard, you may eat all the grapes you want, but do not put any in your basket" (psst: take a big paper bag, in the bible it doesn't say you cannot). Deuteronomy 15.1 "At the end of every seven years you must cancel debts."

In my book ("The Book According To Me. Chapter 1 Verse 1") I think there is a bit of cherry picking going with or without a basket.

I investigated to see if, since my week in the barrier room, they had changed their attitude to blood transfusions. Nope. Well er :

"The Watchtower Society has issued new instructions requiring
Jehovah's Witnesses to offer greater resistance to court-ordered
blood transfusions.

The June 15, 1991 _Watchtower_ magazine (p. 31) suggests that
JWs "avoid being accessible" for such a court-ordered transfusion by fleeing the scene, or else follow the example of a 12-year-old girl who had been taught to "fight any court-authorized transfusion with all the strength she could muster... scream and struggle...pull the injecting device out of her arm and...attempt to destroy the blood in the bag over her bed."

The _Watchtower_ article states that this course is to be
followed even if such action might make the Jehovah's Witness "a lawbreaker or make him liable to prosecution" by the authorities. While medical personnel generally agree that adults have the right to refuse treatment, hospitals routinely obtain court orders when children of Jehovah's Witnesses require transfusions and the parents refuse to consent. In the past, many Jehovah's Witness parents appeared content to leave the matter there: they were freed of responsibility in the eyes of their leaders, while at the same time the child's life could be saved. (Watchtower rules mandate the punishment of shunning for any who accept blood willingly.)

But now hospitals can expect many more Jehovah's Witnesses to follow the headline-making course that only a few took in the past. Obedient to the new instructions, Witness parents may either physically intervene to obstruct treatment or else abduct the child from the hospital and flee -- regardless of whether this will make them lawbreakers liable to prosecution.

-- David A. Reed"

It looks like they also need to wake up to another one of their "current beliefs" as that is how they strangely worded it in answers to questions on their mail bag web site page. To the question why they do not kick out child molesters they answer that to be " disfellowshipped .... the present judicial process demands that there must be two witnesses to such crimes". Well what about, where there is only one witness, at least a bit of shunning which is the punishment dished out to those members who are found to have committed the despicable offence of accepting a blood transfusion.

Anyway back to me. A cardiologist would arrive in the early days wheeling in a little trolley carrying a portable ECG scanner but then:

"It was just like any other day in the barrier room. But for one man things were about to change for the worse. From a distant part of the hospital complex, just after elevenses, approached a member of another sector of the medical professional that was to make his life hell for the next few days. Little did he know that just out of sight behind the reverse barrier room door a woman was slowly but efficiently putting on!!: Her white gloves and then!!: Her white mask? Suddenly, without warning the door to his room swung open and his quiet life would end forever. It was: The Physiotherapist! Then he was to hear the immortal words:

"Oh hello Michael how are you today. I must say you look much better. Already you are getting a sign of healthy looking rosy cheeks. Looks like the kidney is taking well. Had any visitors today?"

But I knew what was coming: torture. It was imperative that I did not get an infection in my chest but I could not cough properly because the scaring made it feel as if my insides were about to rip open. Anyway we had many very pleasant sessions together when she said "come on you can do better than that" and I would say "it is all very well

114

for you but you do not know how painful it is." It is very strange. For me it is as if there is a built in mechanism to stop the cough just as you breath in and about to go for it. I could have put my hand in a fire or done something that would not take a few seconds to prepare for but coughing or clearing your throat was extremely difficult to carry out. You would start, then at the last second your body would remind your brain that telling your mouth to cough was a really dumb idea because you know how painful it was going to be if you continued the process. I do not think that if someone put a gun to my head and said "cough" I could have done a fully fledged cough. I am sure other people who have had an abdominal operation would know what I am getting at.

It was, however, very important because unlike my previous operation I was now immunosuppressed and more likely to get an infection. After my bilateral nephrectomy I was out of bed after a few days and forced, sorry invited, to walk around. Now I was stuck in the reverse barrier room, unable to walk around.

I began to make some subtle enquiries as to when I would be off the dialysis diet but for the first few days it was not allowed until they knew I had a successful transplant. I was producing urine again which was promising but not conclusive. On each occasion a meal arrived I, at a glance knew I was still on my dialysis diet until out of the blue a nurse offered me my first cup of coffee, explaining the doctors had just sanctioned it. I was off the dialysis diet. This strange drink did not arrive during the normal meal and drink times so it arrived in a small plastic cup. A treat from one of the nurses with further encouragement to drink lots. It was easily the best cup of coffee I had tasted in ages for one simple reason: it was the first time I tasted and drunk coffee for just under two years. I was now to go from the medical advice of do not drink very much to drink loads.

Having a catheter into your bladder was arguably more painful for men than for women especially in the morning when .... (Oh it doesn't matter.) During the rest of the week all the tubing was gradually removed from my body, the first being the heart monitors, then the catheter to my wound and then the painkiller drip.

When the seven days were up I was moved to a normal room and began walking around the ward with a nurse holding me in case I fell over, still with my bladder catheter. Then the biggie :on my own up the ward corridor. The trick here is not to forget you still have a catheter attached so when you stop to talk to someone such as a nurse, cleaner, fellow patient or you simply need a breather, you must remember to pick it up before you continue your expedition or ....eck.

Dr Phil Hammond mentions this in his comedy stage act when medical students played a certain sporting activity. Footballs were original made from animal bladders. Well these students apparently used the bladder as the goal, not the ball. Inserting two adapted catheters together and they would pee into each other's bladders. Was it worth it fellas? Look at the discomfort enjoyment ration. I just hope they had to insert a normal one so they learnt what patients had to go through or pee through.

I was always apprehensive about the day the nurse came to take the catheter out but once done I felt sort of human again. Also gone were the calcium, iron and vitamin tablets. In had come the steroid and immunosuppressive. I was still to take blood pressure tablets for a while until they were, hopefully, no longer needed. The steroids and immunosuppressive were to be gradually reduced to a maintenance dose assuming there were no complications over the coming weeks and months.

Once they took the catheter out I was faced with the rather easy task of peeing when my bladder was full. I had not peed for over a year, my bladder muscles were very weak and I now had to build up those muscles to be able to pee naturally again now the catheter was out. When I had my first historic pee it wasn't as if I was going to fill a water tank. My bladder had been empty for a long time. I was therefore advised that every 15 minutes I should try even if I did not feel the need. This way I would build up the bladder muscles. So I brushed away all the cobwebs and got to work. It was very strange seeing what most people never take a second glance at.

Pointing Percy at the porcelain. A very common euphemism for when blokes go to the loo. Although I have just had – so far, anyway -a successful kidney transplant, it will take sometime before I could pee without walking away from it. I now have to collect it on a regular basis so that test can be carried out to monitor the kidney as the first few weeks and months were the most trying. Also my input and output was measured to check I was not retaining any fluid that would be a concern and of course I was regularly weighed.

The medical school from another part of the hospital asked me if I would mind having photos taken of what turned out to be classic acne symptoms brought on by steroids. The symptoms would reduce over the next few weeks and months and they wanted the photos quickly for their medical journal. So I then went to the dermatitis ward to be photographed with the reassurance that my face would not be included in the publication. I had my first ever photo shoot and thought of asking if they wanted my worst side, then returned to my ward.

I was able to meet up with my Dad. We went for what seemed like a long walk in the hospital grounds. With all the groans emanating from both of us I reckoned if we had a drum machine and a mixer we could have made a few ambient records. Although we were in the hospital grounds I knew I was not out of the woods yet. These were the crucial days: to see if the kidney would take. Doctors had noticed that with all transplants, towards the end of the second week the body seems to have get a second wind, a new burst of energy to attack the alien kidney. What ever happened I would not be regularly peeing blood ever again. Or so I thought.

One late evening I was in my room and lay on my bed hearing this weird buzzing noise in my ears. It was very strange and I hadn't experienced anything like it before. After an operation or after just taking a new drug or when really ill you expect something new. A new pain, a new symptom but this was completely out of the blue. This was a new one so I waited in anticipation. After lying there for while I had this urgent need to go to the toilet, I walked across the hallway to the toilet locked the door and as I sat down all hell broke loose: I simultaneously bled from every orifice apart, I think, from my ears. I thought: so this is it then. I slipped off the seat, fainting, collapsing on to the toilet floor. I don't know how long I was unconscious for, probably a few minutes but when I came around I thought: crikey I am still alive. I heard female voices. They were the nurses banging on the door asking me to unlock it. I was lying on a NHS hospital toilet covered in my own blood with what must have been pints of it all over the toilet floor. You will be sad to learn that I did not shake my head vigorously to bring myself round quickly like in the movies but I stood up, managed to open a door, the nurses grabbed me and walked me back to my room across the hallway whilst the doctor was called. (An angel of a doctor? A saviour of doctors?)

I was very quickly put on a special type of drip because there was no time to get blood nor get it cross matched. They had to get fluid into my body as quickly as possible not only to save me but also to try and save the recently transplanted kidney that was going through a bit of a roller coaster ride itself. They then had to put one of those drips that go up your nose. As seen on cheap television programmes for dramatic effect but for those lucky actors it would just be placed under their nose. For most real patients they usually had it inserted while they were still unconscious. I unfortunately remained conscious but there was no time for pleasantries. It went up my nose and down into my stomach so as to drain out all the blood. Was this a stomach pump? It was very uncomfortable especially when it had to change direction at the top of my nose; I was constantly sipping water trying to help the process. I then lay on my bed while I was cleaned up but for the rest of the night I could not really sleep thinking how lucky I was and that had I previously been sent home and this happened anywhere but a hospital I would have clearly not survived.

What had occurred was that with my weak stomach (my dad told me I inherited a weak stomach off him. I also answer to the name of lucky) and the high doses of steroids, I had severe internal bleeding, known as huge hemotemisis. How the nurses found me was pretty lucky and a tribute to their dedication to their duties. Maybe someone was looking for me or noticed a sound coming from the toilet that was like the tap was on full. "Michael what are you doing in there." and that's when I must have come round. If they had banged on the door I could not have done anything while it was all happening and was just disgorging. I was just a mere observer. I could not have spoken. If I could I might have said something like: "Sorry spot of bother with the old internal bleeding. Must splash"

It was also the night that a newly qualified doctor was in charge of a ward for the very first time as she told me afterwards. She must have been thinking gosh they couldn't all be as eventful as this.

In the morning during the doctors round I smiled at them as they entered and was jokingly asked why I was smiling. As they left one of them said " Michael we nearly lost you last night"

I joked later that I thought my kidney was rejecting, that somehow it had slipped its moorings down in my lower abdomen and somehow passed through a blender and then out. You always hear even then about the dreaded "r" word from other patients and the risk with all transplants. I had got my first, and it was not to be my last personal experience of it.

I was eventually discharged and put on a drug to help protect my weak stomach lining, warned against taking aspirin, being sick and retching as both could bring on internal bleeding. I went home with a big bag of exciting new drugs. (Something for nothing eh?) And a:

"STEROID TREATMENT CARD

I am a patient on STEROID treatment, which must not be stopped suddenly.

•If you have been taking this medicine for more than three weeks, the dose should be reduced gradually when you stop taking steroids unless your doctor says otherwise.

•Read the patient information leaflet given with the medicine.

•Always carry this card with you and show it to anyone who treats you (for example a doctor, nurse, pharmacist or dentist) For one year after you stop the treatment, you must mention that you have taken steroids

•If you become ill, or if you come into contact with anyone who has an infectious disease, consult your doctor promptly. If you have never had chickenpox, you should avoid close contact with people who have chickenpox or shingles. If you do come into contact with chickenpox, see your doctor urgently

•Make sure the information on the card is kept up to date"

The information refers to your present dose, which is written on the inside of the card.

The steroids do change your appearance and there are a few possible side effects. Taken from "the patient information sheet" that I guess most never read we have the possibility of the delights of indigestion, peptic ulcers, increased appetite, weight gain, swollen abdomen (just like old times but not as severe I hope); ulceration or thrush of the throat; severe upper abdominal pain, unusual growth of hair, fatigue or drowsiness, swollen feet or ankles (ditto for my ditties); high blood pressure (oh referee!); muscle weakness, brittle bones, tendon problems; acne, thinning of the skin leading to bruising, stretch marks , broken veins or slow healing; mood changes and insomnia ; problems with your eyes including glaucoma and worsening of eye infections , increased likelihood of infection and thrombosis. There is mention of slowed growth for a child patient and stopping of, or irregular periods for women. The changed appearance brought on by weight gain is more pronounced for women because, I am lead to believe, of their different fat /muscle ratio compared with men.

Now the good news: these are just possible side effects. Now weight gain and voracious appetite are guaranteed. The latter ensures an increase in the former and even more likely because for the first time in many years many patients can eat what they like.

In one book written for the medical profession mention is made of weight gain, swollen abdomen and thin arms and legs, the latter not mentioned above, and describes the a patient as "A lemon on two matchsticks." Now I have the utmost regard for the medical profession in their work to keep my fellow renal patients and me alive but I do not think these jokey descriptions helps the new generation of medical students. When they put the book down and enter the ward it does nothing to remind them that they are dealing with other humans and not a fruit cartoon character. I think we can all work out what a torso could look like given the above side effects with arms and legs that can be thinner than usual.

To the author who probably chewed on the end of his glasses as he thought of a funny catchy description, remember the occasional patient may read your stuff. They have had years of looking in the mirror each morning, seeing how unwell they look. Occasionally the finger may well be pointed at patients that may have, in part, contributed to their particular organ failure, whether it be the liver, lungs, heart or even skin but the kidney is one you cannot even begin to protect by a slight change in life style. Now after a possible new life they have to cope with an overnight different set of appearance changes. So remember do not mock appearances over which people have no control over. Four Eyes!

Please note that these are not to be confused with anabolic steroids that the ridiculously looking musclemen use. There were several unpleasant side effects such as a permanently swollen face very noticeable in the early weeks before your dose could be reduced. It is the side effect that concerned me the most.

Before being discharged from the hospital I visited the dialysis ward at the other end of the hospital complex and my Dad, rather considerately, suggested we took a box of chocolates for the nurses in that ward who had helped keep me alive before a kidney became available. The doctors used to work in both units and the nurses in the transplant unit were there for the happy times. These nurses appreciated this gesture and commented that they were often over looked at this happy time once the patient was freed from the regular attendance at their unit.

I discovered the surgeon was a Rolling Stones fan and a friend of mine had a bootleg of one of their concerts. So I sent him a copy. Hopefully it would be more appreciated than the many bottles of drink he must get. He will probably never have to buy one for a party or meal ever again.

"A New Beginning"

Along with hundreds of other students, law graduate Michael O'Sullivan this month began a new academic year. Nothing unusual about that you may say, but there is something very unusual about Michael. This 26-year-old law finals student under went a kidney transplant only two months ago, and has recovered well enough to be able to enrol on the course he had hoped to complete last year.

Michael suffered with the hereditary condition polycystic kidneys, and after years of treatment and special diets, had both kidneys removed in August 1981, because they had grown so large. This operation resulted in hospitalisation for two months and dialysis treatment every other day. Michael heard of the necessity to remove his kidneys in the same post as he heard of his degree award. He began his Law Society course, but the operation took its toll on him and with such side effects as loss of memory, he felt unable to complete the course.

It became apparent that Michael would need a transplant, and the quest for a donor began. His father proved to be partially compatible, and a transfusion test was needed to see if his blood would be rejected. Fortunately it was not, so the transplant went ahead. This was successful, and was followed by a period of "reverse barrier nursing", where Michael was ensconced in a germ free room, allowed no visitors, given high dosages of drugs to combat infection. This was a trying time for him, but well worth it, apart from one slight setback, Michael has progressed since then, and is now feeling much better.

Apart from one or two side effects of the drugs, Michael says it is a marvellous to be able to abandon the restricted diet he has followed for the last three years, and is obviously delighted to be able to start on his Law Society course. His father has also recovered well from the operation.

Mike is a great supporter of the kidney donor scheme, and although he obviously is unable to contribute in that way, he carries a card indicating his willingness to donate any of his organs to those who need it. He hopes that readers will be inspired by his story, and he will be carrying cards to distribute to those who feel they would like to join the scheme. It would be one way of paying tribute to the marvellous work done by the kidney unit at our own XXXXXXX hospital, where all Michael's treatment has taken place, and may ultimately represent another "new beginning" for a fellow human being."

When the Polytechnic found out about my story I was asked if I would like to be interviewed for their internal newsletter. If you have been paying attention you will spot some errors in the resulting article above and all my own fault:

1. There is no treatment for polycystic kidneys. Yes you can reduce the symptoms but no treatment in the sense you can cure the problem or even slow down the deteriorating function .You will not hear "the treatment has worked" which can be the case with other conditions.

2. They were not removed because they were too big but primarily because otherwise there would have been no room for a possible future transplant

3. Before the operation I was already undergoing dialysis treatment.

4. I was told I would have to start dialysis – not have my kidneys removed - the day I heard I had got my degree.

5. I lost my memory when my kidneys were removed and had recovered before I attempted the course but left it because it was impossible to continue with dialysing three days a week.

6. Became apparent? I had no kidneys. It did not become apparent. We somehow knew already I needed a transplant.

7. On a more medical note, the blood was not going to reject but how it reacted in my body would indicate if a transplant from the same person would reject.

8. The drugs were not to combat infection but to stop the kidney rejecting .The side effect of the drugs was to increase the likelihood of infection.

OK a bit pedantic and anoraky but I needed to put the record straight. Also some reader (not you of course) might question inconsistency in the book. I do feel I am being slightly unfair to the journalist who interviewed me as I was shown it before it was published. I am responsible for these errors as, I recall, I just scanned it. I must have overlooked them in all the excitement and not wishing to criticise the piece, being so grateful that anyone wanted to write about and publicise the plight of kidney patients. I was primarily concerned about not appearing a fool and the piece was not going to be a load of sentimental old twaddle.

Although I was still a regular visitor to the renal unit I was no longer going to the dialysis unit. Soon, if I stayed lucky, I would be slowly weaned away from the renal world, until then being nearly half my life. Sometimes I felt like a prisoner on early release. I felt an underlying duty to speak out for my recent fellow inmates. I would possibly not see some of them ever again but I felt a bit guilty being so fortunate. I felt then I had a tiny inkling of what it must have felt like when those falsely convicted prisoners were eventfully realised from prison having met fellow prisoners that they felt were also innocent. Their years of incarceration having been brought about by the shenanigans of a few members of the West Midlands Laughable Crime Squad. For a time they had introduce into the English legal system the new maxim: Innocent until proved Irish. "Release the UK 5,000!" Nowadays the figure on this old banner will need to be quadrupled.

This publicity might make people aware of the need for not only carrying cards but also relaying that decision to their next of kin as they own your body after death and it is their decision to donate should anything happen.

Could you imagine the possible confusion caused if I carried an unamended kidney donor card and was initially looked upon as a potential donor? Normally my next of kin, maybe my Dad, would give consent "Yeah sure any organ but if you see a kidney that's mine." Otherwise they would go for my kidneys and some one should notice I have not got any in the usual place (" Hey this guys got no kidneys. No wonder he's dead.")

No one asked me for any cards as hinted at in the article but now and again, behind my back, I would hear someone whisper: "Hey isn't that the bloke who had that transplant"

I did carry the new organ donor card where you could cross out the organ you did not fancy someone having after your death It reads something like: "I would like my heart/kidney/cornea /liver/ soul to be donated after my death. Please erase ones that you do not wish to be donated". I crossed out kidney but felt like writing in: "Find the kidney and win a prize!!" If it could be transplanted again, it might be hundreds of years old before it got any rest.

Going around at the time was another card. On one side it said:

"DO NOT CARD – I do not want anyone to make political capital out of my misfortune." Turn it over and it continues: "I request that if I am injured in a plane accident or train crash, I shall not be visited by Mrs Thatcher"

That reminds me of a story I was told where British Rail had set up an "accident" to train its staff in case of a real crash. Unfortunately a real doctor passed by and not realising it was all pretend entered the scene of the "train crash". Naturally everyone else let him through. He opened up his bag and injected this "casualty" in the bottom who then turned round and said, "Do we really have to go that far?"

"Shoulder to shoulder...back to back, "

Fighting fit father of four Mr John O'Sullivan donated one of his kidneys for surgery so that his 26-year-old son could live a normal life.

The operation, carried out at XX hospital entailed both Mr John O'Sullivan and his son lying back to back in the operating theatre before surgeons lifted the healthy kidney from father to son in a carefully timed manoeuvre.

Mr Michael O'Sullivan, aged 26, was born with cysts on his kidneys and, after a lifetime of suffering, was told last year he would have to have operations on both.

Since the operation - which ironically he underwent on the day he was awarded a law degree at XX Polytechnic - he was being kept alive by kidney dialysis machines and other treatments.

Until a fortnight ago that is... when his father, John, was rushed from the family home at XX, to XX hospital in XX to play his part in back-to-back transplant surgery.

John, the managing director of his own pharmaceuticals exporting firm in XX, said: "before the operation Michael was a patient at XX General Hospital and he had been in XX awaiting a donor since August."

"I know one can live happily on one kidney alone, for it was never a decision for me to give mine to Michael. It is a fantastic experience to be able to give him a new life. I would recommend it to anybody."

"My only worry was that the kidney was not going to be good enough. It is not every day that you get an opportunity do something worthwhile although at first Michael did not want me to go through with it", he said

Michael's father, who returns to work come Monday after three weeks' convalescence, said he felt very well. Michael, former XX College pupil, plans to continue his law studies and go on to become a solicitor.

Another would-be donor was Michael's sister, Susan a 24 year-old teacher at XX school. Like her father she went for tests but was told he was more suitable for the transplant.

Michael's doctors in XX said they were pleased with the progress he has made since the operation on the 26th July

"His condition is satisfactory and we expect him to be discharged some time next week" said a hospital spokesman.

But for 3000 the wait goes on

Since pioneering surgeons at London's Hammersmith Hospital in the Sixties first carried out kidney transplants, the number of patients receiving treatment has grown steadily.

Last year, about 900 people under went kidney transplant operations. The average success rate is between 60 and 70 per cent.

Though there are believed to be nearly 3000 patients awaiting a donation a recent national poll showed that only an estimated three per cent of the population carries kidney donor cards in Britain.

At XX General Hospital 15 kidney transplant operations - most of them successful - have already been carried out this year by surgeons Professor XX and Mr XX.

Of the 145 patients currently receiving kidney dialysis treatment at the hospital, half are on the transplant waiting list."

I did prefer their "fighting fit father of four" alliteration to mine: "fucking fourth fish finger". What about: "Sickly son's survival sessions cease...supposedly"

Once again a few errors, which this time I cannot be responsible for as I was 120 miles away. Must change my out of town agents.

Anorak time again:

1. Operations on both? Yes in the sense you have an operation on your appendix when it is totally removed. See: once again people cannot believe you can have no kidneys. I bet the journalist was told I had no kidneys for a year but probably thought s/he had misunderstood and amended his/her notes accordingly.
2. No. I did not have operation on the same day I got my degree.
3. Rushed from the family home? OH give over. So dramatic. We had been planning this for months!
4. It was not back-to-back. They took my Dad's kidney out while I was outside of the operating theatre

getting prepared when I was told my Dad's operation was already under way.

I love the bit about " a carefully timed manoeuvre". Well I am sure my Dad's kidney was not removed and then a member of the medical team holding it would slowly turn round and see me sitting up in bed talking to the nurses showing them all my operation scars.

In the general information article under the one on me it stated there about 3,000 awaiting a transplant. At the time of writing the figure is now 7,000.

My Dad made a claim on his private health insurance policy that he had taken out as he was effectively self-employed and the sole family breadwinner. The response: because it was "a self inflicted wound" he was not covered. I am sure a campaign could be started to persuade these large companies to change their standard policy agreement to incorporate. Such a variation would not exactly break the bank and it is pretty easy to prove you were not trying to con
them. Maybe the government could introduce a compensation scheme for potential donors. After all does the government want to save money on the NHS or what?

The students and lecturers commented on my healthier look and that I had put on weight ("it 's the steroids"). One lecturer commented that my eyes were more alive and sparkly and if some one spoke to me which meant that I had to move my eyes to make eye contact they would instantly dart across whereas before they would apparently move slowly to their intended view point. I even had my eyes tested during this time as I then wore glasses and was actually prescribed weaker lenses. Clearly my eyesight had been affected by lack of good kidney function over those preceding years.

It is very difficulty to explain how you feel after a transplant .At first you are recovering from the major operation itself and in my case I had that extra complication. So you do not realise how ill you were until once you are discharged and realise you are doing things that you could not do before. A good analogy, I would propose, is eyesight. Eyesight fades gradually over time and you are not really aware of it deteriorating. However when you try on your nice new pair of glasses you realise what you can now see and are struck for the first time how bad your eyes were.

To some extent the kidney and my resultant better health was improving at a rate that was tricky for accurate drug prescriptions. I was in the Poly library reading a paper in one of those very low comfy seats when I got up too quickly, as it turned out, as I went hypo - my blood pressure dropped- and I fainted banging my head on the side of a computer monitor and landed, thankfully, back into a seat, somehow facing out from the seat I had just attempted to vacate. I looked around and no one had noticed my failed little circus act. I checked my head to see if I was bleeding. I kept my hand up there to cover my mouth as I was in a very public place with lots of students roaming around and knew I would be wearing a stupid grin. This is a very common side effect of going hypo: you go light headed as if you are stoned.

I was not bleeding. So I decided to have another go. The only safe way was to get up in stages: first sit upright on the edge of the seat, wait a bit, then stand up slowly, ready to fall back into the seat if I felt woozy. It appeared it was time to reduce or possibly come off the blood pressure drugs altogether. I then went off to buy a salty snack to try and bring my blood pressure up.

Afterwards I pondered that while I was fainting and descending whether, by the time I landed and had head butted Mr PC Monitor, I was now still fainting or whether the fainting stage stopped as soon as I banged my head. I may be getting a bit obsessed comparing reality with films but I thought this because you always see in films people being slapped around the face when they are unconscious.

It was a long repetitive haul in the first few weeks after the transplant. My check-ups were during the day, which meant missing lectures and tutorials, making plans to get back to the Poly very difficult because of all the waiting in the transplant unit for the doctor to see me. You hand in your 24-hour urine collection and simply wait in the ward. If there's an emergency on the ward you have to wait some more. Your obs are taken. Your blood is taken. You end up going home having possibly missed all the days' lectures and tutorials.

There was very little space in the renal transplant unit, an expanding NHS sector therefore these check ups took place in the ward corridor (the corridor? We use to dream of check ups.) I recall some time before that the head of the unit had his office in a cupboard (laundry cupboard? You were lucky) but eventually the doctors were based in a portacabin. (They get spoilt you know)

Even taking into account the steroid side effects some of the nurses were surprised that in the following weeks I had not put on as much weight as was expected. I put that down to my immediate return to a vegetarian diet after the transplant. Apparently vegetarians are 10% lighter than non-vegetarians of a similar height. Then again we may be back to looking behind the bare statistic. For instance vegetarians are possibly more health conscious and generally lead healthier lifestyles.

Ask in a café: "Is there anything for vegetarians?" and you will be amazed at the varied answers you get back. "Do you eat fish?"; "Well we've got chicken?" (Oh is that vegetarian chicken then?).

I do not impose my vegetarianism on anyone but some people seem to want to have a go as soon as they find out. "Do you wear leather shoes then?" People with no apparent principles trying to catch out people who are striving to have some. I will defend it and will point out things in cafes. For instance in one north London pub all the apparent vegetarian meals come with oyster sauce.

I challenge people who say they are vegetarians but clearly are not. These lot cause all the confusion in the cafés and restaurants. "I am a vegetarian but I eat fish". (Well then you are a non-meat eater.) "I am a vegetarian but every so often I cannot resist the smell of bacon." But I do know how they feel. I am a pacifist but every so often I feel this urge to beat someone up with a cricket bat.

Anyway my visits to the corridor were less frequent. Initially I had to come in every day and then the time period was slowly extended to every other day moving on to twice a week, then once a week, a fortnight.

I did not get further than that. The blood test showed I had an antibody in my system. My body had effectively recognised the foreign kidney. Excuse the football analogy but it was a bit like being two nil down in a Cup final with five minutes to go. Something had to be done quickly. It was only a question of time before the kidney was attacked, rejected and I would be back on dialysis only a few weeks after having the transplant.

What I am going to tell my parents? After my Dad's tremendous courage in going through the pain and discomfort that came with giving a part of his body away and my Mum no doubt feeling guilty (ping) that her hereditary condition had brought this about. I was not feeling too good myself knowing how they may be feeling (pong) were I to tell them. I toyed with the idea of not doing so but when asked a direct question about how things were going I could not very well lie.

The unit had a super-sub. (Sorry. Sorry). One of the consultants had just come back from the US having been introduced to a procedure involving what is known as anti-lymphocyte immune globulin. I was told it had only been used in England twice before, as I understood it, for the first time in that hospital so I was to be the third person to have this groundbreaking method of rescuing a transplant in such a situation. The idea was that I was to have plasmapheresis.

This meant all my blood was to be removed. Crazy thoughts entered my head about how it was to leave my body: What? All at the same time? My imagination has its moments: me "sitting" in corner of the blood transfusion with the doctor in charge of the long progress.

"Dringggg. Dringgggg. Dringggg. Dringgggg"
" Excuse me Michael. Won't be a moment"
" Hello"
" _____, _____.
_____ "

"Yes darling I'll be back about seven tonight something cropped up."
" _____. _____.
_____,_____
_____ "

"Oh really."

"
———————————————, ——————————————————.
———————————————"

"Lovely. That's my favourite."
"
——————————————————.
———————————,———————————............"

(Dried prune in corner attempting to tap fingers impatiently but fails because of a haemoglobin level of exactly nought)
"........———————————————,
————————————————. ——————————— "

"That's funny. So what did you tell her?"
"
———————, ——————————————.
——————— "

" OK Bye."
"
——————— "

"Yes. Love you"
"
————————————————— "

"No you put the phone down first."
"
——————————————————————.
———, ——— "

" I love you too"

Blood is made up of four constituents: plasma, platelets and red and white cells. The antibody is in the plasma. So the red and white cells would be taken out with the plasma and separated by use of a centrifugal spinning machine. My plasma would not be returned but chucked away and replaced by donated plasma.

I therefore had to attend the hospital blood donation building and for most of the day sit in this chair and have needles inserted into both arms. My blood would come out of one arm and go through the machine. My other arm would eventually receive the returning red cells with the donated plasma.

As you may have spotted it would be impossible to take all the plasma out in one go and so traces of it would be left and this is where it got clever. The antibody would be put in a horse and the horse would create an antibody to my antibody. To get rid of the all traces to stop them reproducing again, the horses anti body would be injected into me and hopefully kill off my antibody. I.e. all the traces.

Simple really but would it work? And no the horse was not in the adjacent bed or anywhere in the hospital.

As a bad impressionist of the poet John Hegley might have written:

"I am linked up to something medically fangled,
So all of my blood can be carefully mangled,
In the hope that the antibody can be strangled,
And my fears and hopes for my transplant disentangled."

So after the blood change I was moved back to the transplant unit and told I would be receiving several injections over a week containing the antibody. They could not be normal injections into the arm because the drug was so powerful that if I had it directly into my arm I would get thrombosis. The entry point was to be into my main artery just below my heart.

I waited in my own room expecting to have to go to theatre or something. The consultant came in, produced a six-inch needle and said "I thought we might as well do it here in the ward". I unbuttoned my pyjama top as requested, got my thumb and fingernail ready and waited. With the weight of his body he carefully eased the needle down into my artery in my chest. As he did this a nurse arrived with the pre-med. She looked at the scene realising she may have been a weeny bit too late. I looked at her, the consultant looked at me looking at the door. Then he looked down to me and said: "Oh haven't you had your pre med Michael. I am sorry."

This was to be the first of several doses of the horse antibody. A tap was going to be fitted into my chest, known as a sub-clavial line but beforehand I was given the option of having a permanent one, which would mean I would have to stay in the hospital for the rest of the week. Alternatively there was the temporary one, which could mostly be removed between transfusions, I could be temporally discharged, having to return to hospital for each dose. I jumped at the chance of being discharged.

Although a line remained inserted it seemed well protected. This was important as I was told if it was knocked there was a slight risk air could get into my artery and I could die from air embolism (air bubble blocking main artery). So I had to be very careful. They did not say don't go to nightclubs but then for that matter they didn't specifically say do not go scuba diving either.

Looking back I was a bit of an idiot as I continued to go down the nightclub. However depending on the result in the next few weeks this could well be my last opportunity to drink there.

I was with some friends who met some nurses and to make conversation as you do I told them I had a sub claveal line in. The nurse I was talking to didn't believe me and because I was beginning to get fed up of not being believed whenever I ever explained my medical condition to anyone, I pulled back my shirt. She looked incredulous and appeared to sober up very quickly

The local press somehow got notice of this transplant as a news story and contacted me and I agreed that they could interview me in my room. Early into the interview I told them of the rejection episode I was going through and their heads dropped. I actually felt sorry for them because they had clearly come for the nice little "Ahhhh" the "And finally some good news" story angle. They said they were sorry to hear the news and mentioned that they had hoped they could take a photo of me jumping for joy. Fuck that.

They eventually had me sitting at my desk with all my drugs alongside me, which I immediately regretted. I wonder what would happened if they went to interview a women who had, say, just been badly beaten up by her boyfriend only to discover that when they arrived they had made up. Their heads would drop and maybe one would suggest, "Hey would you mind knocking her about a bit. We came all this way hoping to take a good photo..."Well you know the old saying: some journalist will never let the truth get in the way of a good story. This was what was printed:

"Kidney patient sits his exams

Plucky law graduate Michael O'Sullivan, aged 26, has enrolled at XXXX Polytechnic for his Law Society finals, just two months after having a kidney transplant.

Michael, of XX, who has an hereditary complaint, polycystic kidneys, had both removed shortly after he graduated in August last year.

His father, John, aged 52, was found to be a suitable donor and in August both underwent operations in an adjoining operating theatres at ****** hospital's kidney transplant unit.

He said last night: "I feel very well and intend to become a solicitor."

"I have missed so much of the course already I may have to postpone it, but if I do it'll only be for a year."

"I am very lucky. There are some people much worse than me and some people can never have transplants."

(The article went on to mention an 18 month-old child having the kidney of a three-month-old and in the article directly after this followed)

"Dole doctors "

"Nearly 1500 doctors were unemployed in Britain last month"

As you may have spotted the article made no mention whatsoever of the fact that I was going through a very trying time as my kidney could well reject and I would be back on a kidney machine. I flinched when I read the "I feel fine and intend to become a solicitor". Admittedly during the interview I said I felt fine and when they asked later on what was the purpose of the course I said it was the solicitors' finals course. But the sentence appeared as direct quote with no dots between the two parts. It made me look a pompous idiot. I bet people thought that if I was introduced to them and they asked me how I was I would reply: "I feel fine and intend to become a solicitor".

Another article appeared in its sister local paper running the same story angle with the headline: "Big law test for kidney patient"

I always found local newspaper headlines intriguing. Especially the way as few words as possible are used to create an interest but it sometimes fails and becomes hilarious. For instance in some local papers you would get desperate attempts. Something not far away from: "98 year old man dies", "eleven year old girl goes to school" or "pregnant woman gives birth". There are the old classics like the one during World War One: "General goes back to front". Recently a very popular web site has published a book of the web site pages caricaturing local newspaper stories. The Framley Examiner has news headlines like: "The best kept best kept village sign"

I also crave stupid notices:"Caution, no warning signs" and "Do not throw stones at this notice". I actually spotted this one myself: "Danger unconcealed entrance". Recently the New Scientist magazine has begun to publish them and has found a name for it: semiopthy.
Here are a few they discovered: "Police Club visitors"; "Extra thick baby wipes" (This is a headline as well) and "Touching overhead wires causes instant death! Penalty $200"

"Dead man wins case over time off for treatment". Change of mood required now as this initially just looks like a silly headline. But it comes from an Employment Tribunal case where a man was sacked for having to go on a kidney dialysis. The comparatively new Disability Discrimination Act 1996 allowed him to sue his ex employer for being made redundant after taking time off work to stay alive by attending his dialysis sessions. He died aged 27 of a virus five months after receiving a kidney transplant from his father. His parents carried on the case after his death and it is thought to be the first successful dismissal claim on behalf of a deceased person. His mother said: "People believe that people undergoing dialysis sit by a machine and that's it they are fine, but there's far more complications that can arise."

"A new beginning" Well after a bit of an early scare; "Shoulder to shoulder, back to back" Well not quite; "Law student sits his exams" and "Big law test for kidney patient". Well er no actually.

The new innovative treatment worked and the kidney survived but I did not survive on the course and for the second year running I had to jack the course in. I had to sign on and consider what to do. However keeping the kidney came before anything else.

****

CHAPTER SIX:
Rejection Episodes, Rejection Letters

I am lying on the bed. I feel as if I am in a bath that is slowly filling up. I feel a pool of fluid in my bed. Then I suddenly shoot up, stretched out my left arm and was about to hit a button on the side of my bed when I realised I was not in the dialysis ward but in my own bed. I had been dreaming. I had dreamt that while on dialysis my needle had come out and my bed was filling up with my own blood. I had that dream more than once in the next few months after my transplant. In fact even between dialysis sessions while sleeping I would have to take a double check before turning over in my sleep in case if I was on the machine because if I was and attempted my intended nocturnal manoeuvre I would wrench out both blood lines and set off all the alarms. This still happened weeks and months after the transplant.

After the near loss of the kidney after only a few months I was constantly searching for a fail-safe system to ensure I could never forget to take my steroids (prednisolone) and immunosuppressives, (azatharprin). It seems to be taken for granted that you will always open your drug bottles each morning as regular as clock work and place the requisite amount in the palm of your hands and swallow then with the aid of your small glass of water. I could not rely on this as it would depend on me remembering and these drugs were more important than the ones I had ever taken before due to the potential avalanche of consequences if I forgot. It was one thing if your kidney rejects through no fault of your own but to know you may have contributed to it was something I would find extremely difficult to cope with.

This at first all appears so obvious: of course you can remember. You have to take them every morning and evening. You take them every day so you are bound to get into a routine. It is not that easy. It is because you take them every day that you cannot always remember if you have taken them. That quick five-second procedure is just like the day before and the day before that. Usually taken at the same place whether you "drop" them by your bedside; in the kitchen or from your bathroom cabinet. An analogy could be lending money to a friend. Everyone remembers money was lent but not sure if it was repaid. This is because the original deal takes longer .How much do you want to borrow? I can lend you money if you want. Are you sure? When can I get it back? A full on discussion. Giving it back takes a few seconds. Here. Oh cheers. The end stage happened so fast you do not readily recall it but you never forget the fact that money was at one stage borrowed or lent.

I thought of counting the number of the tablets in each bottle so that if I could not remember whether I took my drugs that day I could count the remaining ones. That's not fool proof because the extra drugs in the bottle could be there due to forgetting days beforehand I would then be at risk of taking a second dose. I was aware of weekly tablet container products on the market. Ideal if you are always at home and have a regular life style routine. I did not.

This was a discussion I once had with one of the doctors. I was not able to convince her how easy it was to forget or not remember you had taken them and risk taking a double dose just to be on the safe side. You could lie in one morning, take your drugs, go back to sleep, wake up again and think did I take my drugs, or am I remembering yesterday's drug consumption, or did I dream it. Or worse: you take them again oblivious to the fact you had already taken them. Taking twice your dose is not a good idea considering how powerful the drugs you are dealing with are, causing a further reduction in your immune system and an increase in the steroid side effects? I should have asked her how often she scratched or blew her nose. Bet she could not tell me. But you do it every day.

I was still sharing the house with group of young blokes from many walks of life, one of which was a very small time thief. One day I went into his room and saw him with an old bubble gum machine. He was going through each mini container, eating the sweet and chucking the round mini plastic containers aside together with the little toy such as a plastic black spider. He had just stolen the whole machine that was usually chained outside the local newsagent. The proprietor had evidently neglected to secure it and, get this: my housemate put it under his jumper and ran off with it down the street with the stand sticking out from under his jumper. Now known as the infamous bubblegum machine heist. Thankfully he was only a threat to shops, building sites and other commercial places. He was not a risk to his housemates.

On another visit to his room for a chat he showed me a copy of a recent local paper that he had actually bought. He pointed out a front-page story containing an article by an angry journalist who had just visited the local pop festival. The journalist's hysteria, no doubt contrived, was over his visit to the site where he saw many youngsters settling down for the weekend to contravene the Misuse of Drugs Act 1968. I always find that a curious title: surely it should be the Abuse of Drugs Act. Misuse conjures up images of youngsters trying to get off on cannabis by putting the joint in their ear. Anyway, this streetwise journalist had seen a tent where the occupiers were openly selling "recently stolen knives". He had seen a sign outside the tent advertising "Hot knives for sale" If you do not know what this means, well I have been told it's when the drug users press two red hot knives between a piece of cannabis resin, thus creating a bellowing of smoke from which they lift a make shift funnel over it and take it in turns to inhale the resulting THC drug contained therein. Apparently.

A few days later I noticed the sweet machine in a nearby skip, next to it a plastic bag full of the little containers. I thought they might be a solution to my problem so I grabbed them, took them home and poured them out on the table to await inspiration.

They were all different colours, just the right size to keep my daily stash in. Then it hit me: snooker colours. White, yellow, green brown, blue, pink and black. Seven balls; seven days in the week. The only snag was that there was not a black one. But hey: replace with a red one, have the white for Saturday, red for Sunday and the rest can follow the standard snooker sequence. They could then be refilled at the beginning of each week. I could double check the colour for that day to see if I had already taken my drugs. The only problem would be if I went out for the day and lost my bauble. I do not usually loose my house keys so why should I suddenly start losing these?

From then on it was reassuring that whenever I had a mild panic (if that's not a contradiction in terms), that I may have not taken my drugs, I could check the colour of the bauble and check it's contents. As time went on I got so expert I could do it without any one knowing I was consuming drugs on their premises, whether it be a pub, a café or at the law centre. I would take it out of my pocket with my hand completely covering it. If, when I shook it next to my ear, there was no sound: empty. OK for today.

Be warned, however, the information sheet that accompanies every pack or bottle of drugs always warns you not to remove them from their original container. Otherwise there is a risk that you will confuse the different types of drugs and if there are children around they may mistake them for sweets where as in, say, a bottle they have safety caps. Nowadays most of the drugs I get are individually wrapped and some even have the days on the week on them. Nevertheless that still requires you having to walk around all day with several crackerly small packages bursting out of you wallet. So the burbles still have their advantages.

My check ups got further and further apart but my socialising events got nearer and nearer. I thought I had some catching up to do. Also I had no idea of knowing how long the kidney would last. The procedure at each check up was as follows: previous day collect all urine; after early morning pee end collection and measure volume; take a sample, write on container amount of urine produced. Go to hospital with it, do a lot of waiting after which you give another urine sample, mainly testing for infection; the usual obs taken, weight recorded and several blood samples. Sometimes it seemed like it was nearly an armful.

Once the check up is over you try to put it behind you. You do not really want to because if the next one presents bad news you are not prepared and you realise you have started to take you transplant for granted which is a dangerous strategy. The longest gap between check ups slowly extended to four months. I would get tense coming up to each check up because you thought so much could be happening inside you over the long period. The tests spot trends and signals months before you get any kind of symptoms.

It is a bit like a tollgate on a road. In the distance you see one. It's miles away but you cannot remove it from your mind knowing all too well it is ahead of you and cannot be avoided and you'll have stop and interrupt your journey. You travel along, with something gnawing at the back of your head ("it could be rejecting this time"), carrying on as you were but every so often you look up and are reminded you have something coming up. It gets nearer and nearer until you have to change down a gear, thoughts that your results are ahead constantly spring to mind. These might show a deteriorating kidney function that could be start of a spiral downwards with the possibility of returning to the machine. Soon you will see nothing but the large tollgate coming into view. You get nervous. You cannot think of anything else. Until finally you change right down to first gear and have to concentrate on getting through. Then you drive off. Glad to be away on the open road again. Until the next one. Not a perfect analogy as any time you can turn a corner and there is an unexpected tollgate on the road that is not marked on the map: a rejection episode. No warning.

This is like getting through a Nazi boarder guard border. You turn a corner and there it was. You cannot turn back. You have to go on. You know your papers are forged (your body is also being conned into think everything is legit) but how good is the deception. You wait. You are told to wait some more. Further inspection of the ID papers takes place by way of a magnifying glass. (The lab technicians are examining the tissue taken as a result of a biopsy by way of a microscope) The phone goes. The tension is mounting. You are told everything is OK and you can go on. Till the next border guard encounter.

If the next one went well then it would be the see-you-in- four months routine unless of course you noticed familiar symptoms such as pain or swollen ankles or you stopped peeing. There might be a problem that you are only aware of the day of the check up or the resulting test results given by phone later on that day. At each check up mention can be made of good figures but that was from the previous check up: not the one you are at.

I was trying to get fit or should that be fitter. That summer my parents and I went to the Transplant Olympics, which were held in Newcastle that year. To qualify you needed an organ transplant so I had no fear of meeting Elton John or Frank Sinatra in the badminton finals. No hair transplant recipients. Sorry

I partook in badminton, 100 metres sprint, cycling and played in a five-a-side football team for another hospital, as mine did not have a team and this one was one player short. So the free transfer went through very quickly without any problems.

The hospital paid for my stay at a hotel for the weekend including meals. It was the first time I had ever had a hotel room to myself. I had heard about the bible in the bedside cabinet and the toilet paper folded into a nice little triangle but not the chocolate on the pillow. What's that all about? So you have a nice wash, clean you teeth, go over to your pillow, you spot for the first time just what you really feel like: a piece of chocolate. What if you come back from the hotel bar, do not put the light on and crawl into bed. You then wake up with all these strange dark stains everywhere and the chambermaid does not rate you as one of the hotels more sophisticated guests anymore.

I even got into the semi final of the cycling which encouraged me some months later to do what I had being considering: I would cycle to see my folks who lived 120 miles away. Initially everyone thought I was mad attempting it in a day or that it was even possible. This only increased my determination to do it.

I set off at about seven in the morning at a steady pace. I had planned the most direct route in advance. Equipped with a list of every town, village and hamlet that I had to pass through, I would not waste time looking at maps or getting lost. I had three water containers on my bike frame to be sure I would not get dehydrated. This could damage my kidney. I near enough cycled non-stop, stopping only to refill the water containers and to now fulfil the now familiar need to empty my bladder.

Traffic lights. You'll be cycling along, slow down, balance the bike on the two wheels when hardly moving so to avoid having to take you left foot out of their peddle clips. Eventfully you will realise you cannot balance while stationary anymore but as soon as you bring your foot out and it touches the kerb the lights change. I have this theory about kerbs just before traffic lights. I reckon that there is an invisible sensor so whenever it is touched it triggers off the green light to come on.

People's attitude to traffic lights, how they obey them strangely interests me. Very few of the obedient pedestrians look at the traffic, just for the green lights. If, say, I cross a road I also check that the red light is on intended for the car drivers to obey. After what I have been through I am not relying on some stupid light system. Such is my newly developing survival instinct. If there is no traffic and the little red man appears, these obedient pedestrian will still not cross. I feel a bit guilty if I disobey the system when, say, a mother is with her young child as I am setting a bad example. However you could look at it another way: the child says, " that man is very naughty" and she is taught not to follow someone's bad example which will be safer in the long run when she is allowed out on her own for the first time.

Recently I have seen a new design of traffic light. The green man is now at waist height at your side of the street and not across the road at the top of the pole. No doubt a cheaper design which I think risks more limbs being damaged because there is no longer any need to look up and out and see cars within you peripheral vision. You'll just glance at only your side of the street and walk. Furthermore most people wait on the kerb. To check the lights you now have to hunt for the green man which can be found by stepping back and looking at the other side of the pole. Recently I saw more construction and thought silly me they haven't finished building it yet: something was going up on the top of the pole on the other side of the street. Green man? No. A camera. Maybe to save more money they have a deal with some cable television channel and have a new series entitled something catchy like "Pratestrians"

It was a sunny summer's day, I had brought a pair of headphones and several music tapes if I was to find the journey monotonous. I found myself playing an album by Captain Beefheart and the Magic Band. The one track that I discovered by pure chance that went very well with plodding up the hills was entitled "Bat Chain Puller". This tune has a rhythm like a steam train engine. The idea apparently came from listening to the rhythmic movement of car windscreen wipers. The words suggest an attack on chain saws while they destroy the countryside.

" A chain with yellow lights,
That glistens like oil beads
On its slick smooth trunk
That travels behind on tracks, and thumps
A wing hangs limp and retreats"

"Bat chain puller,
Puller puller"

I was amazed how much my stamina had improved, even since the Transplant Olympics. I would be cycling up a hill with a slow gradual incline that was over a mile long. I had no hint from my body of needing to stop or slow down, which was just standard practice before the transplant. I could not even have attempted such a journey then.

"Bulbs shoot from its snoot
And vanish into darkness"

"BAT CHAAAAIN puller,
Puller puller"

Once at the crest I did not need to use the hill descent to get my breath back by not pedalling and just sitting there. I would now want to carry on peddling and get some real speed up. I could cycle without having to concentrate but just move on up the hill as if on automatic pilot and look around, hardly out of breath.

"In the hollow wind of its stacks
Ripples felt fades and grey sparks clacks"

Taking in the countryside, moving around under my own steam and actually feeling fit for the first time in many years, making real head way on a long journey. I felt not only that I had a new kidney but new lungs, new heart, new, which is sort of true, leg muscles.

" Lunging the cushioned thickets.
Pumpkins span the hills
With orange crayola patches.
Green inflated trees
Balloon up into marshmallow soot"

Looking through the hedges I would often see what I thought a strange site. A little wood, usually on a little hilltop, right in the middle of well manicured field. Left possibly, so their roots would bind the soil during rainfall, or maybe to encourage wild life to remain and not give up vacant possession.

> "Pulled by rubber dolphins with gold yawning mouths
> That blister and break in agony
> In souls of rust"

It looked to me as the remaining trees had been ordered to congregate in the middle of the field with their hands up. ("We are the millet tree. Nobody move and keep your arms up. Someone give the sycamore a bucket and the willow a tissue. Don't know what they're doing in this neck of the woods?")

> " They kill gold sawdust into dust"

I got to my family's home at about 6:30pm and remarkably I didn't feel tired. When I awoke the next day I thought my muscles may have seized up but luckily I only felt aches when I clenched my leg muscles. Walking up and down the stairs, my biggest concern was a cinch. I then discovered that my Dad had just started redecorating his office and what I thought was going to be two lazy weeks ended up with me as a painter and decorator.

At this time Mum's kidneys appeared to be holding steady although she was keeping the symptoms at bay by taking blood pressure tablets and fighting off the occasional kidney infection, very common with people with Polycystic kidneys.

I did the same journey back, which took me a bit longer and was less of a challenge because I knew I could do it.

A few weeks later the local-authority were having second thoughts as to whether or not they should give me a full grant to take the Law Society Finals because of the problems with the previous two attempts in not being able to complete the course. They wanted confirmation from my doctors that in their opinion I would be fit enough to complete the course in the next academic year. When I next saw my kidney surgeon I showed him the letter and he replied in to his dictaphone while I was with him which ended with the sentence: "he is clearly very fit as indicated by his recent one-day cycle ride to ......".

A few months later I was standing in front of an actual urinal during the interval at an Alexi Sayle concert. Confidently using the facilities without worries I might pass blood while visible to all around me. I looked up and who was standing next to me? Non other than the surgeon. He looked over and said "Still working then?" I may be able to complete this course at last.

On one hitchhike to see my family the driver of the car who picked me up noticed my fistula arm. I must have neglected to button my shirt's long sleeve. He could, to some, be classified as being of the hippy persuasion or as one of my doctor once described me as being bohemian. I then heard the immortal words: " Hey man what do you fix with a bicycle pump?" I have to say at the outset that I know the hippy community due not partake in such heavy drugs.

The Law Society Finals (the LSF), as it was then known, was nothing like the degree course. The exams were nothing like ones where you could revise certain areas and choose, say, four questions out of ten. You had to revise the whole course because you could not choose any of the questions in the exams. You had to answer every one on the paper, which meant you could not overlook an area in case it came up because if it did you would simply fail that exam. And before you ask no, at the start of the course you could not pick options. There were seven "heads" containing the following subjects: conveyancing (buying and selling houses and flats), wills and probate (death law), civil litigation, criminal litigation, company law, partnership law, accounts, solicitors practice, family, welfare benefits, consumer, employment and evidence. If you passed five or six heads you could retake the one or two that you failed within a three exam sitting cycle as long as the ones you failed were not failed abysmally. If you passed less than five or failed one badly you had to take all of them again, even the ones you passed. A friend passed six heads in the first sitting so he had two opportunities to pass the remaining one otherwise he would have to take them all again. He failed that examination head twice and so had to start from scratch.

I finished the course and took all the exams, which was a mild achievement in itself but failed and had to do them all over again the following summer. After the course ended I began to volunteer at an advice centre, which would, unlike the earlier law centre experience, allow me on the front line, and I would be able to advise clients directly. This would mean having to learn welfare benefits law properly rather than as a small adjunct to family law, which was the case on the Law Society Finals course. I was to hear about benefits I did not know existed before.

It was an eye opener as to how little the academic world of law studies prepared you for the real world. For example:

-I discovered that a pensioner renting a flat was using her savings to pay her rent not realising she could claim housing benefit;

-A woman who had wanted to sell her house at a large discount to a relative enquired whether it was the law that she had to get an estate agent;

-Several people who came into the centre saying they had a letter that they did not understand when it became apparent they could not read and you had to explain it was indeed confusing to allow them some dignity in having to ask. Sometimes people would just hand you an unopened letter and I tried to work out whether they were now scared of official letters: had given up the charade of pretending they could read or were just lazy and had become too dependent on the centre.

-We had a visit from an incensed man because a Scottish firm of solicitor had written to him to ask if he was the same person that had lived there years before. He wanted help to complain about the cheek of this nosy firm and to tell then to mind their own business. When he confirmed to me he did indeed have distant relatives there I suggested he might be a lost beneficiary under a will. This carefully placed thought somehow changed his attitude completely.

-A welfare benefit appeal. Only after the hearing, before which I got "my client" to wear my jumper because of the state of his worn dirty clothes, did I realise that he had a history of mental health problems but at the time I could not see how I could have asked.

- On one of my days off the centre had an off day. During the winter a pensioner arrived with her mother who was confused. I heard that she wet her herself, took her bloomers off and put them on the centres sole radiator to dry

Once you had worked out the problem getting all the relevant information out of the client could be difficult. In the academic world all the facts were clearly laid out in front of you on a piece of paper. There were no red herrings. Sometimes it could be difficult explaining what was relevant and was not.

The setting: an interview with a couple that probably knew each other a bit too well:

Me: "So when did you get this summons?"
Her: "Well let me see now. Well I remember when it arrived I put it in a safe place behind the clock on the mantle piece .... or was it the jar..... because I was going to open it later."
Me: "So when was that"
Her: "Oh after breakfast"
Me: "No when did it arrive?"
Her: "oh when did it arrive. I think it was last Tuesday"
Him, quiet until this point: "No it was Wednesday"
Me: "Just roughly when"
Her: "No darling it was definitely Tuesday because I remember we were going to have blackcurrant pie and custard that night and you said...."
Me: "It doesn't..."
Him: "We did not have blackcurrant pie last Tuesday. We had apple crumble"
Me: "Excuse m..."
Her: "Oh yes we did"
Him: "No we had blackcurrant pie last Friday"
Me: "Let's..."
Her: "Where do you get your strange ideas? Last Friday our Mable visited and we went out to that nice restaurant. What's it called?"
Him: "Oh yes I know the one you mean."
........Etc

Oh all right. A slight exaggeration but you get the point. You had to develop a new skill of carefully extracting all the relevant information.

At my next check up I was shown a noticeable slow but steady downward trend in my renal function, the dreaded kidney figures. An early sign that the kidney was rejecting. The possible treatments (at least there was a treatment unlike with my own kidneys) was to be given a boost of increased steroids

150

to hopefully knock the kidney function back into line. Another one was to investigate the kidney itself by ultrasound - commonly associated with pregnancy – to see if everything looks OK or a biopsy which involves the extraction of a tiny piece of the kidney to look at it under a microscope to see if the kidney was indeed rejecting.

I became an inpatient for about a week and had an intravenous steroid drip. The noticeable symptoms being a further increase in a chubby face, which would reduce again, once you are hopefully returned to your normal low maintenance dose. It seemed to do the trick and I was given a bit more time and was left hoping this may be the last rejection episode. The kidney may now settle in and I would have no more such scares.

My Mum's kidney started to deteriorate. This was indicated by the fistula being fitted, the low protein diet and the blood pressure tablets. She also had the classic symptoms particularly the swollen ankles and the painful cramps.

She told me once, and this is as good a time as any to tell you, about a time she was in a general ward, before she was upgraded to a renal patient, when in the middle of the night she heard and saw a very elderly patient fall out of bed and crack her head open. Apparently caused by the lack of a side to the bed or someone forgetting to pull one up. Mum shouted for the nurse but none came and although she had been restricted to her bed had to go to the nurse rest room at the end of the ward and found the only nurse in the ward. Asleep in a chair. To me it looked like the situation where a night nurse has called in sick and so a nurse in a nearby ward has to call by through out the night to check up on the sole ward night workers.

The student type parties were always the best. No one cared if you were not recognised as long as you brought a contribution. Far better than the exclusive ones where someone would say at the door "who invited you". I did not want to be with all the familiar faces. I wanted to meet new people. Even if you found your way into the more exclusive parties you would often get the who's –the- stranger looks as opposed to a free for all when every one was easy going.

Occasionally you would accidentally intrude into a snotty student party, arriving with plenty of drink only for the host to challenge you.

-The hostess came up to us after we had deposited a substantial amount of cans and bottles on the kitchen table. She had with her male students for support with their arms raised and clenched fists asking who had invited us.

-Another time we were in a hall of residence where all the double bedrooms on one floor were opened up for the party and one particular host was miffed that he did not recognise anyone that was partying in his room. So, meticulously, he went round the room asking everyone who had invited them. "This is my room and I do not know you." I had to think fast so went to the door and read the two names. From overhearing an earlier conversation I took a calculated gamble as to which one was his. I nonchalantly walked up to him with a big smile on my face and said hello Darkwin, or what ever his name was, and spoke to him as if he was a long lost friend. From the slightly embarrassed and bewildered look on his face I thought I had got away with it. He didn't ask me or the person I was with to leave but carried on asking everyone else to. After mingling a while to my horror the room slowly empty as his jackboot style inquisition continued. Then he was left talking to someone in a now practically empty room realising his folly, and not wanting to talk to this bloke he must know but could not place. We were therefore left in the room both of our tactics failing miserably.

-I remember being flummoxed as to how we were going to get into a toga party. The Roman centurion on the door reminded that it was fancy dress only. I said we are Romans in fancy dress.... and he let us in.

-One bonfire night we were actually invited to a party, which did happen occasionally, and had to get a lift out of town to a farm. What was so remarkable was that there was a massive bonfire and we thought our ears where playing tricks on us as we felt the music was emanating from the fire itself. I think one record was "Fire!" by Arthur Brown but it was possible I thought it such an appropriate song for that occasion that my yearning to hear it then has overawed the accuracy of my memory banks since. Eventually we twigged. Someone had got some old speakers, placed them in the base of the fire, ran a cable under the surface of the ground and so for hours the music blared out until very late in the evening there was a sudden muffled silence. The brilliant format was over for another year and until someone was willing to sacrifice another pair of old speakers.

I got gate crashing down to a fine art I am embarrassed to say. I met many people, some who were up to the same pastime. We would bump into each other at parties and mockingly berate each other for being there. It got silly. At one stage friends would ring me up on Friday evening expecting me to have a party ready to go to. If I got a phone call at that time in the week I would simply pick it up and immediately say:

"Hello Dial a gate crash. Can I help you?"

Getting in to the social even was our main concern but for one friend of mine getting out was one he had rarely accounted before. Not a party but a pub. He left us all to go the loo and an hours went by and there was no sign of him. We were outside the pub scratching our respective heads as to where he had gone. We were on our way to a party up the road and he did not know where it was. After about twenty minutes or so he suddenly staggered out of the pub.

He told us his peculiar story .He had mistaken the cellar door for the gents. He walked into an abyss, tumbling down the stairs, knocking himself out as he landed on the concrete cellar floor, as the door closed behind him. When he came round he was in pitch-blackness. He could not see a thing and what seemed like ages groped around the room to see if he could feel and identify something to discover where he might be. Then he saw a bright light. He looked round and for a millisecond spotted and door in the sky and steps down wards. Someone had just made the same mistake. I was thinking: his unwitting saviour could have also gone flying down the steps and as he left said "cheers mate" leaving the next victim unconscious on the cellar floor waiting for the next person to make the same mistake, or worse, until someone decided to lock the cellar door.

I had been going through several distinctive periods: polycystic, anaemic, stoic, academic (reprise) and now hedonistic. Born again piss head? Not true. I would never over do it.

My first three priorities were fluid, fluid and fluid. Drinking when you weren't thirsty is difficult at first but I had already experienced it when my own kidneys were on the way out and drinking was the only way of getting out some of the toxins, which was supposed to be the kidneys task.

Pee at last. Praise the lord I can pee. When I would visit an all female household and would often be met by the cry: "Please put the seat back down after you use it." Most of the time blokes get told off for not putting seat up to start with!. And then there is that hilarious notice: "Gentleman. We aim to please. So please aim." There are many loos where putting the blessed seat up is not that easy. You have to use the knee technique: lean back and side ways. And action. I had forgotten all these hassles of having a working kidney

In hot whether I would take a bottle of water with me. Once I took it to football match and I, like everyone else was frisked. The police were in attendance. On its eventual discovery I admitted to being the owner of the said bottle but pointed out it was made of plastic, not glass. I went onward to the terraces and was pursued by a police officer. They had second thoughts. I was told that I couldn't keep my water bottle as it might contain alcohol. I pointed out I had not opened it yet. It was still sealed. This was not a satisfactory argument and so it was confiscated while others looked on as if I was a member of some notorious hooligan gang and "the old bill" had just confiscated my flick knife.

If I was away from a water tap I would not wait but buy a drink in the nearest shop such as those little box cartons of orange juice. Why not go for something healthier than those sugary drinks or watery squashes. Sometimes in the rush I would grab a familiar looking boxy container but on the first sip I would realise I had accidentally gone and purchased flavoured water. But it was no accident that they looked the same. It's interesting that manufactures are informed of this but never the consumer.

I have a similar problem to this day with shampoo. You go into a shop, turn the aisle corner and are met with shelves and shelves of bloody shampoos. You brain tells you they are really all the same but the brain washed part tells you there cannot be and one is the best one for you and your type of hair. Frequent wash, for dry, for brittle, for coloured, for greasy, for fine, for normal, for Christ sake! I just want to wash my hair. You eventually grab anything, get home and later notice you are not getting any suds. Oh no I've done it again. I've once again bought a bloody conditioner by mistake. Although the companies go to a real effort to get the bottle size, design and shape to stand out from the crowded shelves they always seem to forget to clearly distinguish shampoo from conditioner. They are near enough identical apart from the word that is there but not in bold print. I am convinced they do it on purpose because they sell more conditioner that may.

Anyway, these watery drinks are about the same price as the natural juice. I am sure they only starting arriving on the shop shelves after the orange juice. Then there was a plethora of different named drinks but which ones contained the healthy natural juice. You would be facing such names as orange drink, juicy orange squash, and orange juice drink. But which one? I, sad person that I am, did some research and discovered if the product name ended in the word "juice" then and only then, you were safe as it should contain 80% juice, the natural stuff that comes out of oranges as opposed to mangy flavoured water mix that comes out of a man made concoction. If the product, however many pictures of bloody oranges there were on the pack, did not end in juice then it could contain 80% water. And all I wanted was some fluid when I was out and about while not getting conned.

Vegetarians are helped more these days with those green v signs on some food labels but people, even those who work in the catering industry, don't seem know what a vegetarian is. "Have you got any vegetarian sandwiches" gets the varied responce "Do you eat fish/white meat/ eggs /cheese?" when I come back with "You what?" I get "Well some of you do". "No. They are not vegetarians. They are non meat eaters or vegans." (My PC doesn't know what a vegan is either)

In one London pub the vegetarian "options" all come with oyster sauce. At one small restaurant I visited there were two vegetarian meals on offer: cabbage curry and vegetarian curry of the day . I asked what was the vegetarian choice of the day and was told cabbage curry.

As you will see I am getting a bit obsessed with this. I thought my restricted diet days were over. I now try and prevent these unnecessary restrictions imposed on vegetarians. On all five million plus of us in the UK. I have had some correspondence with a manufacturer of crisps. If you looked at all the flavours they produce you would be surprised to discover that the vegetarian sign was on beef, prawn and smoky bacon etc but not on the cheese and onion one. The one flavour the non-anoracky vegetarian would buy thinking it would be one of the few flavours that was vegetarian when in fact it was the only one that wasn't. I got a return re mail from these manufacturers saying ....Only recently, to my amazement when, I was trying to point this out to someone the vegetarian sign now appears.

I would think it would fairer if anything that would seem obvious was vegetarian should have a big warning sign if it would seem odd having meat or fish in it. For instance, let's not put the v sign on bread or a carrot getting people to thing hang on have I been eating bread with fish in it. No, there should be sign warning on pudding like those single desserts where one ingredient has pork gelatine.

**

One chocolate product boasts about having the chocolate full of air and rather than keep it quiet they market the air: the lack of chocolate in the chocolate! I remember one famous mint product. Can you imagine the conversation at there famous marketing and advertising meeting.

"Right everyone. Today we need to do some brain storming. Over to you Darren."

"Hi. I've called you all together today because you are our brightest marketing brains as we have come upon a bit of an impasse in how to sell our world famous product. So any ideas. Anybody. Why do our customers keep on buying our product. Yes Tarkwin"

"Habit? Our brand name?"

"Yes but a bit more than that"

"The mint flavour?"

"Anyone else?"

"The hole"

"What did you say?"

"The hole. It was a joke."

"No hang on. I think young Samantha might have something there.

So they begin to market the sweet by concentrating on the nothingness part of their product. Incredible. They can sell trapped air and a hole to get us to buy their stuff. It is now getting even craftier. When before brand names had to pay to advertise now they get you to pay then for advertising product by walking out of the shop with the name emblazoned on your new shirt and, get this, you are charged more because it is a fashionable expensive brand. Brilliant,

In my quest to avoid expensive squash and buy healthier fluid in the immediate vicinity to constantly hydrate I've invented one all of my own. "Powdered Water. Just add...." Not there quite yet. Still working on the packaging. What do you think?

I was socialising and making up for lost time. At the back of mind I always had the uncertainty over how long the kidney would last. I would always drink at least a pint of water before I went to bed, I knew what damage or risk I could make if I over did it. Remember the huge hemotemises when I redecorated the inside of the renal unit toilet? I was warned not to get into any situation where I might retch as that could trigger internal bleeding from my weak stomach. I was still on the steroids but not as high a dose as immediately after the transplant operation.

I developed a black humour over being sick but only if I was no longer the pukee. Here were healthy people overindulging.

- Travelling along a country lane in North Wales with a convoy of cars driving to another pub in another village. In one car the single back seat passenger is seen learning forward between the two in the front. Next scene three occupants get out and the two in the front have vomit all over then but the disgorgor is spotless as it went forward towards the windscreen and the front two became immersed.

– Nonchalantly looking through the records in a shop on a Saturday morning after the night before. Suddenly a feeling of sickness relating to drinking too much several hours earlier. Empties contents into record rack and carries on flicking through the same record. For the next potential customer commenting that this particular punk band has gone a bit too far on that record cover.

-Upstairs at a party sitting on the open window ledge and suddenly a head juts out from the other window in the same room and something rains down the two innocent women in the garden sitting on a wall. ("I do not remember eating that?"), then I see them running up the stairs to do what with the ill young man I do not know.

CLICK.. WKQ= 0+1+1=2

When Mum was hospitalised to begin dialysis I went to visit her but was initially over come by a feeling of guilt of no longer being on dialysis myself. Everyone in the room was sympathetic and concerned for her, whether it be the rest of the family, the doctors or the nurses. I must have been the only one who actually felt guilty. A total irrational feeling. The worst thing to do if you visit someone in hospital when they have something seriously wrong with them is to show your shock on the state they are in or how they look. That only makes them even more worried. They already know the score. They do not need to have the situation made even worse by being responsible for bringing on this emotional response on some one who was kind enough to visit.

Once I recovered my composure I looked around noting the differences between the hospital practices. The dialysis unit insisted on plastic covers over shoes from all visitors. I at one stage even made a suggestion to a nurse, which she took up, sadly indicated how much I had learnt on the subject myself. As with all such patients Mum had her "honeymoon period" after a few weeks on dialysis. Your health actually improves as the backlog of toxins in the body is removed, your weight is controlled and the ankles are no longer swollen unless you broke your fluid restriction limit.

Eventfully a routine was established and I visited the unit during a few of her sessions. The same unit I attended several x-mases ago. She began dialysing at home. Dad became her carer and an expert on the subject himself. The room they chose to install a machine was my old bedroom.

Even though I had failed the exams it was still worth applying for articles. Several friends had been promised positions within solicitors firms before their results and very few were dismissed after they failed again. Usually they were given two months off prior to the repeat week of exam hell.

In the search for articles I had a few obstacles to overcome and years to explain away. Dad told me that when he came over from Ireland and tried to get digs there would be signs outside saying "No blacks. No Irish. No dogs" I doubt if my surname in this day and age would be another negative factor but two friends had applied for articles for the same vacancies. One had a foreign sounding name and got 2.1 degree while the other had a typical Anglo Saxon name and also had a 2.1 but only the latter got any interviews. It must have been something else in the application. Surely. When my dad applied for promotion once he came across notes made on him before the final decision was made and spotted: "Has a strong Irish accent"

I was therefore going to be very fortunate to get any interviews. I applied to nearly all the firms in the area who specialised in legal aid work and lodged my cv on the register at the local Law Society. This did not achieve very much. I could see why: I had completed the LSF course but failed the exams. I was now signing on and was likely to be seen as a real risk to employ having had a transplant, which for all anyone knew, could reject at any time and so then carrying on a full time job would then be difficult. No doubt they imagined I would be in out of hospital all the time when I should be earning "profit costs" for them. Profit Costs is the term solicitors use when they mean earnings. To me it sounds like an oxymoron such as original copy, pretty ugly, holy war or business ethics.

I surprisingly got several interviews. At one the partner interviewing me mentioned at one stage that there were six F.I.O.N.A.s in his firm. Not being acquainted with this acronym but being familiar with a FILEX – Fellow of the Institute of Legal Executives –. I thought what's this one Fellow of the Institute Of .. no..Fellow in er of...no hang on. I was on the verge of asking him what a FIONA was when I realised he was saying, in a very posh voice, fee earner! This is a term solicitors use for those in the firm whose legal advice results in them getting paid as opposed for example administrative staff who help with earning only indirectly. So I avoided making a real buffoon of myself. I did not get the job either.

At another interview it did not take very long before the proceedings quickly focused on my transplant and the lost years. There was no way of avoiding the period of unemployment; before and after the dialysis; the rejection episode, the attempts to complete the finals course. To avoid being seen to be hiding something and get them all suspicious I got bogged down in explaining the ground breaking American medical procedure. After I explained, one of the partners asked how the horse was now. Not appreciating whether he was making a genuine enquiry or being extremely flippant, my retort was "Well all I can say is that we are both in stable conditions." I am not sure if they got my quip. As I was leaving

I was faced with a welcome-on-board-old-chap type handshake. The human attached to the hand then said "You know we had someone here the other day and he was as black as the ace of spades". I immediately felt ill at ease having flesh contact with this individual and hoped they were not going to be the only firm to offer me a job. It was quite amazing that he would think this let alone verbalise it. Not because of what it portrayed as I knew these opinions were about specially in small towns with small traditional firms possibly called Bigot, Bigot & Bigot but that it was held by someone based in a city.

I am starting to lose heart about getting that particular job as twelve years later I have still not received my rejection letter. The same applies to two other solicitors firms who interviewed me during that time. I realised the only time to seriously try again was when I had passed all the exams.

I moved into a different flat. The present inhabitants had lost one of their co-tenants and were pressurised by their landlord to get another one in quickly or they would be paying rent for an empty room. On checking what household bills were in whose name I came across the phone bill addressed to a Miss D Noma. I then discovered that because this is usually the biggest household bill, in the past none of the tenants wanted it in their name so they made a name up. We had some fun with it when I was there. The pretend name was even in the telephone directory but certain commercial enterprises relied on it and we learnt which inquiries resulted from just ploughing through the telephone directory. On several occasions I would answered the phone and was met with a female voice who wanted to speak to Ms Noma. I even answered the door to an Avon lady type and she wanted to speak to her. I said, "No Denise is out at the moment. Can I take a message?"

I now had quite a collection of rejection letters. I was not going to secrete them in a folder in a drawer so I decided to pin them all up on my bedroom wall.

I recall there was about forty rejection letters in all on my wall. When friends would visit I would simply elucidate on my situation. I refused to hide them out of embarrassment. I had done nothing wrong. Many students had begun articles having taken the course but not quite completed the exams. In fact I would go so far as to say that after what I had been through I showed some degree of determination to still want to pass my exams, get articles and qualify as a solicitor. I had by then some experience away from the lecture room, in the real world of the advice centre in a poor urban area. But alas these firms could not see it that way.

I see something of a comparison with asylum seekers and even what are termed economic migrants. They are accused of being lazy, coming over here to live off our welfare benefit system. I do not think if you were like that you would totally uproot yourself and family; pay out your life savings to get out of your own country; travel half way around the world, for part of the way in an rickety old leaky boat; hide in a big container lorry for days; risk your life in other ways, coming to a strange foreign land where you do not understand the language and culture just to spend out your days on the dole. Jesus, Mary and Joseph. Weren't they asylum seekers?

When I attended the Poly to retake the exams the following summer there were many familiar faces. All failures together. Some were clinging to their present articles and by now, although they had been there for a year, only six months counted towards the two years. The clock would only start to tick again after passing the exams. If they failed again they could stay in their job and probably give up the ghost and decide to become legal executive, a FILEX, or leave and change career or do the retakes from another job.

It was a hot summer and all the windows were open to try and get some air into the room. Probably due to the steroids, my regular bout of hay fever was hardly noticeable which I could not say that for some of my fellow candidates. However the windows really had to be kept open.

It was the same intensive week of three or two hour-long exams. Wednesday afternoon. Thursday morning. Thursday afternoon. Friday morning. At this stage you just wanted to come in the next day and carry on and get them all over with. There was very little you could do over the weekend so as to suddenly learn four areas of law. A few decided they had already failed more than two exams or one very badly and next weeks weren't their strong areas so they did not return after the weekend. Monday afternoon. Tuesday morning. Tuesday afternoon. Wednesday morning. And collapse.

I always remember the first exam but like being a hospital patient the exams, like the days in hospital, all seem to merge into one another when you try to remember actually being there. A candidate two desk ahead of me to my left had earplugs in. He had the old affliction of forgetting he could not hear himself so well and his sighs during the exam were highly audible. I just hoped he did not have an upset tummy from nerves, always more prominent during the first exam.

What I remember even more clearly was the wasp who would not be returning after the weekend. He had already failed Direction Sense Law and next week he had his two worst exams to face: Half Open Window Leaving Law and Danger Law

A considerate invigilator decided to take some immediate action. That's consideration for the candidates; not the trespassing insect. She rolled up the magazine she was reading at the time. I do not know, The Invigilator Enquirer or may be even The Examiner Examiner and waddled over to the window. Where upon after a few ridiculous misses the wispy wasp flew down the room ending up against yet another windowpane and yet another open window directly below. The invigilator chased after it.

"Please finish the flight path you are on. Put your wings down. Do not move and stay where you are. Thwaack!"

I failed the following summer resits. I can give you lots of pathetic explanations or excuses if you want: most of the law subjects were areas of law I now knew for sure I was not interested in and did not want to practice. By working at an advice centre I found the type of clients I wanted to help and areas of law I wanted to work within. Consequently I was less motivated as I was only learning for the exam, not to bring on and forward in to a job. However the two-year articles would probably leave me with no option. The subject matter of the course was mainly business based. There was a simply explanation for this. It was where the money was. The jobs in the private sector, from the private paying clients, were available because the firms got their money, their profit costs, to be able to employ. Several friends of mine were beginning to call it a day after also failing again and complained about this bias. Unfortunately the only way to qualify was to get past this exam hurdle. If you moaned about it, having failed, it would appear to be just sour grapes. The only way to get anyone to listen was if you passed and then criticised the course contents constructively.

Let me give you an illustration of the kind of exam question you would have to answer. I cannot recall them exactly but they are not far off from being verbatim......I think.

CONVEYANCING
Question 1
Here's a load of pretend title deeds and other conveyancing documents. Read them. Then answer the following questions:

(a) List and explain the requisitions on title that you will raise on the epitome of title. (55 marks)

COMPANY AND BUSINESS CLIENT
Question 3
D and C want to set up a company. C, who is D's brother-in- law, has the expertise, having worked in the trade since he left school at sixteen, and D has the money. D, without informing C, had taken independent legal advice because he wanted to be sure his money could be as safe as possible in the new blossoming business venture. C had gone along with D's apparent expertise with all the "paper work."
The business went very well with the experience and knowledge of C and so they were able to expand and employ more staff. However C's marriage with D's sister was going badly. With this excuse D was able to slowly

squeeze C out of the now profitable business. You act for D.

QUESTION: To the nearest foot, from what height should D crap on C? (5 marks)

WILLS AND PROBATE
Question 7

Lady Pomfrey – Smythe has recently inherited off her late husband £2,800,000.00, not including the country estate, which has been in her family for centuries. She wants to make a will so as much as possible of her hard earned inheritance would go to her son, Jeremiah, and not to the state, which might spend it on hospitals and other sectors of the welfare state. Jeremiah, a keen tiddlywinks enthusiast, wants to set up a national tiddlywinks championship and needs some extra money, as his grandfather's trust fund, of which he is the sole beneficiary, is not sufficient for him to maintain the standard of living he demands.

At present he is at a public school where he is being educated beyond his intelligence. The family has many valuable parcels of land; stocks and shares. They have a medium size business employing 2,400 workers and want to sell soon and make all the workers redundant because they wish to go on a world cruise to recover from the stress of making a will. They have come to see you for advice as to how they should organise their financial affairs.

QUESTION: Giving precise details, where would you advice them to shove their obscene wealth? (25 marks)

My final excuse for failing again, if you will indulge me for a moment, was that I was always thinking: what am I doing spending all my time revising all this stuff during the sweltering summer months. I could be back on a kidney machine this time next year.

My parents sent me a cheque for £50 to pay-off my small overdraft of about £35. I popped into the bank to get back into the black but when I went to the counter the cashier dealing with me glanced at my paying-in book and said "just one moment Mr O'Sullivan". She went off behind the screens on the other side of the counter and on returning said "the bank manager would like a word with you." He came out of his heavy-duty internal door and invited me into one of the interview rooms. He then went through his file and commented that "we have been helping you out in the past," which presumably meant while I was a student and when I went overdrawn occasionally particularly during the time my grant check was returned.

The nuts and bolts of it were that they wanted to close my account. Clearly I was a liability having no articles of clerkship. They had lost patients with me and knew they were not going to get a nice fat grant cheque or wage packet going into the account in the near future. I then went back to the cashier; they processed my cheque, rather surprisingly didn't wait for it to clear, gave me the balancing cash and confiscated my chequebook and escorted me to the door.

A few months later I applied to another bank to try and get an account, more as an experiment than in hope. I failed but on passing the same bank a few weeks later someone had, during the night carefully writing in massive letters along side the exterior corner wall: " – BANK, WANK BANK." And I 'll tell you now it had nothing to do with me. More likely a businessman whose business was collapsing and his loan was called in. Hopefully D from question 3 of the Company and Business Client exam paper.

Once Mum had enjoyed the delights of the "honeymoon period" where the dialysis machine was able to remove some of the backlog of toxins that had previously been left for her failing kidneys to contend with, she was due to have both her kidneys removed. Like me, had they remained they were too large to allow a possible transplant any room; would continue to cause problems and continue to grow even though they were not working. It has been known that polycystic kidneys have grown so large that it was impossible even to bend over. Thankfully unlike me she had a standard operation with none of the other complications that I had. She was discharged after a few weeks.

I went to my family home to look after her because the rest of the family, who lived nearby could not. She had just been put on the transplant waiting list because she had fully recovered from the bilateral nephrectomy. Her doctors decided she was now strong enough to put up with another major operation if an offer of a kidney transplant beckoned.

My visit coincided with the day the miner's strike ended. They were marching back to work. I must have watched all the news programmes that day containing the same piece of film footage at least five or six times. During the evening the phone rang. I answered it. It was the hospital. They had a possible kidney for Mum. Unbelievable. She had only been on the list for two weeks! As a fellow kidney patient I thought "you jammy...." but as her son I thought "you jammy...."

She did not look that happy. She rather grudgingly took the phone off me and stated – with some pressure from me - that she was interested and would arrange to come up to the hospital as soon as possible. I then arranged for a taxi to get her there as all the car owner members of the family were away. I was still perturbed that she was not as excited as I had anticipated and she was having second thoughts. She was clearly concerned about how quickly things were moving. She had only just got over the pain and discomfort of a big operation and was about to go through it all over again. There was no rest. I reluctantly conceded that she was right. Yes you would have to go through it all over again but this was a possible once in a lifetime chance and you simply have to take it. There are hundreds of fellow kidney patients waiting, no, dreaming, for this phone call. How many more years before she would get another chance like this and in the meantime, all that time constantly feeling worn out on a strict diet and regular dialysis three times a week? I warned her that if she did not take it she was bound to regret it in the months and years to come. She relented and reluctantly realised she had to continue but was wary of the pain that would lie ahead during the next few days. I was able to point at myself, how ill I used to be and looking at the change in me now, it was worth going for it.

Having phoned for a taxi earlier, because it did not arrive with the time promised, I phoned another firm. Eventually a taxi turned up and I had to let her go to the hospital on her own as I was told I should not come as the operation, if it was to happened would be the next morning. I consoled myself with the knowledge that there would be many familiar faces when she got to the ward.

After she left, for what may be her last dialysis session for hopefully some time, the phoned went again. It was the other taxi firm complaining that one of their taxi's had been outside and were waiting. I explained the situation and apologised for my panicky double booking hoping they would understand but they did not. They put the phone down on me.

I could not understand why they did not ring the doorbell. If they had I would have handed over a fiver so chuffed I was that my Mum could be possibly having a transplant in the morning. In fact I would have probably given them a tenner. May be I would have even gone up stairs and pulled out the kidney machine out of my old bedroom and brought it down the stairs on my back and said "look you take this as well. You can get kidney machines out of this family for a while." But then I would probably get a "is that a kidney machine. Are you on a kidney machine? I'd rather be...." Then I might have slammed the door in his face.

When I replaced the receiver another one of those sepulchral atmospheres descended all around me. The house was now very silent and I was in a sort of limbo: I was at my parents home to care for my mum, now I had to wait for the rest of the family to return and await news of the developments at the hospital. All I could do was watch the telly and for about tenth occasion that day see the miners go back to work, wondering if the operation would go ahead and more importantly would the kidney take. Also hoping that my mum would not return the next morning meaning the transplant was off, kidney not compatible. No news was good news. It was quite a day for the NUM and Mum.

To this day many people think the strike was a pay claim when it was about keeping mines open for future generations. The families could begin to sort out their rent and mortgage arrears that had accumulated over the previous year.

I friend of mine who I did my law degree with joined the police force and told me that during that year police were earning lots of overtime and the headquarters of the NUM received, especially during the summer months, post cards from various parts of the globe, personally addressed to Arthur Scargill thanking him for allowing them to afford such an expensive holiday.

I also heard that year that as well as strikers once picketing a nuclear power station to stop the coal from arriving, there was an odd confrontation in a normal picket line during the winter months.

One picket brought a child's policeman's helmet and when they built a snowman they put it on his head. The police repeatedly asking the miner to remove the helmet but they refused. One officer got in the police range rover and rammed the snowman, only to then realise that it had been built over a concrete pillar and the range rover was a right off.

I do not know what the offence was, possibly breaching the Impersonating A Police Officer (Snowman) Miscellaneous Provisions Act as amended by the Emergency Provisions (Child's Toy) Act.

CLICK...WKQ: 1+1+1 =3

Parity for the first time in years. You guessed. The kidney transplant operation happened and was a success. And Mum could have one of her favourites food again. Beetroot.

There is an NHS policy of only removing the home dialysis machine on the anniversary of the transplant. It is assumed that by then it was a good indication that it was a going to be a good transplant. A year later my old bedroom no longer was a mini hospital ward but a bedroom again which I occasionally slept in during my later visits.

After a year or so my flat mates left and I was once again left living in a property with a landlord who wanted me out. He was not interested in getting the place filled with new joint tenants of my choice. He just wanted me out, vacant possession, and no doubt increase the rent for the next batch. I decided to have an eviction party ("Please bring an axe"). On the evening of the party I was in the local pub and members of our gate crash syndicate told me of my own party. They had to have the evening off as they were now officially invited.

I moved all my stuff out, fitted the music system in a now very empty wardrobe, which had the added advantage of preventing people from accidentally pouring beer over the electrics. Also I had a key so no one could change my tapes so I stayed in charge of the music. If a tape finished, someone would have to get the resident DJ who soon was not going to be resident much longer. Unfortunately during a tape switch the key snapped in half while still stuck in the wardrobe lock which was locked. There was a party type crisis because unless something was done there would be no more music for the rest of the evening. So I gave permission for the back panelling to be unceremoniously removed. Music was soon restored.

A few days later I was involved in the humbling experience of showing the landlord round the property to prove I was entitled to the return of my deposit. When he came into my room I was hoping he wasn't going to spot a half key in the wardrobe lock. Thankfully desperate to justify holding on to my deposit, he started to focus on a little tear on the wallpaper where I had previously had my fine collection of solicitors' firms rejection letters. I got my deposit back.

I always wondered how the new tenant would react to going to the wardrobe. Maybe when it opened he would look in and be met by one of my guests saying "hey man I have been laying in this dark hall way waiting for you to come out of that toilet for ages"

This brings to mind an incident years earlier involving a previous flat mate from another flat whom, as I was to find out, slept in the nude. A few days after moving in he went for a night pee and thought he was in his old flat. He left his bedroom, sleepily took the first right expecting to be in his usual toilet but on hearing a heavy clunk behind him suddenly turned and realised he had walked out of the flat. The door had shut on him and he was without his key or anything else for that matter. He was in the landing with flats above and below. His only hope was to wake me up but could not shout, as I might not be the first person to hear him and answer the door. Luckily for him I heard this little sparrow constantly knocking on the door, whispering "Mick, Mick" I opened it saying something like hey what type of party did you go to but I was pushed out of the way as he rushed back in.

"What's in the bag"?
"Do you really need to know?"
This retort appeared to get the nightclub bouncer extremely interested, as I had not obediently opened it up for him. I admit it was a reasonable request but I tried to avoid having to give the slightly embarrassing explanation as to why I was lugging around all my recently passed urine. I should have simply stayed in that night and gone to my hospital check up the next morning like everyone else does.

Remarkably my hesitancy seemed to get him to over look his earlier order and I was let in. Maybe he thought I was dealing in grass! During the first half-hour or so many people asked me what was in the bag so I decided to hide it behind one of the space invader machines which was the rage at the time. (That's the computer game not collecting 24-hours worth of urine)

When I spotted nature walking up the driveway for a call I retrieved the bag, headed for the gents and quickly got inside a cubicle. If you were lucky you found one with a door attached and even, more optimistically, a lock. Afterwards I would once again re-hide the bag and return to my friends. On the second visit some time later I went to pick the container up. It had disappeared.

I needed to present an accurate 24-hour collection for the hospital as otherwise they would have the wrong readings. This could possibly result in a temporary incorrect diagnosis. I was impatient to avoid becoming an in-patient again which might happen if they needed to keep a closer eye on the next few results. I needed to empty my bladder quickly. Nature was now ringing the doorbell incessantly.

I scurried around the game machine area in a panic and came across the bag with the container still inside ..... with the top off. Oh No! Somebody must have thought it was cider ("God this stuff tastes like ...) I grabbed the container, found the top on route to the gents and returned to a cubicle. I went into one putting my back against the door because there was no lock. As I was filling the container a head appeared over the top from someone standing on the adjacent toilet seat. I felt a bit of a weirdo, being caught peeing into a bag and then I thought: hang on who's the pervert round here! After getting a strange look from the head it disappeared as quickly as it had arrived. I then went back to see my friends but this time decided to put up with all the dumb questions.

The recent rediscovery of drinking was good for the kidney because the regular flushing out and empting of the bladder reduced the possibility of infections. However drinking to excess would be stupid for two reasons: firstly a hangover effectively means headaches, which means dehydration; your brain is squeezed dry for lack of fluid. This can damage my kidney or should I say my Dads. I would joke that we had a great understanding: I drank and he woke up with the hangover. Also if you ended up being sick with my weak stomach that could set off a chain reaction possibly leading to repeat huge hemotemisis. I do not want to be in the middle of a red cell shower ever again.

Leaving that nightclub another time three blokes ran up to me and said in an intimidating manner:

" Have you been mugged yet"

"No I only sent the application forms off yesterday". I heard someone say. Oh no what have I said. It was me. Maybe they didn't quite hear me. Oh dear I might have had it this time. Well at least I am not going to get a ruptured spleen. Surprisingly they walked away which was a relief as my next intended hospital visit was in a few weeks not that night in an unfamiliar ward.

Maybe my unorthodoxed response completely threw them. Obviously it could have just been a joke: to see me scared. Had I acted as if I was easy bashing up fodder or been aggressive and challenging they would have to stand up for themselves and defend their insulted macho ego. So in retrospect I may have done the right thing.

I tried to get back into sport but contact sport could risk my kidney but I thought 5- a-side football would be OK until I realised whom my team was up against. One particular player could not play but he compensated for that by fouling you. We had no referee so it could get a bit scary for my kidney and me. He had been in the army and participated in Falklands War and had now gone AWOL (Absent without leave) from the French Foreign Legion (I am not making any of this up you know: it's all true. Cross my kidney and hope it rejects). When he challenged you - and I mean that not in the sporting tackle sense of the word but in the war theatre sense- he would go for the man every time and if he ended up with the ball it was a bonus. If he came to tackle you some of us would cowardly just pass the ball to him. I unwisely tried to tap the ball away from myself, when the human jaugernaught went by and attempted to go round him and hopefully collect the ball. Well that was the plan anyway. Once he realised I may be taking the piss, he tackled me with extra vigour. His next tackle resulted in the law of gravity being temporally suspended and I was similarly suspended when the law returned like a switch being er switched back on and I came back to earth with a bump. I reminded him I did not have any Argentinean ancestry. I then feared for my kidney and played in goal for the rest of the season, safely ensconced in the "D" area where "out field" (but we're indoors!) players are banned

I was able to arrange these games at the university as I still had a student union card but non students had to pay the full whack but as most of the "squad" were signing on it was difficult to get them to turn up and pay to get in. One bright spark waited until the game began and banged on the emergency fire exit so we let him in, he got away without paying. Gradually over a period of weeks, everyone else copied him, so for a game requiring ten players three or four would enter the court officially. The attendant would then open up his cubbyhole into the court and scratch his head, as he couldn't recall that many students passing through the main entrance.

One time hardly anyone turned up but we – or rather I – had paid. We then asked the students who were coming off the pitch if they would like a second game. They agreed but about 20 minutes into the game we heard a tapping on the fire exit. We could only look at each other in a silent questioning plea. What could we do? We now had a team to play and our regulars were excess to requirements. Would the students twig and grass us up. They did not.

Down the nightclub I was able to put into practice my possible future potential cross-examination skills you always hear about which you have to learn if you want to become a lawyer. However the first time I tried it I was to breach one of the golden rules of cross-examination: do not ask a question you do not already know the answer to. I saw a watch on the floor and went down to pick it up when a young bloke, with all his mates in tow behind him, said
"Hey that's my watch I've just dropped it." I knew this was rubbish. I wasn't really bothered who ended up with the watch I just wanted him to know I wasn't going to fall for that. So my retort was:

> "OK then. What make is it." I covered up the newly discovered timepiece in the palm of my hand.
> Him: "I don't know it's new as it's my birthday today and I got it as a present".
> Uniform chorus immediately behind him: "Yeah"
> Me: "OK then. What's the date today?"
> He looked at me blankly and all his allies behind him didn't seem so confident about backing him up.
> Me: "So you don't even know the date of your own birthday"

Then all his posse turned on him, took the mickey and walked off. It reminds me of the so called football fans who were always loyal supporters when things were going well but as soon as they are losing badly towards the end of a game they would quickly leave the ground in disgust, only wanting to be associated with success. Well anyway I breached one of the golden rules of cross examination but from the look of the witnesses face I was pretty sure he did not even know what day it was let alone the date. Hey this cross-examination malarkey is dead easy. Gizza job.

Once when I was queuing in a grocers shop, the woman in front was insisting on only paying the amount on the item, not the correct price that was being pointed out at the check out. I was getting fed up with all the delay and rather sheepishly explained that legally the wrong price was only an "invitation to treat" and the shop couldn't be bound by it. The offer was only made when the correct price was mentioned. Both looked at me as if I was very strange indeed. I was expecting someone to say but these are not chocolate, but biscuits. Luckily I got the argument stopped and made my purchases and quickly left. This law stuff can be helpful sometimes. Pity no one would give me a job.

I continued to receive benefit without any problems. At interviews I explained my situation and that I was available for work, explaining my voluntary work; the fact I was retaking my solicitors exams and pointed out my recent medical history. This appeared to satisfy them. Living on the dole was financially restricting but as long as my kidney was behaving itself I was OK.

Another rejection scare. This time it was not going to be just being pumped with a high dose of steroids but the full works: ultrasound and biopsy. The kidney appeared to be rejecting big time. Back to hospital again.

Nurses have to do all the meal chores once the food arrives from the kitchens: deliver the food, clear up afterwards, collecting all the dirty crockery and putting them in the big metal trolleys to be shipped back to the hospital kitchens You get the meal you choose by completing the meal cards you were given clearly marked distinguishing transplant from dialysis diets. Occasionally the nurse would have to fill it in for you, which happens when you were not around, in theatre, on dialysis etc. I was sitting at the four-seater table in the day room and a bowl of oxtail soup was placed opposite me. I thought nothing of it until a woman patient who I recognised as being a kidney dialysis patient due to her general demeanour such as her complexion and prominent working fistula. She sat down and started to eat it. It was difficult to communicate with her so I looked up, around and questioned whether she should be eating a high potassium meal. When the nurse returned I told her about the soup, its location and it was immediately switched with the meal she should be eating had she not sat in the wrong place.

The results of all the investigations. I – or rather my kidney – had survived again as the drugs had stopped the trend and the rejection episode had ended for another time.

These rejection frighteners got me out more and more and revising less and less. What was the point of sitting indoors-reading law books if you were not sure if you would ever use the qualification assuming you were eventually going to pass the exams and get a firm of solicitors to take you on with my poor medical history? I was in a clear dilemma: to concentrate on passing the retakes or make the most of a precarious renal function. I was coming up to the third attempt which meant I had to pass them all in one sitting.

After a few years away from the disability of renal failure I merely had to cope with getting through the check ups and overcoming the rejection scares, I became more aware of how people treat anyone with any form of disability. The physical aspects are easy to spot: the wheel chair, the white stick, and the missing limb. But not all physical disabilities are clearly visible. When I was experiencing End Stage Renal Failure I was the hypochondriac as there was no part of your body to point to indicate a real physical disability. The same applied for mental disability or impairment unless behaviour in public is outlandish.

On the other hand a friend of my mine had been blind from birth and experienced what I would classify as patronising disability awareness.

We were in a pub and in looking around for a couple of seats. Spotted what looked like two spares by a small group, one was spare but the other was "taken". In loud pubs these seat enquiring conversations can go on forever where the resident Keeper of the Seats says "yes" and you do not know if that is an answer to what they guess is your question "yes" you can have it or "yes" it is taken. Anyway as only one seat was available I went back to my friend and a few minutes later one of them brought the seats over once they realised "he" was blind. I returned it politely pointing out that just because someone cannot see doesn't mean the legs do not work and he cannot stand up in the corner of a pub.

Going into another pub on another occasion I am told by the bouncer "he cannot come in." I then told him "don't tell me tell him." Just because I was his eyes for the night did not mean I had also become his brain.

On a more sinister note I was at the night club I keep going on about and when I returned from the bar with our drinks he told me that while I was away someone came up to him and kicked him telling him to stop staring at his girlfriend. I fathomed out what must have happened. His eyes were open not looking but appearing to be staring out and not moving. They unfortunately must have been facing the direction of this blokes girlfriend and he had not worked out my friend could not see. On returning from the bar we could not for obvious reason identify the moron so I could challenge him.

Even more bizarrely on another occasion he was walking with another friend and coming towards them on the same narrow pavement were a group of young men. He did not drop his shoulder as they passed and as he had not realised how narrow the pavement was, they knocked shoulders. He swore, they turned round and on realising he was blind beat up the person he was with. I do not know what kind of Citizens Charter boneheads have but there must be a paragraph hidden away.

Sub section 6.7: Saving Face.
"If your mate, like, knocks me or any of me mates and he's, like, not all there or disabled sort of thing, then we'll leave him out of it and kick your bleeding head in. In it"

Or maybe they had badly grazed their knuckles on the pavement

Sub section 6.8: Staring at my pint.............

You would be lucky if as a youngster you did not at least hear of a Mugging or an assault on someone you knew. I heard of a few.

-At a bank dispensing machine at a late hour with no one else about apart, of course, from you friendly neighbourhood assailant. Once the muggee was about to tap in his pin number, he saw a knife. A mugger suggested he ask for more than he had originally intended. The display said sorry we can not dispense your request, the mugger then began a series of demands for the next amount down to be tapped in while, looking over his shoulder getting a bit agitated that this simple plan had failed and he had the misfortune to have accosted an impoverished student. Eventually he gave up cursing his bad luck, the overdrawn student in the final analysis welcoming his.

-I lent to a friend the novel, The Fatherland, by Robert Harris. It was about life if Hitler had won. On walking home he was mugged by two black men and when he showed them the book he was fearful they might mistake him for a nazi. Luckily they did not but stole the book.

-Just before x-mass a friend of mine was challenged by a knife wielder at a very infamous mugging spot and ordered to empty his pockets. On doing so the mugger saw an item covered in silver paper, thinking it was his lucky day he snatched it assuming it to be a big lump of cannabis resin. Later on when unwrapping it was found to be a mince pie.

If ever I was to be mugged and someone picked me up off the ground - after the first seventeen passers by, walked past, as they did not want to get involved; nothing to do with then or couldn't stop because they would miss the start of East Enders – and I was asked if I was OK, I would be one of the select few of males who would say I am fine and relieved but it would totally depend on where I had been hit. As long as it was nowhere near my kidney.

So I'm being cynical. I was walking down a city street with a friend at the end of the night and noticed everyone ahead of us on the same side of the street either looking in or slowing down at a particular shop doorway and then quickly walking on. When we got there what we discovered was what initially looked like a young man sitting there drinking a can having split some of it whereupon a pool had formed. On closer examination I noticed that he cut his wrist with a razor blade that was still in his hand and pool was his blood. While I tried to talk to him, discovering that his girlfriend had just left him and getting him to hand over the blade, my companion phoned for an ambulance. My attempt failed as he crunched it up in his mouth and swallowed it. We waited for the ambulance to explain what he had just done.

One night I was walking home after getting the booby price in a pub team quiz: a Max Bygraves album and what really concerned me was that I might get mugged. How would my assailants react to what I was taking home? "Max Bygraves? Hear mate. Have this tenner. Go and buy some proper music" In fact I was keeping it for a joke question in a music pub quiz that at the time I used to occasionally set.

My seven little tablet borbles containers can only assist very slightly in avoiding the kidney rejecting. The longer the transplant survives does not mean there will come a time when it will have settled in for life and you no longer need to not take the drugs. If you do it will not take long before your body twigs the kidney is foreign and attack it. Here is atypical question and answer session I have been involved in from time to time.

Q   I thought it was dangerous to be on steroids?
A   It is but I am on a maintenance dose. You're probably thinking of those idiots on large doses of anabolic steroids without having a medical need for them. Some of us have no real choice in the matter unless we want to go back on a kidney machine and that is hardly a healthy state of affairs. Anyway you can talk. You're smoking a cigarette. Passive smoking is my real risk at the moment as I am immune suppressed.

Q   Drinking. Should you be with a kidney problem?
A   My kidney works. I have not got a disfunctioning kidney. Alcohol affects the liver not the kidney. I am OK as long as I do not over do it and dehydrate. Drinking large quantities are good for the kidneys, usually not all made of this stuff as it is a diuretic

Q   When will you come off the drugs altogether?
A   Never. There is always a constant battle suppressing my body's immune system to stop it ever identifying the foreign body, my kidney

Q   Surely it's taken by now?
A   It will never fully take. It is the permanent maintenance dose of drugs constantly in my blood supply keeping the problem at bay. This is why I cannot give blood. The potential recipient, who is probably very ill could have their full recovery jeopardised if the blood, that may initially save their life, threatened the health of the recipient if their immune system was weakened just at the time it really needed to be strong.

When I attempt to explain why I have to drink so much, such as tea at every opportunity I am often told "It's bad for you, you know, tea." But in the whole scheme of things fluid is more important than the vague possibility that tea or coffee might do you some slight harm. It's nothing compared to going back on a kidney machine I can tell you. It is rather cute that some people's health problems are so non-existent that have to start inventing risks because of some research they read about. To me it's as if you are on the front line of a battle. You have to rush back to get more weaponry. You dodge the explosion at your feet and duck the bullets flying around your head and when you pick up the box of bullets you hear some well-meaning person well back from the front line say "No. No. No. You should never lift like that. Your have to bend your knees."

Taking drugs day in and day out when you are transplant recipient is to my mind completely different to most other prescribed drug taking. People with a minor complaint will take a drug on one or two occasions for, say a headache. Others will take a course of drugs for a week or so for infection. Others have to take drugs for a lifetime for unrecoverable condition like say a heart problem or diabetes. They are all to help your body. If you forget it there could be a problem but not necessarily an immediate catastrophe. With a transplant the need for the drugs is to deceive your body. If you forget to take your drugs your kidney might reject. If you forget a dose or are late you are told not to worry but just take the drugs as soon as you remember.

But how serious is it? If you forgot it might be OK as you had enough of the drug remaining in your blood stream but what if you forgot on two consecutive occasions. Would that be it? Is there an optimum residue in the blood stream below which it is curtains for the kidney?

I have heard of maverick patients refusing to take the tablets or just stopped taking them because they have had enough of all the side effects, obviously contrary to the doctors advice, but for some reason the kidney does not reject.

As I have explained before as time went on my checkups went to what was at the time the longest gap between check ups: four months. If your kidney was rejecting the test would show a trend of reduced function before any of the familiar symptoms returned. So when you attend your check up everyone looked at the previous results but that was four months ago. Anything could happen in that time. So the wait for the results became excruciatingly painful. In the early years you phoned in for the results and be told if you need to alter your dosage. With the immunsopressive drug, azathaprin it can sometimes knocked out too many of your whites cells so you become too susceptible to infections. Your immune system was too suppressed, you then did not take the drug for a few days to give your body time to recover and raise the white cell count back up again.

The unit eventually switched the duty to a don't-phone-us-we'll-phone-you responsibility. This was due to the continually growing number of transplant recipients. Initially I would get really concerned that they might have forgotten, as the next check up was not for ages. The reassurance of the phone call under the old system was, well, reassuring.

Check ups are clearly a very nervous time. I would have been in hospital most of the morning and when my phone went for the next few days, or I retuned home to a flashing red light on my answer machine, it would concern me that it could be the hospital. It was during this time that if anyone phoned me they may well have been pleasantly surprised how pleased I was that they had called. After the first few days it would not be that bad if the unit contacted me by phone or letter as it was going to be less serious, ie not the possibility of rejection, but that I had a slight infection and was advised to see my GP for a prescription for a course of antibiotics.

For me it was always tempting fate if I planned something after the next check up as I was arrogantly assuming all would be well. After a few rejection episodes I had some justification for taking this attitude.

What have a shoe, a curled watchstrap, marmalade and marmite jar all have in common?

I was concerned about changing my habits in case one of them or even a combination might be the reason for my kidney's stability. For instance I was a vegetarian, not stressed out by a strenuous fulltime job, who drank lager. If I started changing my life style and my kidney rejected could I forgive myself. These three practices or habits could quite possibly be affecting my well being without me knowing and which one, if any, was helping. Who knows? Talking to a young doctor she was explaining to me that in theory, according to the textbooks all transplants should reject but somehow they do not so. For the medical profession this line of it is not science but an art form. Last time we did that and it worked.

I did not want to rock the boat as I did not know what I was doing right or not doing wrong.

CHAPTER SEVEN: Back and Forward

I eventually passed six of the seven heads which meant I had two chances to pass that remaining one which turned out, irony of ironies to be the only head I had dragged into the real world: family and welfare benefit law. A possible sign, I suggest, of being overconfident and neglecting it in my revision. But then the bombshell and not just the shell.

At the next check up I was informed that my function had deteriorated to such an extent that I would soon have to have a fistula fitted. After a few salient questions it became apparent that my doctors knew I was having chronic renal failure for years, possible from the time of the antibody. I did not. During all those regular check ups I never knew what the doctors were thinking or knew themselves. I always assumed the kidney was not rejecting, may be not as stable as you would have preferred but definitely not rejecting. It was however not acute rejection but chronic rejection. I got annoyed with myself for not spotting this. At your regularly checkups you usually see the same consultant but not always and somewhere along the line I was not told. They must have all assumed I knew. So I thought everything was OK. It is always better that when you see a big wallop coming your way that your move your head back to lessen the power of the blow. I now had to get my head down and get through this last exam.

The hospital checkups became, once again, more frequent and the fitting of the new fistula loomed. My previous fistula from years ago had slowly died a few months after my first transplant. As you iron count increases your blood becomes more viscous, gooey rather than runny and that increased thickness sometimes results in the fistula slowly clogging up. Being right handed my first fistula was in inserted in my left arm so I could use my right hand to easily insert needles. This time my fistula had to be in my right arm so it would become more difficult using my left hand for the forthcoming regular dialysis needle onslaught.

During one of my check ups the doctor was alert to the fact that I still had to sit the remaining solicitors finals exam. If I passed I would have finally got through the academic part of qualifying as a solicitor. Only the two years articles to do but for a small problem. Hang on. How come I never got such an offer last time just before my law degree finals? Oh I remember. No one really knew me at the hospital then. I was just an in and out patient. I would have regular check ups and be seen very quickly. When I say quickly I mean the consultant saw me quickly but I was not quickly in and out of the hospital. There were hours of waiting. This time the consultant who I saw knew I was trying to qualify as a solicitor over the last few years and making a real dogs dinner of it.

The consultant suggested a series of blood transfusions to increase my haemoglobin level, building it up to coincide with the date of this exam resit to help me get through it as all the familiar symptoms of renal failure were returning such as anaemia, low iron count.

≈≈≈
≈≈≈
≈≈≈
≈≈≈≈≈≈≈≈≈≈≈≈≈≈≈≈≈

Now imagine a few wavy lines. We are going back in time. You will recall those months during the last year of my law degree when the kidney failure symptoms grew: the cramps, ≈≈≈≈≈≈≈≈≈ the change in skin complexion, ≈≈≈≈≈≈≈≈≈the tiredness, ≈≈≈≈≈≈≈≈≈the swollen ankles, often feeling sick, ≈≈≈≈≈≈≈≈≈ being sick, itchy skin, ≈≈≈≈≈≈≈≈≈ poor concentration, ≈≈≈≈≈≈≈≈≈≈leg cramps, ≈≈≈≈≈≈≈≈≈restless legs, and headaches. ≈≈≈≈≈≈≈≈≈The "Come on Mick. Can't you walk faster than that? We'll be late". Well it all happened all over again. This time I remember not being able to eat very much. It was due to the build up of fluid in my body pressing against my stomach. Strange how I did not recollect that symptom the first time round and then I had two very enlarged kidneys.

≈≈≈
≈≈≈
≈≈≈
≈≈≈

I'm on my way to Wembley .....to take this one exam, which is where all the lucky law students who only had one or two exams were allowed to re take at a winter sitting. I even felt like a cheat, a bit like those sportsman and women using performance-enhancing drugs. Looking back it was a dangerous time for blood transfusions, just at the time of the AIDS scare when blood transfusions were only just being scanned and heated to prevent the virus spreading. I passed but events had moved on and once again an exam pass was not a time to celebrate.

CLICK .... WKQ: 1+1+0 = 2

My first day back at the dialysis unit as a dialysis patient was not one of my better days. I was back on the day shift, three five-hour shifts actually on a operating dialysis machine but much longer in the unit setting up and clearing up. The day shifts are for training on new developments in dialysis medicine. The machines had improved and were more sophisticated. They now had more sensors. For example if there was an air pocket in the lines a buzzer would sound and the machine would stop. This extra safety system prevented any possibility of a big air pocket going into your blood steam that can be fatal.

I remember getting the corner dialysis machine and been "plugged in" by a nurse who didn't want to talk and treated the whole operation as if he was servicing a car. Once settled in I was left with a meal, my first dialysis meal while on the machine for several years.

After a few mouthfuls I threw up and pressed the buzzer. The unit was silent. Once all the meals are distributed the nurses have theirs, leaving us all to tuck in to our mouth-watering dialysis meal. A nurse came rushing up to my machine and on realising who was attached to it called back towards her colleagues "It's OK. It's only Michael." This first day back was getting worse by the minute. However, on later reflection the comment was a backhanded compliment: Michael can look after himself. Cannot be anything serious, as Michael would not have blundered in that way.

The non-dialysis diet meal in the first hour had to wait until I began my longer hours in a few weeks time during the evening shift when I could "put myself on" and "take myself off" the machine and not normally really need the nursing staff. Hence the reduced staff in the evening.

A couple of sessions later another nurse asked me how long I had had my previous kidney. When I told her she suggested I "was lucky and that's good. Let's see if we can get another kidney that good for your next time." Maybe I expect too much but I wanted one that lasted for the rest of my life. I can dream and anyway I was not lucky. Maybe a lucky kidney patient but not a lucky person.

My mate Morris mentions:

> "The return to dialysis after transplantation is a difficult period for the patient and the nephrologist. Not only are there understandable emotional difficulties, but also there are frequently physical problems. Early graft {transplanted kidney} failure is less traumatic for the patient who has not enjoyed independence from dialysis" p42

I hope s/he did not mean it as it was worded. I cannot just ignore the part that there is a "difficult period for the patient and the nephrologist" I am not knocking my doctors, all of who I always had and still have total confidence in but come on. The situation is not exactly the same is it? It's like saying: "Professor Plumb was found in the parlour having been plunged to death after repeated stabbings and lost a lot of blood. This was very distressing for Professor Plumb and Karla Klarke the carpet cleaner.

There was no proposal to arrange for someone to talk to me about what is clearly going on in my mind: I am back on a kidney machine. It is times like these that some doctor or nurse trained in psychology should check patients out. They should do it the first time you go on a machine or better still from the moment your know you are heading back to one. I wasn't. If the NHS ever get more than enough money just to keep us alive they should put some aside for patients about to face the prospects of spending the rest of their life on a kidney machine. A little bit of, or at least an offer of counselling would not go amiss.

I saw a psychiatrist when I lost my memory after my kidneys were removed. The trauma, possible worse for a younger person, is obvious and every patient should be offered someone to talk to. The renal nurse training should incorporate the knowledge of what to say as well as what not to say rather than the patient having to gleam things from over worked doctors and nurses and wanting to ask lots of questions yet feeling guilty that you may be keeping the doctors from a more needy patient. You just wanted you anxiety relieved.

And I do not want one of those new age counsellor. "Well Michael. Imagine you are a tree. Yes? Are you with me Michael? Yes you are a tree and these dialyses machine tubes are your new branches and the artificial kidney over there that's a bird nest." Yeah right. You're on one of my branches. Now fly away and go and catch some worms. I am doing my own bird: a kidney machine prisoner with no release date. No. I am just requesting I be given the opportunity to talk to someone to talk things through and not come out with glib and unrealistically optimistic clichés or something without really thinking.

An early new kidney did not seem promising. I had already asked my Dad for the other one (but no luck there) and so I had to rely on what is called a cadaver: a dead person, so their misfortunate (a bit of an understatement) could benefit me. I always knew my blood group was b negative which was only 5 % of the population which indicated a long wait for another transplant but a nurse told me that meant you would be on the top of the list if a kidney with that blood group became available. I could not work that out as an advantage. The chances were less frequent unless people with that blood group were genetically more disposed to being bad drivers or crossed roads without looking both ways. New on the scene was EPO, a manufactured form of iron for the blood. When I enquired whether I could "score" some I was told it does not work on polycystic kidney sufferers.

Years before a fellow dialysis patient had gone away for the weekend but had forgotten to give the transplant team his contact telephone number. When he returned and attended his next dialysis session he was told the efforts made to find him, which as I was told included calling the police. He was informed that a kidney had become available for him but they had to offer it to another patient as he was uncontactable and they could not wait any longer. My, did he feel sick. That was not going to happen to me. I would go out of my way to check my phone bill was paid early. I occasionally got paranoid and if the phone had gone off or not used for a day or so I would check we were still connected by picking it up to hear the tone.

Returning to the routine I had left years ago I hoped I would never have to return to again. I had two weekly sessions of dialysing of at least eight hours each on the machine. One day I stayed over because I had not cycled in. That morning I was waiting at the bus stop with the workers starting their productive day, fainted and fell into the road. My very first total back out, without any notice whatsoever. Usually I had a few seconds to plan my descent to the floor remembering to head but the occasional computer monitor if one was in the immediate vicinity. It was only while I was being picked up by two people in the bus queue did I realise I must have gone hypo. Usually I have a few moments notice but this time it was sudden. I was being walked to the hospital emergency and accident department but it took me what seemed like ages in my confused state to explain I should be taken to the dialysis unit. A little battle of the wills then ensued whereby my rescuers tried to frog march me in the direction of emergency out patients when I was pushing us all towards the dialysis unit that was in the other direction.

Eventually they relented and when a familiar face belonging to one of the nurses took me off them I got what I interpreted as a who's-been-a-naughty-boy look and felt embarrassed that I had let the unit down by allowing myself to go hypo and having to be rescued by these two members of the public who were now late for work and quite probably in trouble with the boss. ("Why are you late?" "You'll never guess....")

My blood pressure was taken and found to be very low. I was told I had to drink 6 litres of fluid and that I could not go home until I had drunk it which took nearly the rest of day.

What must have happened is that I had dialysed too much fluid off the night before and not noticed my drop in weight. So when I got up and walked to the bus stop I took my blood pressure tablet and that had dropped my blood pressure even further so while I was waiting for the bus the tablet took affect and then I fainted. I was so lucky as it was the rush hour. Buses and cars were passing along that road at quite a speed. Just think I could have been run over by a bus. What a cliché way to go. I just hoped that it would have been a taxi that had run me over, not so common don't you think?

A strange one off incident happened to me while coming off the machine on another occasion. I think I must have had a fit. Whilst taking myself off the machine I sheepishly and slowly raised myself to my feet to ensure readiness to quickly sit down again in case I went hypo and collapse into a heap. I made it but a few moments later, although still keeping my balance, the top half of my body appeared to have a mind of its own and was taking quick repeated bows to an invisible audience in the corner of the room. I was then grabbed from behind by a nurse who spotted me and prevented me from falling over.

After my second honeymoon period was over I returned to volunteering at the advice centre and followed the old routine of dialysis, strict diet, restricted fluid content and permanent feeling of tiredness.

At the beginning of one session I noticed that the needle packaging appeared different but thought nothing of it. Before I went on I was warned by one of the nurses that the unit had now to use new needles and once again thought nothing of it. Once the machine was ready and I was about to insert the needles I noticed that they did not behave like the old ones. The familiar ones did not bend. You would put the needle into the little bubble on your skin, which was evidence of the whereabouts of the local anaesthetic you had only just injected into the area. But when you pushed in the new needle further into your arm, into your enlarged vein it would meander and rather than nest in the centre of the wide vein, it would have a mind of it's own and sometimes leave the vein though another wall into your body tissue and then the vein would blow. By blow I mean it became very painful as the vein closed down in that region and swelled up. You had to stop, pull out the needle, press down to suppress the blood flow, hold it there for several minute, as the heparin made it longer to clot, and while waiting look along the arm for another site as this one was now history for the remainder of this session at least. You were now delayed in starting your session and had to continue to press hard against it waiting for it to clot. Alternatively you could pick up a very powerful clamp that you could put on your arm and locate another site so as not to waste anymore time beginning the eight hour session.

I asked if I could use the more reliable old needles again but it was reluctantly acceded by one of the nurses that I could not. We all now had to use these new cheaper ones. I eventually had to devise a new technique, like everyone else, of controlling these less obedient needles over the forthcoming sessions, however long that was to be.

Arriving at home from a different kind of session, at the advice centre, I heard the phone going as I put my key in the door. It was the hospital. A familiar voice belonging to a nurse on the other end told me that there might be kidney available and suggested I might want to come up to the hospital that evening and take tests. I left a note for my flat mate and set off to the hospital.

The Intensive Care Unit (ICU) was literary next door to the Renal Unit. Over the years while walking along the corridor I would often look into the small waiting room opposite where on glancing in I would see very restless relatives waiting for news on their friend or relative.

On this occasion I couldn't look in case I caught someone's eye. This time it was different: I was about to possibly benefit from their loss.

At the unit I was immediately put on the machine, not in the dialysis unit, but in the transplant unit. I had to keep my expectations under control, as I knew there were many hurdles before a possible operation not to mention a successful operation and successful transplant. A short while after a young blonde male joined me in the twin dialysis bay room. We started chatting. While dialysising through the night it became apparent that he had also been called in for a possible transplant. It suddenly dawned on me that we might be in direct competition for the same kidney from what I learnt from the system of kidney distribution. We were rivals because usually if there is a death resulting in a possible donation, most likely as a result of a road traffic accident, one of the kidneys is offered to the UK while the other is offered further a field to, say, the rest of Western Europe.

This was going to be a very awkward, demanding and all night long dialysis session. It appeared to me that for one of us it was going to be a complete waste of time, possibly for both of us. Neither of us could sleep nor even doze. Every nurse entrance could be bringing good news for one of us, or bad news for both. Or it could be night nurse popping to do a mundane chore.

A few hours earlier a distraught group of relatives had possibly just left the same hospital after being told of the death of a loved one, having – as is often the case – to make a immediate decision while at the same time recovering from a family loss where they had already made a decision about whether to keep the life support machines running.

A part of you wants this potential rival to be told he was not going to have the operation because early tests showed he was incompatible. It was a rotten feeling. We must have inwardly have held the same awkward sentiment but as experienced kidney patients at such a young age we were old timers and simply had to behave stoically and see how the night was to pan out. Blood samples were taken and we both began pestering the nurses as to whether the results were back and what were are respective results for the possible contender for the kidney.

It then emerged, after irritating constant questioning from me, that both kidneys of the unfortunate person were in the hospital and for some reason - possible because by chance we were the most compatible patients in Europe, both having the same rare blood group - we were no longer competing for the same kidney. This reduced the tension in this marathon all night dialysis session.

The nurses reported back that the tests were looking good for both of us and unless there was late reaction between our bloods and the two kidneys we may be "lucky". In the morning we were told that we were both compatible and both would be having the operation in the morning.

CLICK .... WKQ: 1+1+1=3

I was getting rather blasé about major surgeries. At this one, while I was going under I looked around me and all I saw was nothing but faces with white or blue masks attached and in my stoned stupor before losing consciousness I remember asking "which bank is it today then lads?"

The reverse barrier nursing room had a few improvements since my last visit: colour telly, remote control and a painkiller drip which, to a limited extent you could control. I was very careful in not being too greedy in pressing the device to allow another mini injection of the painkiller. After years of self-control over diet and fluid intake and dealing with confronting pain I was able to do this quite easily. As you did not know when you would need more you did not want to press the hand squeezey thing only to discover you had used up you limit for the day. Also, some of the previous restrictions appeared to have gone. You could now have a few things brought in from the "outside" such as get-well cards. All in all, luxury.

The ward sister, who I got on with and had in the past lent her some of my music tapes (the one I remember being "Future Days" by Can, very appropriate what?) commented that I bet my parents would be pleased now that I was having a transplant so quickly. She looked at me in amazement when I told her that I had not told them yet or anybody apart from the quickly scribbled note I had left for my flat mate. While I tried to explain that everything happened so quickly, the phone call, the fact that there was uncertainty through out the night, not wanting to disturb the few night nurses from what they were in the middle of to ask for a phone. I did not want to raise my parents hopes up and give my mum her own all night international table tennis tournament until I knew for sure and by then there was very little time before I was made ready for theatre. The sister let out a deep sigh and walked off saying she was going to phone them now. I could not really stop her strapped to the bed with all the drips (see previous transplant) I felt then, as it appeared to be going well, that maybe it was time to tell them.

When my parents arrived they could only come as far as the door entrance and when my mum saw me she burst into tears. I felt like tearing out all the tubes attached to my body and walk up to her to show her I was ok but that would have been a bit stupid.

The kidney did not waste any time getting stuck in to relieving me of the extra fluid that had previously been the machine's job. My urine bag was nearly bursting at the seams. I had my third day x-ray with the little hour trip away from the barrier room and things looked very promising. I was soon off the dialysis diet. Then there was the heart scan and the daily visit of one particular medical specialist: The Return Of The Physiotherapist!

I was soon out of the barrier room and back into a normal ward room. My bladder muscles were not as weak as before because there was only a comparatively short period where I had stopped peeing.

Unfortunately my kidney transplant "blood brother" was going through hell. Initially his transplant went well but due to what appeared to be the many antibodies in his body before the transplant, his body did not waste any time trying to reject the kidney. He was to go on some very powerful drugs to avoid it. One side effect was to cause all is hair to fall out during the few days he was on it in the hope the drug would stop the acute rejection episode.

Meanwhile the doctors were impressed with my new kidneys figures but his plight obviously detracted from the feeling of good fortune I was experiencing.

No room at the ward. So remarkable was my initial successful transplant and operation recovery that one day, without warning, the ward sister came to my room and told me they had to discharge me early. As they were short of beds and as I was the healthiest patient in the ward and had to leave. It was only about nine or ten days after the operation. I was not ordered to leave but I was asked with whether I could cope at home and I explained it would just be me there for the first week. It looked as if I had an option to protest and put my case that I was not sure if I was well enough yet but I didn't. I was in two minds: on the one hand I wanted to get out there with my new kidney and test it out but at the same time I was a bit apprehensive about being discharged so soon. But I had no qualms about going when the time came later on that day. After all someone needed the bed more than me.

I waited for my new supply of steroids that I remained on since the last transplant, to avoid going "cold turkey", but the dose was to be increased. I was introduced to a new immunosuppressive drug called cyclospurin. It was so new it was not yet in tablet form but had to be taken as a medicine and so I was also given a syringe like device so I could administer the correct dosage each day. Before leaving I was reminded, more than once, how expensive this new drug was compared with the earlier azathaprin that I had stopped taking when my previous transplant had failed. I was told several thousand pounds worth of taxpayer's money was in my bag. That's each year mind. Although to keep off a kidney machine would be several times more expensive to keep me alive. What was I suppose to do or say to that? Oh I'll just have the one then.

In the ambulance back to my flat I was thinking about how I could incorporate this clumsy syringe into my systems to avoid forgetting to take the drug and what to do if in the unlikely event I had another huge hemotemises. It was about the same time after the last transplant that I was picking myself off the ward toilet covered in blood. I would be very unlucky if it happened again. So I planned for it.

My flatmate had gone on holiday to New York and I would be on my own. I decided that if I got that funny buzzing noise I could not afford to go to the loo in my own flat but would have to endure the indignity of going out on to the street, possible with a note attached around my neck: "Hello, or rather goodbye. Now stop gawping and get an ambulance".

Once in the hall way I was met with my first obstacle getting up the stairs. For a moment I thought I could do it in two journeys. First, take the drug ladened bag up stairs and then go down for the wound. No that wouldn't work. I must be suffering from the side effect of residual anaesthetic drug still in my system. Leave the wound up in the flat and go back down and get that bag. No. I had devised a plan. To reduce the discomfort I held on to my side and leant against the stairway wall and pushed myself up the stairs holding on to my bag with the other hand.

Once in the flat I looked around. It had been empty for sometime. Guess what: the food cupboard was bare. Apart that is from what to most people would be all the boring usual stuff: the tin of beans, the tin of tomatoes but to me they were to be rediscovered luxuries. I could now make a meal with them without any thought of the potassium contents. I now had to leave the flat again. Walking to the shops had to be planned. I still had my stitches in and so had to devise a speed of walking without unnecessarily attracting attention to myself: not too slow that people might enquire if I was ok and suggest I be in hospital ("Full. Just checked") or just think me a bit weird or walk too fast and make the operation wound too painful. Well it was hardly a big concern but it quickly vanished when I realised I could shop without any restrictions and even went so mad as to by myself a box of chocolates!

Once back at the flat I read while eating the chocolates and was quite amazed how quickly I could read. I had not discovered such a vast improvement in my concentration abilities at the same stage of my previous transplant. This may have simply been because last time I had the poor start; the rush to the Poly to start the solicitor's finals course; the fact I had no time to relax and compare and contrast plus the speed on this occasion of being discharged. I did have certain doubts about eating nearly half a box of chocolate. Part of me thought they were still dangerous and may be risking a cardiac arrest. I felt like I would be up against the Pythonesque "crunching frog" ("if it did not have real frog bones in it wouldn't be crunch would it?") or "spring surprise" (" .. two steel bolts spring out into each cheek..") but I just ended up feeling slightly sick. Apart from that self-imposed over indulgence the only discomfort was getting out of my seat because of my comparatively fresh operation wound when I still had my stitches in.

For the next few days I would be picked up every morning, taking with me the requisite 24 hour collection, spending the morning back in hospital for the standard regular check ups, eventually having my stitches out and dropped back off at the flat. I slumped myself in a chair and gave myself a refresher course in recent law updates. I needed to get up to speed for possible interviews for articles, thinking all the time that I might be ignored because of the now growing list of obstacles : the period on the dole; the inordinate number of attempts to pass the exams; the perceived probability that I would always be ill and requesting time off work and the risk of my new kidney rejecting.

Unlike after my first transplant I immediately felt I had more energy. This time I could, at the risk of sounding Churchillian, afford myself a short period of relaxation. After a while when the wound healed and the hospital check ups reduced to once a week, I fully appreciated my new invigorated healthy body when I walked down the street. It is clichéic but I really did feel as if I was walking on air. But all that indicated was that I was not "up" but just no longer "down". Beforehand it required more effort doing something as mind numbingly mundane as walking down a street. I wanted to collar someone and ask them: "So this is what it is like having fully functioning kidneys all the time and I bet you have not even considered it once in you life or even what they do or even where they are. Bye. Have a nice day."

The Komposite Kid is big and strong,
He's immuno suppressed all day long,
The potential bars: the countless scars
The goodness that's in ...a decent diet.

The milky zits are on me

My teenage acne was back. That's the third time in my life to date. This was due to the increase in steroids. If my transplant behaved and my body carried on allowing it to be hoodwinked by these drugs, the dosages would be reduced to a maintenance level once again. After a time the new very expensive, if I may remind you, cyclosporin was in tablet form. I no longer had to go around with a drug users kit bag including a syringe to measure the exact dosage. When I say tablet form it was still liquid but encased in a gelatine capsule but it was tablet to me. Several large horse tablets.

Morris again:

"Some of the side effects of immuno-suppressive drugs can be distressing, such as the hirsutism of cyclosporin {hairiness} and the obesity that is, in part, due to steroids. The patient should know what to expect with regard to the operation and postoperative period, for example, the possibility of delayed graft {kidney} function and readmission for diagnosis and treatment of rejection episodes. Counselling is required to cover all these points." p56

He also referred to one side effect of steroids as the "brutalisation of the face"p220

I was soon back giving free legal advice at the centre. It had been a while since I was last there. It came home to me when I took my usual short cut. To avoid going down one road, round a corner and back up the adjacent road I would climb over a tiny wall which was part of derelict house and once had a window on it, through the ruins, the unkempt garden and out into the street. This time I was engrossed in thought and lifted my leg intended to climb in when I suddenly to my shock noticed nice new curtains, a freshly painted frame and a windowpane and sharply withdrew. Just in time. Just before the happy new occupants were saying something akin to: "Seems like a nice and quite neighbourhood darling" and some hoodlum puts is boot through their living room window ("Well it was like this Officer.....")
        One day after a hospital check up the phone rang and one of the other workers turned to me and said I had a call from the hospital (Gulp) I went over to the phone fearing the worst. The nurse on the other end said "Michael we have just

had your results back. Please go back on to a low potassium diet immediately as your potassium level results are very high." From the phone conversation I found it strange how my kidney function had not deteriorated but my potassium was high. When I put the phone down I suddenly realised that about an hour ago I had just had a big mushroom pizza. Mushrooms, you will recall are very high in potassium and banned outright if you are a dialysis patient. I could quite possibly have a heart attack soon.

I did not know what the best thing to do. If I phoned the hospital back there is nothing much they could do and if spoke to them or to my fellow workers in the centre everyone might get into a panic and that itself may put my stress levels and blood pressure up which may bring on a cardiac arrest which I could have avoided if I kept calm. I went into the toilet to try and make myself sick. As last years all comers vomiting record holder, the only time I wanted to puke my guts up, I could not. I started to drink more to see if emptying out my bladder might help.

I swayed between thinking that if the potassium levels were or could be dangerously high they would have sent an ambulance for me or at least questioned me about what I had eaten since my tests were taken. Maybe they realised that in the circumstances all they could do was warn me and hope for the best.

I decide there was nothing I could do and calculated that if I was going to have a heart attack it would be in the next two hours and I just had to keep calm. I walked home very slowly and made sure I do not frighten myself by carelessly crossing a road. At home as the evening wore on realised I must have got away with it. The next morning I woke up relieved that I had done so. It was a good job the café did not do puddings like banana splits.

I went into to the hospital the next day for more tests to double check these odd results. I stayed on the low potassium diet and phoned up for the results. And heard this. "Oh nothing to worry about Michael you kidney is fine. The potassium machine was not working properly. You can go back on to a normal diet" More money for the NHS. That's' what I say.

As well as returning to the advice centre, I also started working at the TUC Unemployed Workers Centre which had a weekly "out reach" session at the local Probation Office each Wednesday afternoon. Hardly any of the people on probation were interested in checking their welfare benefit entitlements. People in the area who were from the Asian community mainly took up the session. Gosh I really have difficulty using that word, community in that context for some strange reason that I cannot fathom. Community to me relates to a geographical proximity. I think the user means network and sometimes is trying to avoid the word ghetto. And then you get disabled community or gay community as if there is this little village just on the outskirts of town of gay people or disabled people and by using this phrase you are giving the impression that their whole being relates to their sexuality or disability. What's' next. "News: Mothercare are opening a new branch in the town centre this Saturday. This is very good news for the pregnant community." "Lighthouse keeper wanted. We are committed to equality of opportunity and therefore welcome applications from members of the hermit community"

Well OK then just me then. The first few people I saw had families and their benefits were all wrong and so I was able to get their benefits increased to the amount they were legally entitled to and also claim some back payments. This lead to more people just coming in not for a query but for a full benefit check.

The unemployed workers centre became the TUC Community Advice Centre and my part time job moved from the probation office to a new location and became a centre it self. I set it up with none other than the city Major. I tended to work there full time to get it off the ground. I also gave talks to other organisations. One on Consumer law to advisors from advice centres in the city and a talk on then new poll tax for I think the now defunct Claimants Union, which by definition did not have a lot of industrial power.("Right if you do not increase our benefit we are going to refuse to sign on.")

I also gave a talk to about forty pensioners, sorry members of the senior citizen community, and in explaining their welfare benefits rights realised they come from a generation that see themselves as "scroungers" if they "sponge" off the state. On reminding myself of this and the something for nothing society, half way through my talk I ignored my notes and put the point that they had no qualms about claiming family allowance – the old name for child benefit - when they were bringing up their children so if they are legally entitled to other payments they should claim that to.

On scanning my notes I suddenly realised even I was not claiming for what I should have done. In those days of supplementary benefit- changing its name to income support and then job seekers allowance - I had not claimed for my special diet. It is very common spotting just at the wrong time that when you do not understand something once you vocalise it to someone else it hits you. So I made a successful claim for a back payment and wondered if any others pensioners would now make a claim for what they were entitled to.

On my next outpatient visit I tried to hunt down the hospital social worker to check that she knew this. I eventually found her empty office and was only able to leave a note on her desk. Guess what? This benefit was abolished a few years later.

A local radio had somehow tracked me down and wanted to interview me as they had heard I had recently had a transplant and I think it must have been "transplant week" on the local station.

Here is a transcript of the interview with the journalist. The original transcript is pretty embarrassing for me so for it to be more readable I have it taken out the "errrs" ; the "well"; the "well I mean" and the "I am not a kidney transplant recipient I'm a human being"

Him:" Seven years ago both Mick O'Sullivan's kidneys stopped working after years of deterioration. A year on dialysis followed before tests showed that one of his father's kidneys was a close enough match for a transplant. This kidney lasted six years before failing and three months ago Mick had his second transplant from an unknown donor. I visited Mick at a local advice centre where he works and asked him what he has to miss out on to protect his new kidney.

Me: I just cannot forget to take my drugs. I can do anything I want. I am playing five-a-side football this evening. A few months after my first transplant I cycled from XXX to XXXX in a day and I am just as fit as anyone else. The only problem is that you have got to remember to take your drugs. You also have to make sure you go for you check-ups and you have to drink a lot.

Him: every now and again the media brings up the controversial topic of transplanting animal organs into humans. Would Mick ever consider having an animal kidney in his body?

Me: I haven't really thought about it but the jump from having part of another body, of a human, inside you to an animal is not so great a jump. For most people they have no idea what kidney patients go through. But those people would not like the idea of even having another human part inside them.

Him: with one failed transplant already how long does Mick think he's present kidney will last?

Me: you can never say it. When I had my transplant three months ago a person in the same ward had the other kidney of the same person who had died but last week his kidney had to come out. Of three weeks of having the kidney it was taken out as it didn't take. What I find very strange is that when my first kidney rejected I was talking to my friends and they would say something like never mind, hope you get a better kidney next time.

While back at the dialysis unit a nurse said let's see if we can get you just as good a kidney as last time.

Him: finally if you would like to get a donor card there is one in each copy of this week's information pack which has all of this weeks transplant topics.

At this time a new card had been published. Not just a kidney donor card but a practically anything-you-fancy-passing-on-now-you- have card.

It allows you to put in after where it states "In the event of my death, if possible contact:.. your next of kin. In the event suggests it s like a fire: it might not happen but anyway it also reminds you to tell members of your immediate family that you have this card because on your next of kin owns your body and can override your instructions on the card and not agree to allow you to "help others live after" your death.

**

CHAPTER EIGHT: An Unqualified Success

The solicitors firms were taking me more seriously. Most probably it was because I had finally passed the academic part of qualifying as a solicitor. Hopefully a new kidney transplant may signify a turning point. Little did the firms know about my fear that a kidney transplant can reject particularly after witnessing my kidney brother's quick return to the kidney machine? I updated my curriculum vitae (cv) and was able to include all the practical experience and good grounding in welfare benefit law that was only mentioned in passing on the course itself. I was therefore different to most of the other candidates in yet another respect. To increase my chances of getting articles I also took up driving lessons.

I had one interview where one of the partners was curious as to why I was interested in skull shapes and sizes and how they were supposed to indicate intelligence. The nazi may well have been interested in this "science" but I was not. I had put "graphology" down in my cv as one of my interest but he had somehow confused it with the word phrenology or craniology. At the time my interest was to see if handwriting could reveal personal characteristics. I am still not convinced. I had what I thought was a good interview but got a familiar looking rejection letter.

I received more rejections. One of which I had what I thought was also a good interview but still got the familiar standard rejection letter.

Years later someone I knew began articles with this firm After several months she handed in her resignation but the firm refused to accept it. This meant she could not be released from her "deed of articles" which for a time made it very difficult for her complete her two years and eventually qualify.

I was eventually offered articles. It would have entailed working in three departments within the firm over the next two years. There were subjects I had no real interest in: probate (wills etc); conveyancing and family. Accepting the job would have meant I would have to spend most of my time helping comfortably off middle-class people in their attempt to get and stay even more comfortably off. Assisting the up trodden. Also I would not get a lot of legal aid experience, apart from the occasional family case. Had I been offered this years before I would more than likely have accepted it but my years in the not for profit sector had changed my priorities completely. So I turned it down and hoped I wouldn't regret it.

I had previously decided not to look further than the surrounding area as I did not want to have to change renal unit and see a whole new group of doctors who did not know my full medical history. Not everything is written down in the records and for me keeping a transplant was more important than qualifying.

I had one interview that lasted two hours without a break with just the senior partner and me. I got a bit confused as to when the interview had ended and I had actually been offered the job. On refection it was a good way to interview. A long one to one informal chat meant eventually you would reveal your true self rather than continue to maintain a false front trying to impress.

Only right at the end when the senior partner introduced me to the staff and said see you on Monday did I know for certain that I had been given the job or, should I say, the deed of articles. I was eventually to become what I had been striving for for years: "a suit".

In my first few weeks I just read old cases so as to get to know the firm procedures and practice; how to run a case and how to organise a file. On reading the letters from other solicitor's firms, the opposition in the case, the infamous otherside, I would often come across opening lines such as "Thank you for you letter of the third ultimo" or "Further to your letter of the 22nd inst ...." I did not know what they meant and on asking in the office was told it meant the previous or present month. Why the writers did not just say the name of the month I don't know. I would also come across "the said" when it would have been easier to have just used the word "it". But then again, as you all know, never use a big word when a diminutive word will suffice.

Help .... hereunto .... forthwith .... hereinafter, herein, gulp..inter alia ..herewith...help... aforementioned... nothwithstanding ... help I'm drowning... gulp.. in the linguistic world of legal mumbo jumbo. You do not see so much of it these days. Maybe it is from the previous generation that has now retired. Maybe the Law Society had them all lined up against a wall and shot.

When I got my first wage cheque I had to open a bank account during my dinner hour. I had not had an account for years. Not since I was unceremoniously shown the door after my chequebook was taken from me just after I had paid off my small unofficial overdraft. This time I was treated very courteously. Now I was an articled clerk soon to be very rich qualified solicitor. They assumed. At the bank I was offered many services such as a loan ("Mr O'Sullivan. You may want to consider taking out a loan to purchase a car. Our rates are very reasonable. As we are able to offer you a Rich Potential Plus Account you will immediately be entitled to a special reduction ") and looking around the bank I could see lots of other ways to go into debt but the word being used was the more pleasing one of credit. " 10% off everything in the world! Please read the small print. Offer only available if you turn up at main office before 9.00 am on any weekday wearing a six foot giant bright yellow whelk outfit. (Normal yellow will not be sufficient) in any year when Ash Wednesday falls on a Thursday. "World" is defined as…)." During the spiel I just wanted to say just give me a simply current account so I can put my wage cheque somewhere.

Once while attempting to take £40 out of one of their hole-in-the-wall machines, a friend passed by. As I finished the conversation with him I went to take the money that had been sitting there waiting for me and the machine gobbled it up. I was so startled I looked around for a candid camera. On not being able to locate one I went into the bank. The staff member assured me that the machine would somehow know I hadn't taken the money and my account would not be affected. To be on the safe side I made a note of the date and time. After a conversation with one of the bank employees they said they would credit my account. I was immediately sceptical of this enthusiastic reassurance and was definitely going to scrutinise my next bank statement very carefully. Sure enough when my next bank statement arrived I was £40 down. I could never work out how the machine could have worked out if I had tampered with the cash once outside. Otherwise I could take out a hundred pounds use a pair of tweezers and pull out a few £20 notes and complain to the bank.

As soon as I got the job and a living wage for a single man I of course lost my welfare benefits, free prescriptions and with the cost of weekly train travel I was only just about better off financially. I had the one suit and had to wear it everyday until I could afford to buy a second one. Before then, if I got caught in the rain on the way home, I had occasionally to use the hairdryer on it to be sure it was dry for the next morning.

The cost of all the prescription I had to pay to stay away from a kidney machine meant I had to invest in an annual prepayment prescription certificate. Then about £70.00 pa. Now about £ 100.00. Nye Bevan would be spinning in his grave. He had hoped all prescriptions would be free for everyone. Regardless of income, making them non-means tested. As of right. He resigned from the Labour government cabinet when the principle was lost when the government charged 20 old pennies per prescription. A tax on the ill and the sick.

It is not usually anyone's fault to be ill especially people who will always be on prescriptions of one kind or another for the rest of their lives. I will. However the class of drug will depend on whether I keep the transplant or go back on a kidney machine unless of course I am not working when it will be free again. The Chinese government send to the executed prisoner's relatives an invoice for the cost of the bullet used during the execution to rub it in. They do not really need to do so as it is hardly going to matter in the overall scheme of things. With the UK being one of the largest economies in the world you wonder why the ill have to pay for their drugs, especially those who are on them for their rest of their reduced lives. They have enough to contend with without it being rubbed in such a way.

There was a lot of too-ing and fro-ing about who was handing out the prescriptions, the hospital or the GP. Early on the hospital took up the tab for the tabs. Then there was a period when I got them for a month even though my next check up was in four. So I had to go to my GP who couldn't give a full prescription for the remaining three months so I had to go back again. My GP thought I might be possibly exempt as I was totally reliant on them and recalled that having a fistula was one of the exemptions. However when he checked the exemption was for those with permanent fistulas for such

207

conditions as caecostomy, colostomy, laryngostomy or ileostomy, as you probably already knew about.

Little tip on renewing your prepayment prescription. Do not renew it when it is about to expire. Wait till you need your next prescription because you can back date for a week.

My week was a five day twelve hour day that I was not used to. 7 am to 7pm when I finally got home. The mad morning rush out the door to catch the train once resulted in me closing the front door behind me, only to find the wheels of my bike had been stolen. The rest of the bike was chained to railings, presumably because it was demonstrating for more rights for bikes like "Stronger break blocks for all"; "We want mudguards. When do we want them? Now!" On another bleary-eyed early morning when I looked down as I got on my bike, equipped with new expensive wheels, I noticed that I was wearing one shoe and one slipper. Another time while on the train I realised I had, horror of horrors, forgotten to put on my tie. A capital offence in a solicitor's office. So I had to hang outside a man's clothes shop, and at 9am when it opened buy the first cheapest tie I could find, run to the office and be slightly late. I was to be met with. "New tie Michael?" ("Yes, about one minute new")

In the office my desk was by a window and in the summer when the window was open you could not avoid the sound of the microphone on the tourist open top bus. Every time it turned the corner without fail I would hear: "And this is XXX Street. This is where Lady Di went shopping and bought two very expensive yet absolutely lovely dresses. On all accounts we understand that she enjoyed the visit immensely"

Once I had the strong urge to shout out of the window: "Yeah but with your money!" and duck and hide to see the quaint little tourist scene descend into a classic ending to a Muppet Show sketch. But I couldn't do it because it would have been technical incorrect as most of the passengers were American and Japanese tourists and also my boss had just walked into the room.

My first few legal jobs or rather expeditions outside the office did not go according to plan. One of my first errands was to serve a witness summons on a bank manager. When I got to the address the building was empty. The bank had moved. I then had to ring up my office so they could rush through the telephone directory and trace the relocated office and hopefully find the named individual so I could serve the court papers on him there. I could not go back to the office until I served the papers on the witness, as the court hearing was imminent. I eventually found him at the banks new offices miles away.

It was very common for the articled clerk to go to court and sit with the barrister in a criminal trial in the Crown Court. At the beginning of the day, all the lawyers and the judge would thrash out the order and estimated time of each case. Once, the judge was mighty upset because our firm had not attended a previous hearing on another case and he wanted a full explanation.

On the Judge being told the only representative from my firm, who by the way had no idea what the fuss was about, was only a mere articled clerk, said that was not good enough and demanded to see the senior partner. It transpired that there was mix up by the court with two firms with very similar names in the region.

Many times articled clerks are expected to turn up at court with the barrister, not always having been able to the read the file. Your duty was to represent the firm and take notes while the barrister "was on his hind legs"

Apparently you should never walk on the stairs when there is a Judge walking on it at the same time dressed in all his/her regalia. I discovered this when, due to the lay out of a very old court building, members of the judiciary had to walk from their robing room though the court waiting room to get to the courts. I heard the usually back to front phrase of "be up standing", looked up while descending the stairwell, and got the dirtiest look imaginable from the court usher who was escorting the Judge who did not even seem to have noticed me.

At another hearing the firms barrister was at the front of the court and I was at the back because there was nowhere else to sit. All the white wigged barristers and more experienced solicitors had grabbed all the seats and then he spoke: "Your honour it would appear that my client has not yet been arraigned." He looked across the court to me and all the other eyes in the room followed. I did not know what he was on about. I did not know what he meant by the word "arraigned". Why's he talking about the weather at a time like this. It never cropped up in any of my lectures or tutorials and if it was in the textbook I must have missed it. I was about to walk up to him and ask what arraigned meant when he looked back at his papers and said, "Your Honour. I do apologise. He has been" and sat down.

Well thank goodness for that. He's been arraigned. Now to return to the office and found out what it means. The solicitor at the office who had sent me to court for his client did not know either. I needed to solve this conundrum, out of curiosity more than anything else.

At the office we did not have an extensive law library as the main office was in another town. It was not so much a small branch office but more of a large twig office and every so often, when I came up against an obscure legal query, often a task given to the article clerk, I crossed the road to an academic bookshop with a legal section where I often looked things up.

"Arraigned: arraign-to call a prisoner to the bar of the court by name, to read to him the substance of the indictment, and to ask him whether he pleads guilt or not guilty. (1976 Osborn's Concise Law Dictionary)"

On another research visit I saw one of the firm's solicitors talking to himself in the corner of the bookshop. Initially I thought he might have lost it. So this is what the pressure of work is like once you qualify and you have to reach your monthly profit costs target to get the "bonus" element of your expected wage. Then I noticed he had his dictaphone with him and he was reading chunks of a legal source to help him out with one of his cases. He would then get it taped up by one of the secretaries. If I was to be kept on with that firm after I qualified my ambition was to get someone to swear an affidavit from one of the bible's in the bookshop. Knowing my luck I would probably have to get it sworn twice:

"Sorry you will have to do that again."

"Why?"

"Because you have in your hand Bambi's Bumper Christmas Annual. Top shelf on the left. Right. From the top: I swear by almighty god that this is my name and handwriting....".

One-day an elderly woman came into the office and said she wanted to change her will because of the way she was being treated by her adult children and wanted to disinherit them because, as she said, they knew they were the main beneficiaries under her will and saw her as an obstacle to their booty. She had decided to change the will so that it would teach them a lesson. This is usually quite dangerous because sometimes wills can be contested. It is advisable to have a letter with it explaining the dramatic change of heart establishing that she still had the mental capacity and so knew what she was doing and why.

I have since heard stories of wily rich elderly person having the last laugh. One instructed his solicitor to divulge the contents of the will only after the funeral but it was to take place in northern Scotland. The only person to make the journey from London was his cleaner. In the will it was stated that the estate was to be distributed equally between the people who attended the funeral. The cleaner got everything.

That reminds me of the husband who promised his wife he would mention her in his will but cruelly when she read the paragraph in the will relating to her it just said "hello ***". So he kept his promised.

My family learnt about a will relating to the farm that I used to work on as schoolboy. I discovered that Tide – Welsh for "granddad" – had executed his will which contained a condition that if my uncle did not leave any issue (OK then children, grandchildren) then the farm would go to my Mum's kids equally. These grandchildren, my brother, sisters and me, were chosen in preference to other relatives because, it was suggested, I was the only one who showed any interest in working on the farm in the past. My uncle got married and had a son and so the prospect of the inheritance ended.

One client had begun a claim against the police after two officers allegedly beat him up. I had to interview a witness at her home who lived in a nearby town and on leaving I was initially disoriented as to how to get back to the station. I began walking along the pavement towards an Afro Caribbean man who was talking to a woman in her front garden although he was still on the pavement. As I was walking towards the couple I suddenly realised I should be heading up the side street on the other side of the road and so I crossed the road but when I was in the middle of the road realised I was wrong and went back on the same side of the pavement. Unfortunately my change of mind and direction was directly along side the two. As I continued along the pavement I heard him say, "Look at that. He would not even walk on the same pavement as a black man". It took me a few seconds to realise he was referring to me and I was then put in a quandary: whether to turn back and explain he was mistaken but then he would see my face and probably not believe me and I could not face him looking at me and putting down this particular white honky "suit" as a racist. So I continued walking, glad he would not recognise me even though I was completely innocent of the charge against me. It was nevertheless disturbing that due to past experience he had got so paranoid or maybe it was the only rational explanation for possibly the worst timed change of mind imaginably.

I had to attend a few court hearings with family law barrister over who gets what after the divorce.

"Michael I need you to go to ****** County Court next week. It's a full ancillary relief hearing. Mr H of ******* Chambers will be attending with you. You'll need to read the *** file. It was a quickie divorce.."

"...... which Lady Di enjoyed immensely..."

"The Petitioner is very wealthy and it appears he has not disclosed all his wealth and we have difficult proving this. An application for an Anton Pillar may be appropriate. However there are rumours he has three mansions in England and a retreat in Scotland. We understand that he has recently spent a fortune on his new girlfriend including.......

" .... two very expensive yet absolutely lovely dresses......

We believe he has several bank accounts, the existence of which he is keeping from the court, as he did not disclose them in his recently sworn Affidavit of Means. We do know however that..."

"Ladies in Waiting purchased these as you may already be aware it is seen as rather unseemly for any member of the royal family to be seen handling coins of the realm"

I was given the task of interviewing new clients who were squatting on some open land. I was told to explain the law to them but after the interview decided to research it as I thought they may have rights under the Caravans Site Act 1967.I applied for emergency legal aid, got it and instructed a barrister to attend the possession hearing to get it adjourned so that a separate set of proceedings - judicial review in the High Court in London - could take place. I went to the county court in another town and was met with not only the representatives of the travellers group but the rest of them: all twenty odd! All in the county court waiting room. While I attempted to explain the process I looked up and recognised someone at the other end of the waiting room: she was a friend from my law degree days. I think the last time a saw her was during my half-day release from hospital to attend my degree graduation ceremony. Expecting a comment on my healthier but chubby steroid induced cheeks, I went up to her and asked what she was doing. She said she worked for the local council and was in court on that day because of a new age travellers campsite on their land. I then realised she was the "other side" so I had to rush away as my clients would be suspicious if they saw me being very friendly with a member of the opposing legal team. We quickly agreed to meet up for a coffee after the court case.

Being called into court was very amusing because it took ages before my clients walked into court and settled down. All you could hear for a minute or so was the heavy clod of the boots stomping in. We got the adjournment and the case went to London but the hearing was not to take place for months. Not only did we lose in the end but also it became one of a number of cases that had eventually persuaded the government, a few years later, to abolish sections of the act.

During this time the firm was getting other cases from new age travellers. Once my name was given to the police as their solicitor but not only was I not one but it involved criminal law and I was in another town and they wanted help that day. So many people are scared of contacting solicitors mainly because of the enormous fees they think they will incur when so many are entitled to free advice and at police interviews they are now all free.

New age travellers were getting a bad press during these years and were vilified for being benefit scroungers but my recently acquired knowledge on the subject lead me to believe that they had small rural trades to make a living but were not allowed to trade as they were spending most of their time finding somewhere to park and being told to move on and then getting involved in court cases. They had no option but to sign on. They were guilty of that indefensible and unwritten law of unusualness. During this time of high unemployment with the option of living in a small bed sit in a city suburb – which by not doing so they were saving the state loads in unclaimed housing benefit – and so driven mad by young kids who had nowhere to play and no one with whom they could leave them with for a break - the option of leaving with a big travelling rural, yes, community, I know which option I would go for.

Usually the new age traveller clients had civil cases over their limited right not to be evicted from land but occasional they would get involved in the criminal law. One such case involved a young man who lived in an old Sunblest bakers van. He went to a free festival, parked his van and although there were several policemen around no crime had been committed. They were there to apparently observe the event. This man was lying on a patch of the field with his friends for a few hours having by then consumed a few pints of cider when two police officers asked him to move his van as it was suddenly causing an obstruction. He went to move it. He put the key ignition in, the engine came to life, he was asked to turn it off again and "blow into this bag please sir". Where upon he did and was arrested for being drunk in charge of a motor vehicle.

He was convicted but there were grounds of appeal because a similar case had occurred a few years before and the defence had succeeded. In the other case a businessman type executive was beckoned out of his wine bar to move his car and, as far as I can recall the only difference was the time delay.

The Judge had therefore to consider if there was a sufficient distinguish between that case from the one before him if the appeal was to fail, which he did and it did. The name of this client and the barristers who was defending him was very similar. Like, say, Donald and McDonald. I was always told by my Dad not to let anyone get away with calling me just Sullivan as it was an indication that our ancestors had been enslaved. Apparently that's when they loose the right to keep their "O'" or "Mac" of which the nearest translation is grandson of. When the judge returned to a pass sentence he said "I have listened carefully to what Mr Donald has...", when my client, not realising the Judge was talking about his Brief and not him shouted out "my name is <u>Mac</u>Donald, not Donald." I told him to shut up as this, apart from obviously being disrespectful to the court, may influence the Judge in deciding on his sentence.

I had kept up the driving lessons although I did not really have to as the original purpose of getting my licence was to increase my chances of getting articled. I had spent so much money on them up to then that I felt I had to continue but what irked me was that they destroyed my lazy Saturday afternoon. I liked my two free days and this regular rendezvous with my instructor ruined it.

I had a few mock tests coming up to the big day with different instructors so I would get used to a silent stranger in the passenger seat. The game was not to talk, apart from the instructor telling me which turning to take next. The emergency stops were a bit of a scream. We would be up a quiet side street and my pretend test instructor would look behind him several times and he would exercise the obligatory hand slam on the dashboard to indicate I had to do my emergency stop. I was given so much notice with the repeated looking over the shoulder routine it was not even a pretend emergency as I was already ready, thinking, "ready when you are. Give the magic sign."

On the evening before the real test I had my last pretend one because the car I used to learn to drive in had had a problem: it's clutch had gone and so I quickly had to get the hang of driving a completely different car. The next afternoon during the test it rained. Not too much of a disaster you may think but it was for me. Throughout the many delightful Saturday afternoons it never rained. The test instructor was waiting for me to turn on the windscreen wipers, which I would have done if I knew where the bloody switch was. So what transpired was me turning on and off all the weird and wonderful switches I had not used while trying to keep an eye on the road looking through a slowing non-transparent and very wet windscreen. Ultimately I flicked a switch I had never flicked before and I then heard what sounded remarkably like Bat Chain Puller by Captain Beefheart and the Magic Band.

At this stage I thought I had failed so I relaxed and that was what probably got me through it. The decision I had passed was only relayed to me once I had partaken in little card test while we had parked up back at the motoring school. I was able to give an answer to all of them until I was shown a card with " MSM" on it. I was asked what it stood for. I did not have a clue. Later I realise it was obvious: Mirror, Signal Manoeuvre, which was a bit of an unfair question. If I had been asked what do you do before you leave your parking space or change lanes I would, without hesitation have said Mirror, Signal, Manoeuvre. MSM was the test instructor and presumably, judging by the very nice professionally manufactured cards, the rest of the test instructor community's acronym. It is once again an example of a little cloistered professional world that gets lost in their own world of shorthand.

A few months later I was walking across a zebra crossing and spotted a friend of mine driving a car with L plates waiting for me to cross. I rather unkindly stopped in my tracks and pretending to go back where I had been and turn around again and then bend down to tie my non existence undone shoe lace. But luckily it was only one of her lessons and not her test and she forgave me when I met her next .

During less pressurising moments in my articles one of my tasks was to weed out the old files and on one occasion I found a strange looking small file. I opened it up, scan read it and thought who is this poor bastard, then glancing back at the name suddenly realised it was me; my personnel file. I read the letter I had initially began reading but this time from the top:

"Mr O'Sullivan joined this department in September 1978 to read for an LLB (Hons) degree. I taught him in his first year and came to know him and his work very well. It is, perhaps, something of a miracle that he graduated in July 1981 with a Lower Second Class degree in spite of the most turbulent personal circumstances imaginable. Among other things during his undergraduate days, he was not expected to live to complete the course and his serious kidney problems often made it impossible for him to do any work or to attend any classes. During his final year he was run over and seriously injured. He is probably the most courageous student I have known in over 20 years.

Though I do not see Mr O'Sullivan very often these days, I do bump into him from time to time and know that his courage is undiminished and his cheerfulness still shines through. I cannot predict that he is likely to be robust, but you can be sure that it would take something serious to make him admit defeat. He is intelligent, conscientious, imaginative, brave and determined. I recommend him to you I will be happy to supply more information if you require it."

The lecturer who had written this had made two errors of which I do not blame him in the slightest as it relates to a time when we did not see a lot of each other: one was the time of the car crash as it was some what earlier but the second unfortunately must have been thought by others as well as him, namely that I was going to die. This explains to some extent why I felt there was not much support heading my way at the time. Everyone must have been embarrassed to talk to me as they did not know what to say. Anyway I copied it and sent it to my Mum and Dad, as I am sure it would have cheered them up after what they had to go through during that period.

When I visited home my Mum and I would often compare our recent experiences and drug dosage. She was constantly amazed as to how I managed to swallow (without the aid of any drink) the large cyclosprin horse tablets that both of us had to take every day. It was just years of practice and sometimes brought on by the necessity to take them when there was no drink nearby. I discovered that she was told by one of the junior doctors that if she is concerned by her oedema (swelling around her ankles) she should cut down on her fluid intake. I said this couldn't be right because a large fluid intake to flush out the kidneys was more important than the embarrassment of swollen ankles and she should check with the consultant. She was reluctant but promised me she would at least mention it, even if it was just in passing. I suggested that at her next check up, which was very soon, that she could make out she was a bit confused about this advice rather than being seen to be correcting or challenging the doctors, which she did not want to do.

I was to learn that when she raised the issue she was asked to leave the consulting room so that that the nephrologist could give the junior doctor concerned, to use the medical term, a right bollocking.

My initial fear that, after all this time, I might not be capable of completing my articles through rejection episodes diminished. I slowly learnt the ropes and got the hang of the practical problems of working for a firm of solicitors rather than the academic legal problems that few and far between and appeared to only happen in theory. My kidney behaved itself and my check ups were regularly every four months and this time I had no rejection scares. The senior partner was kind enough to allow me to use the half-day in hospital as time off I did not have to pay back to the firm or use as a holiday. "Michael. The firm would be able to absorb that time", as he put it.

When I had to attend court well in advance of the actual visit I would conscientiously put the date in my dairy. Apparently diary non-entries and missing the subsequent deadline is the biggest cause of professional negligence legal actions. So I would always double and treble check them. Moving through the diary to find the date to insert my entry I would notice ready printed standard important dates such as "Trinity Law sittings begin" and the even more important "Trinity Law sittings ends". And this is just a bog standard non-legal diary. What is the point in putting this inane information in a legal dairy is beyond me let alone a standard one. Anyway, on turning the page for my next court hearing I spotted it coincided with the day before one of my four monthly check ups. The significance of this was that was the day when I had to lug around my 24-hour urine collection. I had to take it with me even though the court hearing was listed for less than half an hour as I may be caught short especially, which is often the case, the long wait to be called.

In the morning the container is relatively empty and light to carry so you tend to allow the contents to whish about so I had to be careful as I did not want it to leak out, so to speak, as to what was in my bag. The name of the case was called out and I had to go into registers chambers – now district judge – so I carefully picked up the bag and concentrated on placing it gently on the floor where I was to sit. I had this awful fear I had not put the top back on properly and it would fall onto it's side or I would accidentally kick it during the hearing ("Mister - O-Sull – i – van. Am I correct in my assumption that you are endeavouring to bring into my court a substantial quantity of a beverage deemed to be of an alcoholic nature?")

Some months later in the same courtroom I had less, not more baggage that is usually expected. I had no file. My opponents stole it while I was waiting for the case to start. I was representing an ex-employer of a partnership that was not making as much profit as they had anticipated so when they sacked her they decided not to pay her for her last few weeks work. I was talking to one of the Defendants and had my file on my lap explaining what I was going to say in court. When my client arrived I put my file down and walked up to her. When I returned my file was gone and down the corridor I saw this Co-Defendant talking to some shadowy figure who had obviously taken it. But what could you do? In court without my notes but what could I tell the judge? That this bloke had stolen my file was an unprovable accusation so I just had to continue, rely on my memory and hope for the best.

I always find it strange that absolutely anyone can be an employer without any real checks. Nowadays there are loads of jobs and services where you need a licence, even selling sandwiches, but as an employer, where you can have so much control over people's lives and their families, you do not have to fulfil any minimum conditions. You could inherit a large company and hundreds, perhaps thousands of families would be dependant on your unproven decision making skills.

I had to attend police interviews of an accused client. They are incorrectly sometimes called police interrogations. This is incorrect as the purpose of the interview is to elicit the truth from the accused person on what actually happened and not just to get a confession. Apparently.

When I got to the police station my client was accused of several armed robberies on banks and building societies. During the taped interview he said it was not him. Then the police introduced into the interview photographs of stills taken from cameras active at the time of the crimes. On looking across at them the robber in the photograph had a scarf hiding his face. The only snag was that it was identical to the one my client was now wearing sitting right next to me. Not only that, but he was wearing the same clothes as the man in the photograph. The police then took great pleasure, and who could blame them, in slowly going through each item of clothing, with the tape running. It was a long and painful interview.

"The shoes in the photographs are light brown and very similar, if not identical in design to the ones you are wearing now would you not say"

"Yes they are but it's not me"

"OK let's look at the trousers this man is wearing shall we? Would you say they are similar to the ones you are wearing now ?"

"Yes but it is not me"

And so it went on: shirt, jumper, and bomber jacket while I was thinking how is my firm going to defend this one. If he does not admit his guilt he will get a bigger sentence, considering the overwhelming evidence and near certainty of a conviction. At least he was not cursed with the possibility of innocence. Eventfully he admitted it and the interview ended and so did the problems of defending the case. A plea in mitigation was all that was left to consider.

In the previous year before starting articles a policeman came up to me and asked if I would like to accompany him to the police station, as they needed people to make up an identity parade. I went along as I had time on my hands; it would be a practical experience for the future and I needed the two pounds an hour they were offering. What got me was that the accused was about five foot three when most of the parade was six foot. Now years later I was about to have to take on the solicitor role, as I had to accompany one of the firm's clients and make sure the correct procedure was followed. He had been accused of "flashing" – I will spare you the exact criminal offence- and the police did not hold back on taking the micky out of him behind his back. When enough men were rounded up to hold the parade I wondered if they would have got them so speedily if they knew the offence. As the witness came in from the other side of the one way mirror they might have expected the command "right everyone if you could all lower your trousers and undergarments." But thankfully that was not going to happen but on eyeing up the parade members I did notice my firm's client wore a strikingly bright red jumper. Some of the other men had long straggly hair. I wanted to ensure this was going to be a fair process so I asked that my client temporally exchange jumpers with someone else in the line and all the members of the line up with long hair have it tied back. That's their hair.

Then the witness arrived with his mum. It suddenly became very serious. He was a young boy of about ten. He picked the accused out with no trouble so it was a fair procedure, which I was there to ensure. So I had been the parade member, taken the solicitor role but I was about to be the witness myself.

I was walking up one of the steep hill streets in the centre of town during a cold January afternoon when I head a loud bang which I took to be something like a big wooden board falling over in the wind so I thought nothing of it. As I got further up the hill I noticed a bloke in a jeweller's shop window collecting all the jewellery which were individually seated on cushions in a window display. Smoke was bellowing out of the top of the door. A result of a gun going off. He was, strangely I thought, putting the cushions as well as the jewellery under his jacket. Clearly not a professional.

An armed robbery was taking place and I looked around to see if anyone else in this comparatively busy Saturday afternoon street was noticing. But the shoppers continued their brisk walk, as they didn't want to getting involved. I cursed the fact that I had for the second time in a month witnessed a crime and had to take on the responsibility of reporting it. While thinking all this I was glancing at the robber continuing his manic theft of jewellery and jewellery cushions. I was making mental notes of what he looked like and being ready at an instant to look away if he saw me looking at him because I knew he had already shot someone.

I crossed the road and entered the first shop I saw and believe it or not it was some kind of Christian aid bookshop. I went to the counter that had a queue emanating from it and explained, " An armed robbery is going on over the road and I need to phone the police as I think someone's been shot". The person at the counter appeared to look at me as if I was a nutcase and had been watching too many American cop shows. The people in the queue seemed perturbed that I had apparently jumped the queue. I got no response, saw the phone and pulled it from behind the counter walked with it to the window as far as the lead would allow, phoned the police and gave a running commentary of events opposite which ended with " he has now come out of the jeweller's shop and has taken a turn off to the left". He was easy to spot. He had put on a substantial amount of weight since I had last seen him. He stuffed all the jewellery display cushions, with jewellery attached, up his jumper.

Just before the phone conversation ended I was told to hand my self in to the police so they could take a statement but on putting the receiver down I felt a bit deflated. I wanted to end it with:"this is Michael O'Sullivan news at 10, the high street". I then went out into the street as advised by the police waiting to be called into the incident van to give a statement. Now there was a crowd when before everyone seemed to have scurried away. Once inside I heard the police radio's running commentary on the eventual apprehension of " the accused". While I was in the van a stretcher came out of the jewellers shop carrying a heavily bandaged person who had been shot in the head. He died a few hours later. I was no longer a witness to an armed robbery but a murder.

And then had to wait for hours at the police station to be seen by a police detective who took a statement in between the long puffs and relighting of his pipe. I think he had been watching too many detective shows.

Over the next few weeks' police visited me at work to clarify my statement and I was eventually invited to pick out the alleged murderer out at an identity parade. The first day was a complete waste of time because the police were unable to gather enough people to make up their identity parade, possibly because of the bad relationship with young black men in the city and only being offering £2.00 per hour for their time.

The second attempt to hold the identity parade worked because the police had put a request out for young black men who were prisoners to stand at an identity parade for a few minutes which was to them probably an interesting day out. When I attended the identity parade I was asked: "could you identify the person you saw on the date and if so to give his number in the row." This was easy for three reasons: I recalled his bad facial scarring; I recognised him and because he was the only one not looking bored and was trying to look totally nonchalant but failed miserably. The tracksuit hoods, ordered by his solicitors and worn by each man in the parade, were a waste of time, as they did not cover his scarring. In answering the question I said, "I think so" and knew as soon as I said it that it was going to be great cross examination material if he was going to continue to plead not guilty. There is usually nothing to lose by doing so because there is only one compulsory sentence for murder: life, although possible release dates are available well before.

My biggest concern was that after taking on nearly every role in this identification procedure that quite possibly one day in the future I might, God forgive, be the ....police officer.

Several months later there was a magistrates' court hearing which was a full committal (defence option, at the time, to see if enough evidence available to go to full crown court jury trial) in which depositions were taking which meant witnesses giving statements while being questioned. I was the first one. I was in a waiting room on my own for some time and left it to go to the toilet and as I did so walked passed two-armed police who were guarding the room I had just left. Part of me wanted to say I just remembered I've got a dental appointment but realised it was not going to be that easy and asked myself if this was standard procedure for all murder cases or whether they knew something that I did not.

When I was called before the magistrates it became apparent that the defence wanted my name and address to be read out in open court. I was about to make it clear to the prosecution that I was not going to give evidence if I had to give my address but luckily it never came to that and my name was sufficient for the record. The deposition was taken by the magistrates' clerk dictating a statement from the questions made and answers given. During the whole time I was in the witness box the accused was on the other a side of the room constantly staring at me trying, in my opinion, to intimidate me. At the end of the day after hearing all the other witnesses the magistrates decided there was a case to answer and several months later there was to be a full Crown Court jury trial.

One witness got involved by walking into the shop with her young daughter in her arms at the time I was on the phone and was met with a terrible sight of the dying shop manager on the floor. She told me that after the incident her daughter would only play in the same room as her at home. Beforehand she would happily play anywhere in the house. A concern that appeared to concern me more than it did her mum. The site that confronted them when they entered the jewellers shop probably traumatised her young daughter and she was not getting any psychiatric help.

I suppose in this country if you ever experience anything that could affect your mental health in the months and years ahead, whether it be a shocking site or other experience or even the realisation you might spend the rest of your life on a kidney machine, the best solution is to experience it with a group of people all at the same time. Not just on your own. That way it may get in the papers, questions will no doubt be raised "in the House", and you will have the added advantage, compared with others who will have to fend for themselves in perfect isolation, of having many available shoulders to cry on as they will be going through exactly the same experience as you. You will get all the support you need from each other. You can even set up your own support group, which could be well funded by trust fund, especially if the press take an interest.

The alert amongst you may have noticed I mentioned that I was a witness to another crime in this short period of time. Well this was in my own home. I lived on the ground floor and there was a communal stairway. Quite often some thing as innocuous as a toaster on level three burn would trigger off the sensitive fire alarm situated there. One Sunday afternoon I was looking forward to watching a football match ("Come on you Spurs") on television when after sitting down with a nice cup of tea the bloody thing went off again. I rushed into hallway, not you understand because I thought there was a fire but because the match was about to start and I needed to quickly reset the alarm. As I was messing about with it the guy who I recognised from the top flat came down the stairs appearing quite unperturbed about the ear-piercing noise and unhurriedly walked past me. I turned to him to point out that this thing wasn't resetting but he completely blanked me and walked out the building. I found this rather strange. So much so that I went into the back garden, ("He's hit the post! Absolutely amazing! Tottenham's defence is all over the place. Five minutes into the game and they could already be two nil down if, er, Liverpool had scored two goals") looked up the building and noticed that the top flat was ablaze. I rang the fire brigade, making a mental note to tell the police that I did not think it was an accidentally fire, irritated that the match had now started. When they arrived I directed them and their hoses up the stairs while I sneaked back to watch the match ("What an incredible save by Walker. This young goalkeeper is coming on in leaps and bounds ") hoping the ceiling would not fall in and obscure my view of the television.

The next interruption came, not with a pitch streaker, but when a fireman showed me some photographs and asked me if the man in them was the one I had seen. It was and I told him so. About 10 minutes later, just before half time, I was asked for permission to allow them to kick down one of the flat doors in because the waterbed had burst and water was seeping down through the building. I said yes even though I had no authority to do so.

After the fire was out I was interviewed by a police officer. They later told me they could not find the suspect and that they had checked the potential local places where people taking such drastic action sometimes attempt suicide. So I went back to watch the remainder of the match glad I was not going to burn to death ("And so the final score here at White Hart Lane: Spurs nil, Liverpool nil")

That night I was the only one in the building and heard a noise and thinking it might be him returning to "get" the only witness. I went downstairs to confront him and luckily for me he wasn't there.

They did find him and a few months later I was witness summonsed to attend his Crown Court trial. A few months after that while at work I spoke to a barrister I had instructed on an unrelated case and he recognise my name as being the witness to an arson case he had been involved in. I was only then to learn that the alleged arsonist's girlfriend had booted him out the flat and he had returned, by using his spare key to burn the house down. This piece of information annoyed me because it meant the case had been finalised and the Crown Prosecution Service didn't have the courtesy to tell me. They did not know attending court and giving evidence would not necessarily faze me. Receiving the summons may have already petrified me and further worried me sick about having to give evidence. I wrote to the CPS explaining this and reminding them that no wonder many members of the general public do not come forward to volunteer as witnesses if you not prepared to reassure witnesses that they would not have to give evidence after all. I have still not got a reply.

And if you think witnessing two crimes in a short period of time, all during my two-year articles is unusual I have to tell you about the third. One early evening after leaving work I went into the train station waiting room, which was empty, or so I thought. I sat down on the settee with a full view of the platform. But as soon as I sat down I looked up and three things simultaneously struck me: there were two men behind the door looking at me and on the platform opposite were two police officers running up and down looking over at me and my right hand had touched something while it was dangling over the settee arm. It was whole stack of computer games.

I just could not believe it: in the space of two months I had now witnessed three crimes. Maybe it was the Law Society putting me to the test to see if I warranted the ennobled title of Officer of the Supreme Court, which is a solicitor's official title.

I have heard of mystery shopper but mystery shoplifter? So I just read my paper. Initially upside down but I nonchalantly pretended I was merely checking the crossword answers. Then the right way up.

When the train arrived I got on and noticed the two guys rushing back to the waiting room to get their stash. They then leaped on the train just before it left and in the commotion of the rush hour stood right by where I was standing. For the whole of the journey they just stared at me knowingly, some may say intimidatedly, but I thought the police would be waiting for them at the next station but to my amazement there was no one there and they walked off with their goodies and Mr law abiding citizen felt a bit guilty.

" She's gone! Free glass of wine with every meal. "On one of my adventurous strolls around town during lunchtime I saw one vegetarian restaurant with all its front windows all covered in white paper and in big felt type was written this message.

I could not resist it. Not one for expensive sit-downs and drinking during the day I nevertheless went in and treated myself. While swirling around what was left of the red wine before rushing back to the office I had a rare moment of sentimentality about what had been happening to me while Thatcher was in power.

When she came to power I was working in the paper mill as a fitter's mate for those three weeks in the year when the power from the mills were shut down to allow their full annual maintenance fit.

Just before she finally buried Supplementary Benefit, together with grants for families by replacing them with a loan system, our KGB tent was buried under the summer mud at the Glastonbury festival.

On the day she had defeated the "enemy within" I was hopefully seeing the last of the kidney machine in my old bedroom my Mum had been totally dependant on.

As Thatcher's policy of cut backs was taking hold I was holding on to my left arm as my second attempt that day to begin to dialyse was delayed as my vein blew yet again having not yet got the hang of the new unreliable cheaper dialysis needles.

As she was about to put into practice the regressive Poll tax, now defunct, I was giving a talk to the Claimants Union, now defunct, on the how the system was likely to work in practice.

Question. What have a shoe, curled watchstrap, marmalade and marmite jar all have in common.

Answer. Where I place my morning drugs – in its special capsule-every morning to ensure I never forget to take them.

So why has this transplant lasted so long? Twice the average lifespan. Could it be I just got lucky and it was the ideal tissue type match for me? The fact that's as a polycystic kidney gene recipient I had all my probably complications – more common with other recipients with different causes-removed when my own two kidneys were? Is it my obsession with a lot of fluid intake every day, my vegetarian diet , or my , in recent years, my even healthy anti cancer/anti free radicals mopping up/pro   diet, my part-time , my less stressful life style or my obsessive drug taking routines?

Every Sunday I have a serious routine which I do so often I worry I may sometimes do it routinely so I have to mentally kick my self while doing it so I don't get complacent and sloppy. While doing constantly reminding myself that if I slip once it might well trigger a rejection episode and lead to kidney rejection.

It goes as follows: I carry together my faithful snooker colour sequence baubles, congratulating them individual on the fact that they have not deserted me over the last few decades since we first met and made full eye contact when I saw them discarded in a skip. I then opened them up making fourteen halves ready for filling. In the past they used to roll around so got into the habit of placing them on my duvet after pulling it up and about creating a channel to sit them in. Nowadays I have an exciting self-made polystyrene block that I have hollowed out fourteen little holes to sit the halves of the capsules/baubles.

First go in the steroids seven half milligrams which means one small white tablet and half a small white tablet which I had to break in half hoping to get a 50-50 break. If the percentage is clearly out I discard it and start again. The next drug is always worryingly another white tablet, for my heart condition, which is fractionally larger than the steroid drugs so I have to be awfully careful I don't get confuse the two. And finally in the other half of the actual go the big chunky horse tablets: 2 100 capsules and 250 capsules.

The seven capsules are now full and the two halves fastened together and go into my magic box ready for the next week. However the occasional break in routine causes some consternation for my little brain, fearful that my omission or commission, however small may result in me spending the rest of my life on a kidney machine. Here are two classics: the change in breakfast routine and the hospital check up. Let me explain.

What has a lid of a jar of marmalade, a wristwatch strap, an elastic band have in common? Give in? They are just some of my pathetic little aids to ensure I take my morning drugs (the two and a half white drugs and the two of the four horse tables if any one is taking notes.) For years I had toast and marmalade for breakfast so the bauble would quietly sit there all night so I couldn't forget to take it in my hand and consume the drugs first thing. Sometimes in my early morning haze I would not check as I poured them in my gob and then I would drop one or was it two. Crisis. Once I had recovered the serious situation I would hold back on the swallowing stage of the procedure until – get this – I looked in the mirror, extended my tongue out, inspected the gooey mess and ticked them all off as being all present and correct before I swallowed. Gulp and the day truly began.

The wristwatch strap? We are now talking about situations where one is sleeping elsewhere. No mandatory marmalade jar you see. You have to have alternative reminder aids. The prerequisite was that you always wear a watch and that the strap curls when plonked down near your night resting place. So – you're ahead of me-the bauble nests in the space created by the curl.

The essential need for an elastic band was rare: the morning of my check up. Lets not forget at this stage only every 6 months, twice a year so the rarity of it made it easy to overlook. The problem here is that in the morning before your tests, to see if the kidney is behaving itself, you cannot take your steroid drug. This always worried me because it was a classic situation when I would forget and so it proved. Hours after I was released from hospital, and sometimes only when it was evening tablet drop time, did I noticed I had not yet taken the drugs. Could this trigger rejection. Doctors will tell you no but if shortly after it I was to trigger a rejection and rejection itself I would blame myself and blame it on this.

So the elastic band must be a tight one or you don't constantly feel it round your wrist and I would have forgotten to take my morning drugs! - albeit later than normal. It happened a few times and so the night before I had to put the days bauble in a strange position to trigger the response hey why is that in a strange position -over night so that when I saw it the next day and pocketed but put the Only day will I get reminders to take the drug .

Law is not my career: my kidney's survival is.

As we don't have managers that decisions are made at the staff meeting. We try and avoid votes and get agreement by consensus that occasionally votes have when there is dead lock. Order is dependent on the skill of the rotating shift. I have occasionally been told I'm good at this but the paradox is that all I want the ease and speed the process up and his only by default that I end up being seen as a good chair. This can be quite embarrassing. But all I want to do is call the meeting there to size because they're the extra power at the meeting when there is a tendency to people to put forward the opinion when he quite often is a repeat of someone else opinion which is used in the form of words, time spent does not result in making the decision. Every hour extra at the staff meeting there is an extra hour I have to work on pay before I can go home.

This reminded me of an incident when I was about six and at less than and we all had to draw a figure. I was saying grossed in parts of the drawing that went all the pictures were collected by the teacher and I took one final look at my tent and it was taken from me and I suddenly noticed in my horror that I haven't put any arms on! Worse than that in front of the class the teacher had my painting in there and bought the plaster ordered to say something and I was expecting to be vilified but to my sheer astonishment she said: "I want to show you Michael is very original drawing. as you will see the person in Michael's picture is standing looking at the sun with his arms behind his back"

I'm getting reports of strange noises emanating from the roof at Tyr Peg: possibly little animals. Suggestions are wide ranging. But unless mice have been keen to wear Wellington the boots or badgers are going around in their slippers, it looks as if we have squirrels, a family of squirrels no less. I felt like letting them be and some of my female friends tried to persuade me to stop thinking about ways of killing them such as putting poison in the roof. I have no real opinion and as long as the illegal residents weren't bothered me then I wasn't. Until that is the locals commented on the squirrels as they had noticed so many of them crawling around the roof. They suggested getting a gun and more importantly using it. They pointed out that if you just leave them they will gnaw into the rafters and eventually the roof will fall in and well be left with bits of some the ships from the Spanish Armada jutting up out of the ground. So we beat off the Spanish invaders but the invading American squirrels got us in the end.

This meant I had to do something. At the time there was a lot of talk in the media about what a nuisance that grey squirrels were and that the nice red squirrels had been effectively lost within the British Isles. There was talk of the red squirrels being the natural squirrels species and the grey ones had come over from America and with far more vicious and less delicate than the red squirrels. Was also talk that not only had the grace is pushed them out of the way and taking over their territory they had introduced and violence that the red squirrels could not tolerate.

The Torygraph suggested putting them in a bag and a getting a big stick and......

Free NHS prescriptions are available to anyone under 16 or over 59. As well as pregnant women who in the last 12 months gave birth to a live child or one registered as stillborn.. At one stage my GP thought I was exempt and I had thought this my self when I had a working fistula. However it has to be permanent one that requires continuous surgical dressing or an appliance..
You are exempt if you are an epileptic as long as you require continuous anticonvulsive therapy.. You are also exempt if you have diabetes but not if treatment is by diet alone. The same applies to any one with the continuing physical disability which means he can't leave the house without the help of someone else but temporary disabilities do not count. And of course the two conditions everyone is familiar with: hypoparathyroidism and hypoadrenalism..

*

CHAPTER NINE: How's Your Kidney Been?

I obviously did not know how long this second transplant would last so decided to apply for a part time job. Hopefully less stressful and so reduce the rejection risk. While I had my health I may as well use the time rather than be cooped up in an office five days a week.

In the latter months of my articles I applied for a part time solicitors post at the very same law centre I had previously volunteered during my first dialysis stint. I wanted to apply without my present employer knowing because I did not know if they were planning to keep me on once I qualified. This caused an application form problem because it asked for names of referees, which I was only prepared to divulge if I was going to be offered the job.

I attended the interview after work expecting an easy time, on account of it being a law centre. It was far more difficult than my chatty two-hour interview for my articles. Once I arrived I was given a twenty-minute test. There were five people awaiting me. Afterwards I retreated back to the waiting room. After five minutes I was asked to return and offered the job, of course, subject to references. As I had seen my ex lecturer's previous one it was all down to my present boss who on receiving the request would, for the first time realise I had applied for the job.

The terms, legal aid, law centre, advice centre, law shop, and law society are often confused with one another. Phrases like community law and community lawyer are often banded about but I do not know what they are supposed to mean. Legal Aid has now been replaced by a similar system run by the Legal Service Commission (LSC), previously the Legal Aid Board. It has the same role of funding cases. It funds initial advice but can also fund what used to be full legal aid, now certificated or full public funding, on a case-by-case basis. This would include representation at court hearings but not if the case involved a tribunal unless it is relates to the later appeal stages.

Most of the law centre specialisms involve tribunals and so without a local law centre or some advice centres, people who could not afford lawyers to represent them at civil court hearings would have to represent themselves, pay lawyers of their own pockets or enter into a "no win no fee" contract. This is also known as a contingency fee basis. This in itself is misleading because if you lose you have to pay the other sides costs so should insure against that possibility. So you have to pay something although not to your solicitor so it is only no win, no fee to your solicitor. OK technical correct but misleading to many. Most people are not bothered whom they do not have to pay money to but if they have to pay anyone.

The standard image of a solicitor is one who works for a High street firm with both private paying and legal aid clients with the intention of making profits, profit costs to be exact. The public tend to think you can have your own family solicitor to help with all legal problems. This is not only outdated but also dangerous. If you are private paying you can take this gamble but with LSC funded work the firm has usually to have a LSC contract in that legal area to indicate their expertise. No lawyer can be an expert in all areas.

As the Law Society is the solicitor's professional body it provides special dispensation to allow solicitors to work for law centres. Without solicitors it would not be a law centre but an advice centre and unlikely to get LSC funding for certificated cases. High street solicitors firms and Law Centres are second tier and advice centres such as the CABs are first tier. The first tier may well refer to second tier and phone for more specialist advice and consultations.

Law Shops have nothing to do with law centres. They are an appendage to a firm of solicitors that will allow you to use their legal information, sometimes for a small fee and may then take your case on if it has merit whether it be funded by the LSC; no win no fee or on a private paying basis.

Law Centre work is usually more likely to be associated with advice centre and CABs than High street solicitors firm but this is to misunderstand its role. Law Centres like Advice Centres are mainly funded by the local council. We can do all the kind of legal work solicitors firms can do as we employ solicitors and barristers. They are more specialised than most firms and concentrate on areas of law the firms do not always do, such as welfare rights, immigration, employment, race, sex and disability discrimination, debt, community groups, community care, education and housing. They do not usually do criminal and family law; have special dispensation from the Law Society not to advice employers and landlords and do not charge. Law Centres are non profit making and in the one I joined there is wage parity where all the staff, whether they are qualified or not, caseworkers or not, get the same hourly rate of pay. We also do not have real managers as we are a "collective" and manage ourselves although a voluntary managing committee makes the big decisions as opposed to decisions for the day-to-day running of the centre.

The sad thing is that the public see a law centre as just another advice centre and that the best place to go is to a firm of solicitors. This is incorrect. In fact you could argue the exact opposite as most lawyers at law centres, whether they be legally qualified or not, are more likely to be just as experienced, if not more so, than their counterparts in the high street firms. It saddens me when now and again a client will decide to take their case to a firm of solicitors based purely on the preconception or misconception that they will get better advice, some how thinking firms of solicitors are always better and if they pay they will get better advice when at the law centre if we believe in a case we will run it even if full "legal aid" is denied or unavailable.

Once you do your two years traineeship you have to wait a few months before the bureaucracy works through before you actually qualify. It was strange: working one day at a firm where you would observe in the corner of your principal's office while he interviewed clients and then, only a few days, later have some one observing you which in my case turned out to be a social science student on a placement at the Law Centre.

I soon got my piece of paper saying I was a qualified solicitor and given yet another chance to wear a piece of cardboard on my head at a ceremony in London which this time I declined to attend.

I 'd love to be able to tell you I was one of the first to "downshift", that is, accept a lower paid job and more modest living conditions in return for liberation from the drudgery of office life, but alas I cannot. The verb, to downshift had only been introduced round about 1994. By then I had already been working part time for several years at the Law Centre. For me it was not really downshifting as I never had a well paid, middle class type job, owned a house, a car, had the annual holiday abroad. Consequently I was never up to down shift from.

I had decided to not even go there. I only had a slight increase in my wage from being a trainee solicitor although now only working part time. I was getting a basic wage for hopefully a richer life. I could not afford to worry about the future and all that career nonsense. I had to simply live for the present and the result of the next check up.

However for the real downshifters it is a hard and brave decision to make. You have to be totally honest with your self and ask: am I working for the wrong reasons? For instance do

I like my job only because it fills a vacuum in my life? Am I married to my job? In slickness and in wealth. Far richer, far poorer. To have and to hold on to. Is it lack of self-esteem? If so should I be solving the root problem and stop hiding behind my position at work. Am I too far up the greasy pole to look down let alone jump off?

What's the point in buying a big dream house you never see with the gnawing threat of a redundancy, not get the expected promotion and resulting wage increase to make the mortgage payments more manageable plus the risk of the mortgage rates going up because you had already overstretched yourself financially to achieve the dream. You have lots of money to buy and partake in expensive things and pastimes but no time to use or do them.

What's the point of having a big pension that you might never see as you died prematurely from stress or retired early through ill health and all those hobbies and interests you promised your self you can no longer take up. Surely it is better to fulfil those promises you made to yourself now rather than gamble that you will have a healthy retirement and delay it until then.

What's the point of earning for the family's future financial security and watching you career grow but not your children. Coming home late from the office when they are already in bed asleep and you do not get all your sleep, get irritable and grumpy, bringing home stress from work.

I have developed a interest in sleep. We are all constantly reminded that we spend about third of our existence asleep. Since my kidney problems I very rarely had a full nights sleep without waking up several times in the night. Possibly because of a weakened bladder, drinking all the time and the side effect of all the drugs? Maybe a combination and concoction of all three.

An alarm clock by a bed is evidence of sleep deprivation. Being woken up before your body wants to cannot be healthy for anyone and now modern living makes it even worse especially with the limited time away from work and the late nights socializing exacerbating the problem. Lack of sleep has been put forward as the cause of many of today's problems

Driving accidents and illness such as migraine and behavioural disorders for young children. As it is a comparatively new science there are apparently many missed diagnosis such as apnea (not sleeping properly because your airways get blocked when your muscles relax in preparation for sleep) and narcolepsy (disorder where you often fall asleep without warning during the day.) In the book Counting Sheep by Paul Martin illustrations are given of how discoveries and solutions suddenly emerge after dreaming once reinterpreted in the real light of day. As writer Arthur Koestler thinks, we are all most creative when our rational thought is suspended. Freud sees dreams as letters to your self when interpreting dreams. REM sleep, the stage when you dream, occurs several times during sleep and always just before you wake up. But this cannot happen, and so you cannot recall them, if you are not getting enough sleep and you do not wake up naturally.

Did you know the average work dinner "hour" is 27 minutes and that some people are now scared to take all their annual holiday. The UK has the worst (if you own your own firm or company please replace worst with best) average in Europe for time spent at work (48 hours week) but hey that's OK as our economy is healthier and leaner but that is not what can easily be said about the people who are now doing one and a half jobs. Nowadays, for some, time off is about rushing around just to be able to do your chores mainly during the one of the two days off a week so you are ready to go back to work for the next five day. Those few weeks in the summer are the only time when you can have your life back but you so concerned about enjoying it that you cannot.

Several friends and relatives asked "But why are you only working part-time. You are now a fully qualified solicitor. You could earn lots of money. Far more that what you are earning now. What was the point of all that effort to qualify, after what you have been through, when you are going to earn hardly much more than you did during your articles." Even now I still get a lot of that. Even now I get news of people I know: "Oh he's very successful now"; "Guess how much he's earning now." What exactly is a successful person anyway?

It is not just me, although I am not your average example with my kidney time bomb but look at these statistics. 1997- 1.7 million downshifted; 2002- 2.6 million and the estimate for 2007 is 3.7 million. So, with these estimates of those trying to achieve their "work-life balance", just you left then?

Look on the bright side of not having those expensive holidays abroad. Admittedly for me, even with lots of money I 'd have some explaining to do taking all my drugs through customs, the spotting of my needle marks in my fistula arms and the threat of picking up viruses and infections because, altogether now, I am permanently immune suppressed. But you would never have to feel bad about being a person from the rich west visiting to gawp at how poor people live on the other side of the world. But you would still politely have to look at all those holiday snaps of others.

I was at a friend's birthday meal. She had hired out a large room for about twenty guests who were able to sit around this massive round table. I went for the one of the cheapest meals and had one glass of wine. At the end of the evening she said, "Well the bill works out at about £25.00 each. How does that sound?" All agreed that it seemed fair rather than working out all the individual calculations; apart, that is, from one person. I was surrounding by well-paid people. I had to speak out and say I couldn't afford it. There was a short embarrassed silence. They had not fathomed on everyone there not used to such an expensive night out. I was not in the slightest bit embarrassed although I had reduced the jolliness quotient down for about half a minute. Once you do not feel awkward at a moment like that you have cracked it, although few people have not heard of a not well off solicitor before.

Similarly I had to turn down an invitation to a stag night where money was required up front for the night in Paris.

On another occasion someone asked me how much I earned and I told him £10.000.00 pa gross. I asked him the same question and I had to squeeze an amount out of him because, I was to discover later, he was embarrassed for me to have to reveal that he earned three times as much but frankly I did not give a damn. I found it amusing that he thought I would somehow be upset. I am not try to earn lots of money. Most of the time when I used to phone him up for a drink he was often too tired, working late or had to travel out of town and stay in hotels in the evening in a bar on his own. Wow.

I'm often asked, so what do you do on your days off then? Well time is money and money is time. You earn a good hourly rate of pay but have no time to do much.

No expensive restaurants for me so I cannot spend, say, £20.00 for a meal. Getting someone else to cook when you do not want to, through tiredness or lack of time.

I have discovered vegetarian Indian cooking. Not only it is remarkably cheap but the varieties and fresh spice combinations and degree of spicy hotness is near enough endless. That's once you divorced yourself of old habits of over cooking, over boiling and over frying everything that you touch which is what the English are often accused of. It took me sometime to stop over boiling due to my history of the compulsory dialysis diet.

My first few months at this ethnic cooking was a disaster simply because I subconsciously would overrule what it said in the recipe book. From years of brainwashing when I saw the words "a few seconds." I would tell myself, it cannot be ready yet. So consequently all powdered spices were burnt and all the spicy flavouring never had a chance to survive and escape from the wok to the plate.

However the other parts of the recipe book got me scratching my head. "A cup of rice." "A piece of ginger." "Two green chillies." So how much is that then? The ingredients are listed at the top. You place them in front of you on your wooden board. You are starving, ready with your sharp clean knife to begin the preparation when you know will not take long, when half way down the page you see "the lentils, having been soaked over night, ..." or " then cover and simmer on a low heat (what else?) for one hour." Or another classic "... with the retained liquid...." But you never told me to retain it at the time. I poured it all down the sink!

I now read the whole recipe from beginning to end with big marker pen on stand by. With as nearly as much alertness as when perusing a tenancy agreement at work.

A friend of mine got into all this different sort of cooking for the first time when he left home for collage. Never having used these strange ingredients, he mistook a clove of garlic for a head of garlic. And for a week after that meal he was not exactly the most popular fresher on the campus. I suppose people would say, once they picked themselves off the floor, "My god. Have you got End Stage Renal Failure?"

I have been reading more books one reason being to see how published authors structure their book and which styles are easy to read and why.

No money but lost of time also allows me to discover new authors. I patrol the second hand bookshops. Even being mad enough to gamble on an unknown author by throwing a die and buying a book for a quid of one beginning with, say, the letter t and it works. Once you have an author you like you go to those website book stores and search for that book and discover what people who have bought that book also read as there taste might coincide.

I have discover a web site for libraries (www.whichbook.net) You type in the condition you like in say a novel, eg happy end or twist in the end or "laugh you pants off" etc. Then up comes certain books and if you choose one the nation system directs you to a copy in the library near to you and states whether it is out on loan or not.

At the law centre my clients became known as users, which gave the impression they had needles hanging out of their arms. And all because of the apparent need to dissociate ourselves from solicitors, who seemed to have got the monopoly on the term client in the legal world. When some of my service users (the latest term) found out I was a solicitor working part time they had difficulty understanding why I worked at the law centre and queried whether it was my sole source of income. They would assume I volunteer there for a few days and for the rest of the week went back to my own practise where the real work began.

Even in the county court District Judges have sometimes asked me if I am a solicitor when my opponent is from a firm and assumed to be qualified and has rights of audience unlike nonqualified advisors. Sometimes I would get the written court order a few days later. At the top it would read. "Solicitor for the Claimant and representative for the Defendant" automatically assuming I am not a solicitor because of the organisation I work for.

I was advising a bartender in her claim for unfair dismissal against a certain religion. I cannot really tell you which one but I understand the pope is a member. She had worked in their social club. She could not get what was then full legal aid for court representation because it was an industrial – now called employment- tribunal and not within the system like all the other tribunals. She could not afford to instruct a firm of solicitors and it would not be worth it anyway because in tribunals – like small claim courts -the loser does not have to pay the winners costs. So most, if not all, of her compensation could go to the firm she instructed. The no win no fee agreements were not around then.

Unfortunately I was the only one at the law centre at that time who could possibly represent her but could not do so on the day of the hearing as I had to attend an "out reach" "drop in". Two pieces of jargon the not for profit sector are guilty of. Out reach – seeing clients away from the office, usually on the outskirts of the town for easier access. Drop in – being able to attend between certain fixed hours each week without the need to arrange an appointment in advance.

I agreed to advise her on what to say in cross-examining the priest. The hour-long session the evening before the hearing involved a quick initiation in this unusual process. In this case one piece of information weakened their defence. If you were to ask a particular question the priest could only answer in one of two ways. I told her that if he answers one way you then ask another specific direct question and then you have him. But if he answers the otherway then their defence collapses.

On arriving at the tribunal she discovered that the church had instructed a solicitor and a barrister for the hearing. She won and, she explained, the tribunal panel questioned the priest's truthfulness under oath even though he had just sworn on the bible.

During an advice line session a young man who wanted a lawyer to help him get a court injunction to get his ex girlfriend to have an abortion. The worker was unwilling to speak to him and passed him on to me. I answered, not knowing what it was about, and he repeated his request. In a situation like this I always wanted to double check that I was hearing it correctly before I responded.

"So let me get this right: you want you ex girl friend to have an operation against her will so you can save money in the next 18 years."

Without hesitation he said "yeah".

"Sorry but we do not live in nazi Germany" and put the phone down on him.

So after all the time trying to qualify I was heading for my first official complaint. Luckily it did not happen, strangely enough, but what got me is that he thought he had a legal right to such an order. He was so engrossed in his own situation he neglected to consider that if he such rights then she must have no rights whatsoever.

"Michael, you Mum has had stroke"

I got the phone call from Dad. Mum's health had been slowly deteriorating. While transplants are doing fine, when other medical conditions introduce themselves, the doctors have to treat the most serious. So the most life threatening conditions was a series of stokes. She would have several further minor stokes but the trend was ominous.

"Occasionally fistulas can burst in which case the artery has to be reconstructed."

I was in goal in a five-aside football tournament. As I had already learnt it was safer in the "D" of the goal area because there was no chance of bodily contact that could injure my kidney. Although, admittedly the ball could, but usually we had a nice soft one and if you cannot save a ball coming straight at you what chance did you have tipping it over the bar in the top right hand corner? A few minutes into the game I saved a shot and after throwing the ball back out, glanced down at my glove and thought I had not put it on properly as the little finger glove compartment was hanging lose. I still kept my eye on developments on the pitch in front of me and quickly began to readjust my glove but on taking it off noticed my little finger was indeed in the glove in the correct place but was hanging down. I had dislocated it.

I ended up in hospital but in an Accident and Emergency ward. Very unusual for me. The last time it happened was that car crash that set off my own kidneys bleeding constantly for several weeks. However I went to the unit feeling proud of myself. It was nothing to do with kidneys but a sports injury. The kind of injury that could repair itself and you would not have to consider the future consequences or begin a drug programme that you had to continue to take indefinitely. You just waited and your body would miraculously heal itself.

I was dropped off at casualty and after a series of waits interspersed with getting my name on a list; being interviewed by a nurse, walking to the x-ray department by following a red line along a series of corridors, waiting there, walking back and waiting again. I was then seen by a doctor who studying the x-ray informed me that, guess what, I had dislocated my finger. But I had not broken it. I was given a local anaesthetic and my finger was "placed" back in to position and I was sent home, walking back along the same route I took many years previously when, after being seen examined by the doctors was not even allowed to walk down a ward corridor let alone several miles home.

I did not feel like a kidney patient for the first time in my life. A very strange feeling indeed. My poor little finger never fully recovered but is only noticeable by me but I would fit very nicely holding my tea at the next Queens garden party.

My next sporting injury was different. Although it happened as a direct result of playing sport it was not an injury most sporting people will ever experience. Once again I was playing 5 –a side football and during the game, when I was in goal, the ball hit me squarely on the lower part of my left arm where my second but still functioning fistula resided. You will recall that a few months after my first transplant my first fistula slowly died and eventfully completely clogged up. A good sign as it meant my blood was full of iron once again. I had a high hemoglobin and my blood was viscous and no longer weak and wishy washy. For some reason this fistula was happily pumping away very quietly years later.

The injury was not that noticeable at first. I then got a slight ache. I thought nothing of it, putting it down to a small sports injury. I went to visit my mother in hospital who just had a massive stroke but remained in the renal ward because she was still predominantly a kidney patient. The doctors told the family that it was very rare for anyone to survive a stroke of that magnitude.

When I visited Mum she had come round although it was not clear if she would survive and if so have any permanent damage to her brain, bodily movement or both.

My arm had now started swelling up and was slowly turning red through internal bruising. I showed my arm to the nurses and they were curious as they had never seen this before and arm was getting rather large. The fact that it was a sport type injury meant I did not get much sympathy as it could have been avoided. My arm was turning a bright red and aching even more. I was advised to mention it at my own unit when I returned the next day.

Back there the doctors and nurses were equally impressed and I was told my fistula had burst. I needed to allow the blood to drain away and then have my arm artery reconstructed. This would involve taking a small vein from my leg and implant it in my arm.

On the day of the operation I had my "pre med" and waited to be trolleyed to theatre. I got as far as the corridor, all nicely prepared in my white revealing gown and Pythonesk Gumby hat. The porter left my medical notes on my stomach and went off somewhere, the loo I think, and I, never missing an opportunity to read these files, picked them up and at the top it read "Rachel O'Sullivan". Oh No! What's going on? I then hoped that the pre med would react like it normally did with me and not send me to sleep, which it often can do with other patients.

When the porter came back I pointed out, what looked like a pretty serious error. "It says here Rachel O'Sullivan." The porter, to be fair, looked a bit concerned and said "I think I'd better check." ("Too right. Do I look like a bloody Rachel?") Behind me I heard a familiar voice saying, "You're not going to sue us are you Michael?" It was one of the doctors. I would have found it amusing in any other circumstances.

It turned out that although it clearly did say Rachel the rest of the form clearly related to me having "male" circled and having my correct date of birth but I think I was entitled to have my little panic considering my immediate destination and that I would be out cold in about ten minutes time.

I can only imagine it was brought about by poor handwriting: the end of Michael is very similar to the end of Rachel and must have been mistransposed when taking the name from the previous handwritten form.

When I came around after the operation I quickly checked all my limbs and that other bits were still present and sort of correct just to make sure nothing was missing. Only one limb was free: my right leg. My left leg was bandaged from having the vein removed; my left arm had a drip in it and my right arm was heavily bandaged because I had just had my artery reconstructed. I couldn't really move much apart from do a half Harry Worth impression.

I stayed in hospital for a few days. A friend, Jaquie, was visiting when I was told I could be discharged and she kindly said I could stay at her place for a few days. I took her up on the offer. She left the ward her phone number in case anyone phoned to see how I was and enquired about possibly visiting. Once discharged two very curious incidents took place. Afterwards I had a theory of how they came about. Let's see if you, dear reader, come to the same conclusion as I did.

I was playing with my new carer's young son, Vinny. (Hey that's amazing: for some strange reason my temperamental home computer keeps on switching from Language "English (U.K.)" to "English (U.S.)" and just then it had played it's a party trick on me and a squigglerly red line appeared under the word "carer" - there it is again - but once I corrected it back to "English (UK)" it went. The American version has not got a word for "carer".

Sorry. Where was I? Oh yes. For no apparent reason Vinny threw his toy car at me. Blood seeped down my face. I had only been discharged a few hours earlier and I was now bleeding again. (Bloody dinky toys. They will be the death of me)

After a diplomatic delay Jaquie then said she had to go out and could I look after her kids for an hour or so. She wouldn't be long. In the middle of my enforced baby-sitting stint the phone rang. I answered it. The women on the other end said:

"Is that you Michael."

"Er Yes."

"Where are you?"

"Jaquie's."

"Who's Jaquie?"

There was a pause and then she hung up. Weird. Who was that?

I learnt about a week later that at about the same time another friend had tried to visit me and phoned the hospital and was told what ward I was in. When he got there it was found to be one of the psychiatric wards. At the reception he explained whom he had come to visit. He was directed to the day room. When he got there all he saw was an elderly looking man watching the TV on his own. He went back to the receptionist and said I was not there (this was getting surreal).

" He was there a moment ago. He must be in the garden." They both went out in the garden. She then looked through the French windows in to the day room and said,

"Look there he is."

"No he is not. God. I must be going mad." Definitely not the most appropriate cliché to use in the circumstances.

It's conclusion time. I think that there were two Michael O'Sullivans in the same hospital for those days and the hospital main switchboard had confused the two. Thank goodness there was not a Rachel O'Sullivan.

A few days later I was back in my own bed and back at work. At the Law Centre we try and be "self servicing" which means you do you own basic tasks, such as typing your own letters, putting them in to envelopes; putting stamps on them and taking it in turns to "do the post". Only occasionally could you justify using a Dictaphone and get someone with proper typing skills to type your letters and statements for you. This would usually only be if you were under pressure with your work load or your arm was in a sling as you had just had your artery reconstructed as a consequence of your old fistula having burst inside you several weeks previously because you were foolish enough to play indoor five a side football. But I had to develop a new technique, as I had to use my left hand to use the thing.

Weeks later I was at a stag night and while waiting for my "go" in a game of ten pin bowling to arrive got involved in a table football game. My recently reconstructed arm went into spasm. I was alarmed and immediately stopped playing and eventually the spasms stopped and the rogue arm behaved itself again. When mentioning this strange episode at my next checkup I was told that I should have continued playing as it was good exercise to get blood bumping into the small erstwhile leg vein as it would get it to grow. Similar process to fistulas. But no one told me.

My arm eventually healed very well and there was not even an unsightly lump, which I was expecting. Even the surgeon appeared please with the outcome. I was even daring enough to wear short sleeve shirts without embarrassment for the first time in years as the scaring was hardly noticeable and by now my fistula and dialysis injection marks were practically invisible.

***

The first few years at the law centre I was not allowed on the insurance policy because of my health history. We had insurance because if any of the caseworkers were off ill for a long time we would need an immediate locum as the other lawyers at the centre would not be suffiently specialist to cover and do to the extra work.

Eventfully I had the honour of being allowed on. I had been told on more than one occasion by one of my colleagues that I had one of the best attendance records at the centre, which probably left the insurance company with no choice especially with the possible threat of action under the Disability Discrimination Act. I would suggest that one of the reasons I did not ever go ill was because I only work part tine and had more time to relax outside work and acquire less stress.

Our insurance policy did not appear to have the far stricter condition as this one I recently came across.

Declaration.
I understand that this application to join "Healthy Profits Now" is on the basis of a Moratorium. This means that any medical or physical condition which was diagnosed or where symptoms were present or for which I received treatment, took medication, underwent test, or sought advice from a doctor or consultant during the 24 consecutive months before the start of my policy or during the 90 days after the start of my policy, will not be covered, until I have subsequently been clear of the condition for two consecutives years.

Even though at this stage I did not have a day off work in years I would fail because of the "took medication" condition, which I will never avoid to my dying day.

My biggest dilemma has always been whether to go for it in life. Take up every single opportunity to do anything and everything I would not be able to do when I returned to the kidney machine but thereby miss the loss of a working kidney even more so when it happened because my life would become so drastically different. Or lead a slow and less eventful lifestyle, with lots of time to relax and ponder and enjoy, if that is the right word, my own company so when the eventual day returns, the shock will not be so great. This later option may prolong my kidneys life but if it did reject would I regret having taken the less active decision.

At one of my four monthly kidney checkups I got a shock. I walked into the consultant's room and saw two trainee doctors sitting there. That's not the shock but how the consultant introduced me. I was introduced as having one of best kidney functions in the unit. Well it was news to me. This is not the fault of the doctor. There are several consultant and these consultations are akin to being on a conveyor belt and unless you have something to report, or there is a strange test result, then it last only a few minutes. Not every doctor knows every detail of every patient. Even if they did they would not know how much detail the patient had or wanted to. I look forward to future observers sitting in to gleam other gems of information.

"Call Mr Michael O'Sullivan.". "Call Mr Michael O'Sullivan". "Call Mr Michael O'Sullivan." "Call Mr Michael O'Sullivan." I was waiting for hours at the Crown Court murder trial. Once called I caused a slight delay in the proceedings by insisting that I wanted to affirm rather than swear on the bible before giving evidence. After a few straightforward questions, setting the scene for the jury by the prosecution barrister on what I saw, I was cross-examined by the defence barrister. As I was expecting he asked me why I did not just say, "yes" at the identity parade when asked at the time did I recognise the person I saw stealing the jewellery rather than the "I think so" which was what came out. I explained it had such serious implications to say I recognised him that I used the less certain reply because I knew I was effectively accusing him of murder and, by contributing to the evidence, sending him to prison for life. He then said in classic barrister cliché " I put it to you Mr O'Sullivan that you are mistaken about that identification" and calmly as I could said "No I'm not". Then a second barrister cliché descended on the court. "No further questions" and he sat down.

What an anticlimax. I was expecting far more that. The Defence barrister probably knew I was in the legal profession and assumed I was unlikely to be intimidated by such an occasion even with a jury and a full press gallery. Presumably he was not prepared to take the risk of asking more questions. He wanted me forgotten by the jury as quickly as possible.

On leaving the court I saw what could only have been the senior police inspector giving me a big smile supposedly pleased with my very short contribution and that I hadn't screwed up. I also spotted, a few seats away, a couple staring down in front of them who could only have been the victim's parents.

The police phoned me a few weeks later and told me I was being given a bravery award and wanted to check over the wording of the press release. They reeled out my name, age, area of the town I lived in and where I worked. I made it clear I did not want all that information to be released and would only allow my name, which was already in the public domain after the full committal. I was already concerned about regular sightings of a person I recognised from the trial. The police employee on the phone seemed a bit surprised at my reaction especially after I said I did not want to attend the award ceremony either.

Only comparatively recently had they stopped handing out money for these awards. I learned that you got a nice plaque to put on your wall. (I will have to add that to the other two plaques not on my wall at the Law Centre) Later I learnt that one of the other witnesses did not want to go to the ceremony but felt she had to because the police had asked her thought she could not refuse. I felt it was not about bravery. None of the witnesses had really put themselves at real risk. It was a device to encourage more members of the public to come forward if they had any evidence which is fair enough I guess considering how so many people do not want to get involved.

When I read the local newspaper article it was quite amusing as the headline was something like "brave five collect their awards" but there was only a photograph of four. Well the other one could not be that brave. I took the bravery award to my Mum when I next visited her.

I always had my own personalised definition of brave and courage. For me to be brave is to hide your fear and control the situation you are in and not panic and keep calm. Courage on the other hand is to walk into a situation knowing the risk and that you can turn back at any time but nevertheless continue. People have said I have been brave the way I have dealt with my kidney condition but my Dad had the courage as he did not have to give his kidney – in fact I tried to put him off - and for him it definitely was the unknown as he had never been a hospital patient in his life.

**

Once again I was being asked to leave my home by the owner of the building. He wanted to relet and wanted all the tenants out. I was not that keen to buy a flat and take out a mortgage but this time I knew I might have to if I wanted some security of tenure. The government had changed the law on private tenancies. Image if you will three tenants of the same landlord living in three separate flats in the same house. One tenant moved in before 15th January 1989; the second moved in between 15th January 1989 and 27th February 1997 and the third moved in after that date.

Assuming no historic complication and that the flat and the landlord is the same, then these three tenants would very probably have differing legal rights when it comes to being allowed to keep their home. The longer lasting one would possibly have something very valuable to sell back to her/his landlord; the middle one may have similar security depending on how the tenancy was originally created but the most recent would have little rights indeed.

By signing any new private tenancy I would have a guanteed minimum of only about six months to remain there and would have no legal defence to possession proceedings even if I were an ideal tenant with no rent arrears.

I did however test the market and phoned up one ad and the landlord said with absolute conviction that all tenancies were now six months. I explained that it was the minimum not the maximum and he continued to bamboozle me with his ignorance. I knew landlords especially that one was only going to offer the minimum so it had to be the first rung of the home owning democracy ladder for me.

It was exciting times in the new world of owning your own bricks and mortar. It was suggested you could not lose. Endowment mortgages were the thing. I doubt, with my medical history, I would get a favourable deal but at one building society I was asked:

" No doubt you would want an endowment mortgage" I said no and there was a look of shock emanating from the other side of the desk. When usual professional composure was resumed:

" Well you should consider it as in the future you know you might settle down, marry and have children and you know things can happen (really) and you being the bread winner .." etc etc.

My reply: "Well if I married and had several children do you not think I would have moved out of a one bed roomed flat by then."

"Oh yes I see you point".

"What do you mean you see my point? I just caught you out giving partial advice. You just want your commission for selling an endowment policy!!" I thought.

I eventually   took the plunge but not after my first serious attempt collapsed and I lost several hundred pounds after the company had a last minute change of mind and pulled out of the deal just before we were about to exchange contracts. The directors had decided the market at that time was not allowing them to sell for a price they would be willing to accept.

Owning your home was the thing. I saw many people come to see me at work after financially overstretching themselves and being threatened with eviction because of mortgage arrears. They had spent thousands, usually by taking out a second mortgage to redecorate and improve their home automatically thinking it would increase the value but this is not necessarily so.

One client wanted to exercise her right to buy her council flat so that her children could inherit and sell it. This was seen to be an investment that would have no drawbacks but it does. It was not easy to get a mortgage to buy a flat in a council skyscraper. Although her children would inherit it they would not be able to sell without difficulty because potential purchasers had problems getting a mortgage. They could only let it out; it may become a burden and be capital they could not "unlock."

Also there were many sad stories when the outside of a block needing renovation. The tenants did not have a problem but the owner occupiers had to pay their share, which would amount to thousand of pounds. If this woman's children inherited the flat they would not be able to sell it easily but they could rent it out but as soon as the renovation bill arrive it could be a financial disaster. I tried to put her off but failed.

<u>"Michael I'm afraid your Mum has now gone back on a kidney machine"</u>

CLICK ....WKQ: 0+1+1=2

Due to the last stroke she was now a wheel chair user and was paralyzed down one side of her body. The need to return to the machine was quite sudden but deep down we knew it was coming. Probably brought on by the most recent big stroke. She had not yet had another fistula fitted, the one from years ago had stopped flowing, and so she had to have emergency dialysis by using a devise fitted in her neck. It is temporary for when the patient has not got a working fistula. You usually have a two-barrelled catheter, one for blood leaving the body, the other for blood returning. The option, which my Mum had, was a single barrel one. This subclavain line is inserted into a large vein at the side of the neck just under the collarbone. At one stage they attempted to dialysis from the leg but it was not working very well and returned to the neck.

The new fistula operation was put back several times and she was told of the postponement just the evening before it was supposed to go ahead. This was very upsetting for her and the most upset I had ever seen her. Some of my operations were delayed for a few hours due to emergencies but I was always kept informed but they always took place on the planned day. But while her dialysis was possible the operation could be postponed until the hospital had more time as more urgent, life-threatening operations took preference.

When she was discharged, after finally having her fistula fitted, she had to continue dialysising from her neck to allow time for the fistula to grow. This second fistula resulted in her circulation being restricted to her hand to the extent that several of her fingers slightly changed colour indicating reduced blood circulation.

"Prednisolone, like many other medicines may cause side effects in some people. These may include .... unusual growth of body hair." (On the sheet inside every drug packet.)

"Side effects that have sometimes been reported in patients taking cyclosporin include........ increased growth of hair on the body and the face" (On the sheet inside every drug packet.)

I had grown more hair particularly down my back and in and on my ears. After a bath or shower I would feel as if I was under water and I was constantly putting my finger in each ear and wiggling it about to try and release the fluid but to no avail. I had to wait for it to drain away over the next few hours. Sometimes it didn't and I was left lugging liquid around in my lughole.

I initially went to the chemist and was given some drops. They did not help but when I saw my GP he advised against these products. They were likely to give you an ear infection and I was advised to try warm olive oil. The medical professions definition of "warm" appeared to differ from mine. When they meant warm they must mean not cold i.e. not from the fridge but I thought warm meant heated up a bit. I heated a teaspoon worth on - yeah you're ahead of me - a teaspoon by using a match or lighter underneath. It felt as if was chasing the dragon. Luckily I did not pour hot olive oil into my ears. Warming it up first didn't work. After several days trying to soften the wax the next syringing attempt failed. It is not really syringing anyway, more like water pistoling. We were getting nowhere. The wax would not budge so I was referred to the ear, nose and throat (ENT) hospital.

Arriving at the reception a few weeks later I must have handed over my GP' s referral letter in which he had explained the problem. He had likened the wax and hair entanglement as something similar to a fiberglass type structure. I patiently waited for the receptionist to read the letter then she said "how did you get fiberglass in your ear?" To which I replied "it's an analogy you great 'nana" (well apart from the last bit) and any moment was expecting her to say. "Well Mr. O' Sullivan if you take a seat the analogist will be with you in one moment."

A strange metal prehistoric looking funnel device was put in my ear and the medic began to pull out individual strands of hair. Seeing a certain flaw in this procedure as a long-term solution I questioned it. She suggested I prevent my ears from ever getting wet. To which my reply was, what? Never wash them? Ever? She indicted that was indeed her advice. I was hoping for a solution not tips on how to grow my own potatoes! I was simply yearning for a bilateral waxectomy.

The brilliant plan we decided upon was that before I had a shower I was to clog up my ears with cotton wool to keep them dry. During these shower experiments after a minute or so of soaping up I would look down and see two clumps of white cotton in the bath.

Back to the drawing board or rather the water pistol gallery. I returned to the doctor's surgery where upon we had another go at softening the fiberglass with olive oil for few days and then syringing. I tried to persuade the nurses to have extra goes because this sub aqua life style was starting to get on my wick (well at least I have a good supply of wax for it)

After one session I started to get a pain in one ear and went back to my GP who diagnosed a perforated eardrum. I had pressurized the nurses to try a bit too hard.

Eventfully my GP came up with an odd solution, which was a solution in itself: twice a week pour in a special shampoo usually prescribed for a scalp problem. It did the trick. I now have the cleanest and clearest ears in town and with no split ends!

***

After getting on the first rung of the ladder of the home owning democracy - beautifully engineered by removing security of tenure in the private rented sector - I saw an opportunity of getting on the first rung of the rope ladder of the boat owning democracy.

Some building societies, it has even been suggested, bribed their membership to get them to vote for the organisation to become a bank. I got £2,000.00 in the scam and rather than risk flittering it away I wanted to employ it for something useful. Buying a boat was my idea, which seemed the most appropriate purchase after benefiting from a floatation. But I needed others to partake in the ownership or should that be ownerboat. Also I had to make sure I could still go out on it if my kidney rejected and I went back on a kidney machine. I concluded that the problem would be more financial than physical.

I put the word out amongst my friends and eventually three of us bought the "Honky Tonk", a twenty-foot, four-berth river cruiser for £3,000.00. Only a thousand pound each and I had money left over to deal with the extra annual fees that otherwise, as a sole owner, my part time earnings may not have been able to cope with it. On visiting the marina, shortly after the purchase, one of the workers said he was always perplexed as to why so few people did not club together to jointly own a boat. Three or four people could easily arrange it. For each joint owner there was a guaranteed use about once a month for about a week and for longer holidays you could exchange your weeks. Who would want to go out on it every weekend anyway?

The running costs would be reasonable. For instance had we got a fourth person it would have worked out at £5.00 per week to run it? That would be marina charges, river and canal license and insurance.

Strangely, you do not need to pass any cruising test before you slip you moorings for the first time as a proud new joint captain of your new vessel. You don't have to pass any form of token test or sign a form to confirm that you had read any basic manual.

This became apparent at locks where people would moor up in a full lock and tie up only to become suddenly aware, as all the ropes tightened, that water is going out and your boat will hang there at the top of the lock until one of the ropes, or something else snaps such as the British Waterway's official's patience

You do, however, have to prove that the boat will not easily catch fire. Sink? Don't be silly. Not that the boat might have a great big hole in the hull or that you do not know your starboard from your port, but that the vessel is a fire risk. So strict is this rule that you cannot get insurance unless you get your safety certificate and you cannot get your annual boating license unless you can produce your insurance policy. Before you get your safety certificate your boat is inspected and if work needs to be done, such as getting a fire blanket, your are formally presented with yet another certificate you can proudly nail on a wall somewhere, a Certificate Of Failure. We were so proud.

In the marina some of the larger boats would never appear to move from one month to the next. I surmised that they were either owned by corporations or the wealthy. In some of the other boats you would see people in them and you would be lucky if your heard the engine running let alone put into gear and taken out for a spin. Others, lived on their boat but never moved it.

We took our boat all over the place. Once you paid your annual fees and got the engine serviced it was a roving holiday cottage with only the expense of petrol and food.

As a part time worker I had the luxury of avoiding the bank holiday weekends where the canal was noticeably busier. When I mean busier I mean more boats then usual. If you were boating midweek you would pass only a couple of boats an hour. Sometime even less if it was not a "nice day" or it was not the peak of summer or you were in the middle of nowhere. If it was an "awful day" I'd like to spend it on the boat, as it would often still have to be moved, as it shouldn't stay moored up along the towpath for more than 14 days in one spot. I would never get perturbed that the weather was not boating type weather. In fact with me it was as if a switch would flick in my head and I would treat the journey as a challenge. After all there is no such thing as bad weather, just the wrong kind of clothing.

We took it on the Thames but at the last lock before entering we were asked for our license. I pointed to the one stuck on the window and the lock keeper said "no your Thames license." We discovered only then that the annual "Inland Waterway" license did not cover all inland waterways. Not included were four or five waterways, that's rivers or canals to you and me, including the River Thames. This is because the Thames is the "Queen's Waterway" I sarcastically asked if the queen was cruising that week because otherwise we could use the bit of the water she was not on and try and not waste very much of it. We therefore had to pay for a visitor's monthly license (we were going to London and back) but you could only have one a year or a few for a short period. Breaching this regulation could mean being liable for the full years Thames licence.

One summer the boat had found itself on the Thames moored up in Reading the day before the WOMAD festival was about to begin. I had to leave early as I, of people, had been nominated as a godfather for a baptism/christening. That is why my suit hung up at the back of the boat cockpit.

The young sister of the to-be-christened was watching me holding her new sister and heard a noise emanating from her lower regions. I was to then make a comment that was to haunt me for several years to come. "Oh, a bottom burp." This intrigued her so much that when she was on the Honky Tonk she wanted to know who the captain was. When she was told it was, she said she would call me Captain Bottomburp. This had dire consequences for my next visit to her family home, as she would tell people such as her teachers that Mick

Bottonburp was visiting. One day I was expected to walk her to school but luckily did not meet any of her teachers.

One night at that visit she was in the middle of her evening meal when she looked up and all seriousness asked me with a certain regal resonance, "Have you always been a silly person?" Quite a question. Well it was a career move in my late twenties.

Young children come up with straight to the point and logical questions that eventually through time their original thought process is knocked out of them. Things similar to, why didn't Goldilocks get arrested for breaking and entering. My favourite is the following:

"Mummy?"
"Yes darling"
"Do you know when baby Jesus made the world in seven days?"
"God. Not baby Jesus"
"Oh sorry God"
"yes"
"Well, on the first day?
"Yes"
"What was he standing on?"

The following year the boat was once again at the WOMAD festival at Reading. We left it there hoping to move it the following weekend but for some reason did not and so rescheduled it for the following mid week.

I arranged to meet a friend at the boat with me having to come from London directly from a "counsels conference" (barristers meeting) When I got there the boat wasn't. I was longing to unload myself of this rather bulky and heavy case file. I waited for my crew to turn up, a bit concerned how he was going to react as I had only just managed to persuade him not to cancel the trip. He had recently come out of casualty after a garden accident and was not totally able bodied as he had injured his arm and it was still in a sling. I had reassured him he would not have to do much work such as doing the locks as we were on the Thames and lock keepers did all that stuff. After all we had just paid a supplemental to our annual Inland Waterways licence.

When he arrived we phoned the police and were told they did not have a record of a boat called the Honky Tonk being stolen but had a record of a boat called the Handy Tank. This boat had been reported as being stolen only a few hours before. I politely pointed out it was probably the same boat. Reading is not exactly an international ocean harbour. How many boats are stolen each week.

Because we were both slightly incapacitated, me with a heavy file and my crew with his injury, we decide to hire a taxi to take us up river to where we were told the boat had been taken to. I explained the west bank was our destination while pointing at a river map. However the taxi driver drove to the area of town but I became concerned when he drove over the river bridge. After travelling some distance and eventually finding a bridge miles up river to be able to get out, we were now further away from the boat than where we started from. The taxi then became lighter by two passengers and we were lighter by £20.00. We decided to locate it on foot but with the many new estates we had now lost sight of the Thames.

By nightfall we still had not spotted the river, which was a bit of an achievement in itself and then a police car pulled up, as we may have looked a bit suspicious. As it turned out we had a nice chat, explained the story and they gave us a lift to the marina. The boat had been severely vandalised. The windscreen together with windscreen frame had vanished. I gingerly walked over the boat debris and damage inside to see if it was possible to sleep on it that night. With my torch I saw what was on one of the cabin cushions and suddenly my right hand clenched into a fist and my arm bent rigidly and I shouted out Yes!

The vandals had found what was left of a small amount of washing powder left in a polythine bag that we had never got round to using or throwing out. There on the cushion was the same white powder carefully placed in a line. The vandals had thought it was cocaine and had attempted to snort it. I had this vivid image of them each being interviewed at the local police station and as their false machismo mask slipped away and they started to cry and sniffle, the police office would say "for the purposes of the tape the prisoner has several bubbles emanating from his left nostril and they are in turn slowly ascending to the ceiling and disappearing"

We discovered later that the vandals had got the boat engine working and with a crowbar they had brought with them had moved the boat up the river and after smashing the windscreen and it's frame did further damage to anything else that looked at them in funny way which was then thrown overboard. Maybe that heavy duty Persil was a bit too pure for them to handle. Several people witnessed all this from the bank and phoned the police and they arrived on the scene. In a car. They then got a vessel from the Environmental Agency who run the Thames. The vandals, realising that the their exciting day was coming to an end, drove the boat into the bank and scappered.

We had problems get the insurance company to pay up. Without even consulting us they made a decision on what they would reimburse and what they wouldn't. They, for instance, initially refused to replace the fire extinguishers that were thrown overboard because they were, get this, out of date. I asked them how they knew that if they were missing. They just assumed, without asking me, that the remaining very old extra fire extinguisher was the age of all of them.

They also did not believe me that the engine anti-theft device was stolen. Admittedly it did indeed look dubious: what is the point of having an anti-theft device that can be nicked. If that's possible it is not very likely to be able to the job it was meant for when someone wants to steal the engine. But sure enough our said device had been removed and no doubt thrown overboard. Maybe we need to install an anti-theft devise for the engine anti-theft device. I produced an old receipt not only establishing it's purchase but it's installation and the company backed down.

Eventually the boat got repaired, restocked with fire extinguishers and an engine anti-theft device and is now back on the canal waves.

I had grand idea of taking my Mum out on the boat but it was likely to be difficult to arrange. She could not leave the house without her wheel chair, having lost the ability to walk unaided since her massive stoke. But it would have been a change for her going slowly through the countryside along stretches that cars could not. At about this time I had a strange dream. We were both trapped below deck in a sinking ship. I could have escaped but she couldn't as she was in her wheel chair. I had to make a big decision. Then I woke up.

In parts of the inland waterway, where they weren't conveniently positioned train stations at either end of our journey, we needed two cars. We would as a crew arrive at where we intended to leave the boat at the end of a leisurely cruise, park one up and all jump into the larger one, removing from the abandoned car all the essential provisions for the day. To me it felt like we were planning a bank job, as it is know within the criminal fraternity.

"Right you all know the plan. We have been through it enough times. I 'll go through it once more so they'll be no mistakes. We take Justin and Chrissy's car to where the Honky Tonk is going to end up at the end of the day .OK? Then we all get into Steve's machine and comeback here. Steve has got the universal inland waterway key. Show everyone it Steve. This gets us to use the British Waterway toilets and water points but what is more important is that we need it for the swing and lift bridges. Have you of all used one of these? It is a standard gauge windlass. The size for all locks in this region. Do not lose it. It's the tool we need to get to our destination. Lose it and we are stuck between locks on the canal. We cannot go back. We cannot go forward. If we get stuck and any BW official approaches I 'll do all the talking OK?. Any questions? No? Good. So, if all goes according to plan we get back to the other car, dump the boat and split. Right synchronise watches...."

The one facility the old Honky Tonk did not possess was proper washing facilities. It did allow you to heat up a kettle and mix it with the cold water from the sink but several days in mid canal, battling against the fierce storms and overcoming the risk of scurvy until we got to the next supermarket meant, we needed something more substantial.

I attempted research in locating the whereabouts of any municipal baths in any town we were due to sail through. However coming up from the below the road, from the underworld, to locate these showers and bathing facilities had difficulties. You usually ended up on the town outskirts and had to read the sign for town centre which were for the motorist. So you would end up walking not actually around the houses but around the town rather than straight for the swimming pool.

The best time was early in the morning. There is always that feeling of accomplishment in leaving the boat in search of a warm shower, especially in the summer on a week day, knowing that you are just a mere observer of the rat race to work. Occasionally you arrived at a jam-packed swimming pool, for the early swimmers, for participators of the water rat race. One person wanted to get some extra training in before the real thing. I would be swimming and would actually be knocked from behind. I was actually being tailgated by someone who not only was stressed out from the five day nine-to-five but doing extra stress training on the eight-to-nine swim.

The Thames has some absolute huge boats that wound never get through the largest lock on any of the canals but I am sure the owners did not mind. Nicknamed Gin Palaces, they never looked hired which is not often the case with narrow boats on the canals owned by the extremely rich. One over took our boat once and the friendly occupants were waving to us but none of them realised that the power and speed of their boat was knocking us sideways and it was only a question of time, if the person at the helm did not do some quick steering, that we would have crashed into the bank. I was not annoyed because they were oblivious to what they were causing. I could only wave back as they had no idea and anyway were impossible to communicate with as they were now well ahead of us. There is a good analogy in there somewhere. About how some of the very rich are oblivious as to how some of their actions affect others and they have not got a clue.

When boating the typical reserved Englishness appears to disappear. Everyone says hello or waves when boats pass each other. In fact at any other time, say in the street if you were that friendly to a complete stranger you would be deemed a weirdo. In the boating world if you do not wave or acknowledge you fellow boater you're an antisocial old bugger.

The same thing to a rather limited extent occurs at Glastonbury, my usual annual holiday. People are much more friendly especially if you leave Babylon which is the nickname for the area containing the two main stages that only the TV viewers ever sees. They are completely oblivious to what happens in the rest of the site. It must be the venue not the booked acts that make it such a success. Why else would this be the most expensive weekend camp site that sells out every year without anyone knowing who's playing. On the site there are seventeen stages and about one thousand acts, a substantial minority not being music at all.

Kids are amazed, not only by the contents of the kids field but by things that centuries ago children would not have given a second glance: real fires, an axe, a saw, a teepee, an outside lavatory made out of wood and a wood made out of trees.

Some of the adults worried me about the total dependence on modern living that they could not leave a lone for a few days. Imagine the scene. It is about 3am .I am on night shift. I am at my post with my tabard on, my torch and my walkie-talkie. People come up to me for directions in the 900 acre site. I point in the general direction. Others are lost and have not a clue where their tent is in any of the many fields. I have to coax landmarks out of them to see if I can at least point them in the right direction. Then a young American comes up to me and says, "Hey do you know where I can get a cab?" Sometime later some one ambles up and wants to know who got kicked out of Big Brother that day.

Up in the "green fields" you meet, apart from other things, complimentary or alternative medicine practitioners. John Diamond's book, Snake Oil in which he wrote that, "..the function of all natural medicines seems not to be to cure but to let you be at one with your own neuroses." He, a life long smoker, was unable to complete the book as he died of cancer, of which he honestly accepts fair a degree of contributory negligence for. He had his fare share of offers from representatives of this sector that they can cure him. I will have more faith in them if at future festivals there is a condition of the licence that, for example, there are tabards roaming around the site with "Aromatherapist" emblazoned on the back or people make way once the crowd hear "Stand back, stand back. I'm a reflexologist."

John Diamond searched for evidence that any of them actually worked and there is one classic anecdote, also referred to by Richard Hawkins who wrote the book's forward. When a scientific method was introduced to look into kinesiology (using magnets, nutrition and contact points to find "imbalances" in the body) the results of the double blind test established it was no good but the supporter said, once he had learnt the result " You see, that is why we never do double –blind testing any more. It never works"

Want to win one million dollars? Then check out the exciting competition at the back of this book. It's has been set by a Mr James Randi. Prove scientifically that homeopathy works and he'll hand it over. Homeopathy believes in the memory of water and that diluting medicines makes them stronger. It is diluted to the extent that there cannot possibly even be a molecule of the original medicine left in the medicine. There have been many experiments. The cynics argue it is just the placebo effect where it has also been shown that the bigger or more colourful the tablet the better the resulting benefits. The believers have attempted to remove the possibility of the placebo effect by producing figures that suggest that homeopathy works on animals.

BBC's Horizon took up the challenge to prove homeopathy works and Mr Randi still has his money

Many people will say homeopathy and other alternative or complimentary medicines work and if it works and alleviates any suffering than that's all that matters. The suggested explanation as o why it works is that a very busy

NHS doctor will see you for five minutes whereas private consultation, whether it be a private or alternative, will allow forty minutes where the alternative medic will ask you lots of questions which will have a pleasing effect and you will feel better in you self simply because someone appears to care more by being able to spend more time with you even though you pay them for their time.

Look what I found on the internet:

"I have polycystic kidneys and although I'm not in renal failure - my kidneys function well - I could progress to that stage. What is the success rate in keeping someone from going into renal failure? Can the cysts be healed and the kidneys reduced to normal size again using Tibetan medicine?"

A: It is very difficult for me to give an exact percentage in terms of our success rate in Tibetan medicine, since we don't have a conclusive document or research paper to prove the number of successfully treated cases. In general, Tibetan medicine has been very effective in treating many problems related to the kidneys, such as renal problems, kidney stones, loss of heat in the kidneys, and weak kidney function. I also am a little hesitant to give an answer about whether your kidney cysts are curable or not since it depends on a few different factors.

My best suggestion would be for you to consult with a traditional Tibetan doctor. The doctor will look into your entire body's constitution at this point in time, do a diagnosis based reading of your pulse and be able to see the total picture of your problem. The doctor will also examine your first morning urine to check whether it is a hot or a cold related cyst, and will ask you questions to determine more about any harmful diet or behavior that is contributing to the imbalance. The doctor will then create a specific prescription for your condition with

Tibetan medicine, which is made out of pure herbs and minerals.

Please also look into the question and answer library for information on <u>renal failure</u> posted on January 5th, 2001.

- Dr. Namgyal"

*

I was reading a small article in a legal periodical warning landlord solicitors how careful they have to be with a particular term of a tenancy. It was to help the landlord rather than the tenant. I read it looking at it from the tenant's prospective and saw it as a possible technical legal defence to repossession proceedings I had just been instructed on. I in turn instructed a barrister. I could not go to the full hearing as I had to give a one-day training course on tenant's rights. The defence failed but we had strong ground to appeal it and so we did.

The tenant was an ex teacher who had to give up his job as he had a serious drink problem and his liver was extremely damaged as he had cirrhosis of the liver. I looked into his welfare benefit entitlement to see if extra welfare benefits with a possible back payment could pay off or reduce his outstanding rent arrears. I applied for one, which meant establishing that the applicant was unlikely to live for the next six months. This was confirmed by his doctor and was one of those rare situations where you could apply for a welfare benefit without the client being aware. He got the extra benefit but it could only pay off some of his rent arrears. The attempt to use this to remove the uncertainty of where he would be living in the remaining months of his life had failed so the appeal hearing still want ahead. It reminded me of the situation I was in years earlier when the last thing I wanted was the real threat of repossession proceedings when I was to begin dialysis for the first time.

The appeal hearing was listed for the first day back after the New Year break. Beforehand I had sent several letters to him – his phone line had been disconnected – to check he would be in court on the day. He did not contact me and on the day of the hearing I received a phone call from a firm of solicitors out of town instructed by his sisters to say he had died. In fact he was found in his flat on the toilet seat some time later, all my reminder letters presumably unopened on his hallway mat. He had died before the holiday period. Where he was found was not an uncommon place. The extra strain when you have a weak heart can be fatal. Apparently, Elvis Presley died in similar circumstances.

Nevertheless it was too late not to attend court and I went along with the barrister to make apologies to the Judge. While we were waiting and chatting he told me a story about an armed robber who had just been convicted and was about to be sentenced. He had already shouted out in court that he had a terminal illness and was not expected to live for more than six months.

When the judge passed sentence he gave him a three years prison sentence. He again shouted out, saying that he'd never make it and the judge replied: "Well just do the best you can"

The judge could get away with what initially sounded like a callous thing to say but during this plea in mitigation there was no medical evidence and so it was merely a try on. It does illustrate how people misunderstand the court process and what evidence is all about. Most things, especially medical assertions have to be backed up with medical evidence.

In my job I find it sometimes find it difficult to explain what is not evidence and what is good evidence. Hearsay evidence is a difficult one. One client told me a police had hit him. After a long chat I said

"Where is your evidence"

"What do you call that then", he said pointing daggardly at his black eye

"That's not evidence a policeman gave you a black eye but that you have a black eye"

There is the classic scene in a court albeit a TV pretend court where the policeman is asked if he can refer to his note book. He will then be asked when he wrote them and depending on the reply is likely to be accepted as admissible evidence if written at the time of the incident. Any one can do the same and take contemporaneous notes and it is admissible evidence unlike notes taken just before the hearing rather than immediately after the incident. Police officers note pads are just as admissible or inadmissible as any other person's notes.

Richard Bransdon, owner of his own airline, sneaked off to the toilet once after someone said something to him. He thought he might need to prove what was said in court proceedings at later date. There he scribbled down exactly what was said and as it was soon after he heard it, it would be more likely to be exact and good evidence. It was later used in his successful case against BA

That's something everyone should do if they are told something that they may have to prove in the future. The contemporaneous note signed and dated would be very helpful.

In court the company you are up against enters with a big, impressive looking file. All it contains are copies of letters and telephone conversation notes. That's all that is in their file even though the cover looks very flash and it has a unique file number. Anyone can make their own file and then you are on equal footing.

"It 's the best present she's ever had. She uses it every day"

Mum was now effectively bed ridden and her life was mainly spent moving between her bed, that had to be downstairs because of the problem of fitting a stair lift on our stair, and the seat in the lounge. It was poignant how there was a complete reversal of roles as to when I was a child. During my visits I was helping her with the things she used to help me with such as putting the lid on the plastic beaker and trying to get her to learn to walk. Being unable to walk made you feel the cold, as you could not move around to warm yourself up. Someone told me once that the kidneys were the body's thermostat. So we had here an unfortunate double whammy.

Looking through one of those mail order catalogues selling things you would never think you would never need I came across something somebody actually might. Those sleeping bags you sit in. To me while examining the picture in the ad they looked like giant socks but looked ideal as a solution for fighting off the cold.

I decide it would be a great thing to send her for her birthday. Then I thought why wait. She is cold now so I didn't wait and bought it by mail order to get it delivered as soon as possible.

This reminded me of a discussion with friend who was going to buy her mum a garden tool for her birthday because she had borrowed it but it broke and felt guilty about not replacing it. Surely you cannot use it as an excuse to solve your gift problem, I pointed out. I wanted to suggest she might want to consider setting fire to her garden shed? That way she would not have a present dilemma for at least the next ten years.

"High blood pressure over a long period can lead to heart damage"

Playing 5-a- side football can be very demanding and the resulting breathlessness I put down to being unfit. On more than one occasion my nepthrologist, kidney consultant, asked me if I ever got a "tight chest". He asked this because it is quite common for people who have had high blood pressure over a prolonged period of time to get a damaged heart. Furthermore Polycystic kidney sufferers are prone to have problems with blood vessels generally. In the past doctors I have looked into my eyes, not in a lovey dovey way, but with a mini torch that can magnify images to see if any of the tiny blood vessels had been damaged. A quick test for high blood pressure damage. Occasionally at my check ups if I was asked about whether I had a "tight chest" I would say no as I felt I did not. When I was gasping for breath after exercising I tended to get a dull ache much lower down and not on the surface of my chest. I had, as it turned out a dangerous misconception of what tight chest meant. To me it was a pain up front as if someone was standing on me, which was an expression I heard before. I therefore had delayed treatment by inadvertently not disclosing it.

I noticed the breathlessness and this dull pain was getting worse when I physically exerted myself but did not know if I was merely exercising more and for longer. I decided to research it on the internet and found I had the symptoms of angina. It was some time since my next check up and so I wrote to the hospital expressing my concerns and very soon after I was given an appointment with a heart consultant and he did think from the ECG scan, taken at my normal check up, that I had angina. From the scan he said initially it looked from previous incidents that I was near to having a heart attack at the time of those attacks. This must have been during my five – a – side games when I was on my haunches getting my breath back aware of the dull ache but not what it might signify.

It is a bit difficult to diagnose angina. It is really a symptom as well as a condition. The fact remains, however that it means you have restrictions in your blood flow, usually your arteries which result in a pain in your chest, made worse when you exercise, during cold weather or during moments of extreme stress.

I was put on heart drugs and given a tablet I should put under my tongue if I felt the chest pain. This will be familiar to those of you who have the misfortunate to be watching a cheap TV episode of some imported American detective series. The elderly person type character has a shock, such as he has just been told he is a bad actor and he is not in the next series, and he, with the aid of his caring wife or daughter rushes through his pockets, as he needs his tablets urgently. Once found and swallowed he recovers practically immediately.

I now was able to redefine the pain and now knew it was angina related. I did not have a bad case of it but in the winter if I were to walk up a steep hill quickly it would return. The irony was that by the time I stopped, got the tablet bottle out, unscrewed the top and put the tablet under my tongue, the pain had gone because I had stopped walking. I could recover quickly if I just stopped. Also I could now forecast the chest tightening and avoid the need to take the drug. The bottle label advised that the contents should be discarded after eight weeks of opening. So usually from each bottle I only used about two tablets before I had to chuck it out. The worrying thing for me was the hospital flowchart sheet I was given with it.

"WHAT TO DO IF YOU GET CHEST PAIN
If you get chest pain or discomfort which is similar to your angina or heart attack:
Sit down, relax, take a Glyceryl Trinitrate (GNT) tablet or spray. Wait 5 minutes.
If the pain is gone, rest, then resume your activities gradually.
If the pain is not gone take another tablet /spray. Wait 5 minutes.
If the pain is gone, rest, then resume your activities gradually.
If the pain is not gone, stay calm, relax. DO NOT sit and wait. Dial 999 for an AMBULANCE. Explain what has happened.

IF, AT ANY STAGE AFTER YOU START TAKING YOUR GTN, THE PAIN GETS WORSE, OR YOU BECOME NAUSEOUS, VOMIT OR SWEAT PROFUSELY, CALL 999 FOR AN AMBULANCE STRAIGHT AWAY"

It is a very helpful sheet especially the bit suggesting buying over the counter if you have to pay for your prescriptions, as they are often cheaper than the price of the prescription if you do not have a prepayment certificate.
Most people I would guess would only read this properly for the first time during an attack. Maybe it is my warped mind but I could foresee this scene in homes around the country:

"Get that sheet. Quick "
"Where did you put?
"It must be there somewhere"
"Got it"
"Read it out. I've taken the tablet."
"Right OK are you becoming nauseous, vomiting or
sweating profusely"
"Nauseous?"
"Feeling sick"
"What does profusely mean."
"I don't know."
"Where's the dictionary."
"In the sideboard where it usually is."
"Well get it. Hurry"
"I cannot find it. Who had it last?"
"You did."
"No I didn't."
"You did you were looking up that word angio something"

Angioplasty is where your artery is blocked and needs to
be unblocked to avoid a possible heart attack. In other words a
cardiac arrest. This operation involves inserting a little
deflated balloon up to the part of the artery that is very narrow
and than it is inflated thereby opening up the blood channel
and hopefully dispersing the substance causing the blockage.

Very helpful sheet but not sure if profusely is that
common a word. What's wrong with "a lot"? "Become
nauseous." What's wrong with feel sick? Surprising they did
not say perspire rather than "sweat."

I see many signs with unnecessary unfamiliar words. My
adage. er, saying, has always been why use a big word when a
diminutive one will suffice. This is especially important for
signs. "Car park for use of patrons only". What are they? Male
senior nurses. "Please refrain from smoking." What's that?
Medical advise? Patrons is another one. "Would patrons please
refrain from smoking in the swimming pool."

Soon the road workers will be turning those red and
green sided lollops which will have to be much bigger to allow
the words large enough so they can be read from afar. Soon

they will need to be lifted and turned by at least two people. "Please refrain from progressing your vehicular journey " and on the other side with green background, "Please continue to traverse along this highway"

And let's not forget "Do not alight from the train until it has stopped completely" Stationery I guess. Why alight? "Do not alight from here" sounds like a posh no smoking sign. What's wrong with "get off"? . Is it to vulgar or something? Can you imagine the possibly confusion when passengers from, say abroad where their English is not too hot and they hear "alight" on the train. Is the train on fire? And what if the train is on fire. Do the staff run up and the down the carriages shouting "Alight! Alight!" "Yeah we know it is mate. Where's the bloody door." "Sorry sir. We don't have them on this service. We do however have exit facilities. Your nearest one is in that direction just beyond all that smoke" While on one train the electronic board showed some improvement as it said: "Please be alert to the safety notices in the vestibules"

Yer wot?

Trains have reminded me of something and I feel another anecdote coming on. It is one of Spike Milligan's and on writing this I have heard of his recent death. I feel I cannot ignore the chance to relay on a story he often told on TV chat shows which may now be lost if it is not written down somewhere if it hasn't already.

Spike Milligan's many little autobiographically books were strangely all contained within his wartime memories. They had gems like "silence when you speak to an officer" and at the begging of a letter back home: "We have moved. I am not allowed to say where we are. We had spaghetti for lunch." His rebuke of unnecessary military discipline was engaging.

He tells of time his friend was returning from India and was suffering from dysentery. Well he had an accident. Not in the journey but within his garb. Having no change of clothes, having no suitcase was not explained, decided to rush out at the next station stop, buy a change of clothing for his nether region and jump back on. His plan worked. He found a clothes shop, waited impatiently in a queue, quickly paid by cash, grabbed the carrier bag and got back on the train just in time.

He then retreated to the train toilet. Once the train was well into the countryside he chucked the discarded attire out of the window, opened up the bag and there he looked down. At a lady's cardigan.

In the rush he had snatched the wrong bag. He now had no clothes for covering up his body between his ankles and his waist but he had a brand new women's cardigan. He then had no option but to experiment on how best to wear it. He began putting his legs down each sleeve that gave him a choice of which part of his anatomy he wished to revel to the world. Sorry I do not know what happened next.

*

In 2001 the civil court attempted to remove some of the archaic words from the court procedure so it would be easier to understand. Plaintiff, the person suing, was replaced by Claimant. Writ (High Court) and Summons (County Court) was replaced by Claim Form. Threatening to serve a claim form on someone does not sound so intimating does it? When they first introduced the changes I was staffing a free legal advice line. Someone on the other end was telling me they had got a claim form. I asked what were they applying for and suggest they just fill it in. Then it struck me they had just been sued. Beforehand everyone knew what a writ or a summons was. So of all the antediluvian legal words why change those we all know?

The trouble is that, in my humble opinion, the change is back to front. The writ/ summons is applied for so it can be served on someone. But the claim form does not sound like something you send to someone but something you do yourself.

Other words were removed such as Subpoena, now Witness Summons; Oral Examination becomes Order To Obtain Information From The Judgement Debtor and Garnishee Orders, you'll be relieved to know, becomes: Third Party Debt Orders (e.g. ordering nice mister bank manager to dip into your account to pay off the judgement creditor.). Phrases not titles. You 'll be glad to that an Anton Pillar Order is now called a Search Order.

However Summary Judgement, which by it's name you get an idea what it is about which is applying for early judgement because the defence is a joke is replaced by Part 24 Proceedings which gives no clues at all. Equally Third Party Proceedings (defendant drags in a third person as they feel they are the really guilty one) is replaced by Part 20 Proceedings. Payment Into Court becomes Part 36 Payments.

Intervening with the jury system is dangerous but getting people more up to speed with their own legal system would help. A solicitor friend of mine was convinced the jury found the defendant guilty of the greater offence of affray because it did not seem as bad as GBH. Take also the story of when a jury chairman said "not guilty" someone in court coughed loudly over the word "not" and the judge, not hearing the drowned out little word, sentenced the newly convicted. It was apparently only the academic curiosity of one jury member that prevented a miscarriage of justice. He asked a court usher why the defendant was sentenced. Had he got other offences?

Bailiff is about to be, or by the time you read this may have already, changed to enforcement agent. One legal journalist commented on this arguing there was no need arguing everyone knows what a bailiff is but went on to take about chattels as if everyone knew what they were.

The Plain English Society have a wonderful website quoting ridiculous pompous quotes from bureaucrats or people who consider the longer the sentence or bigger the word, the more important the writer. The fact that easy communication goes straight out the window is often over looked. Like:

"if there are any points on which you require explanation or further particulars we shall be glad to furnish such additional details as may be required by telephone"

The society turns that into:
"If you have any questions, please ring"
And:

"You enquiry about the use of the entrance area at the library for the purpose of displaying posters and leaflets about Welfare and Supplementary Benefit rights, gives rise to the question of the provenance and authoritativeness of the material to be displayed. Posters and leaflets issued by the Central Office of Information, the Department of Health and Social Security and other authoritative bodies are usually displayed in libraries, but items of a disputatious or polemic kind, whilst not necessarily excluded, are considered individually."

becomes:

"Thank you for your letter asking permission to put up posters in the entrance area of the library. Before we can give you an answer we will need to see a copy of the posters to make sure they won't offend anyone"

This is a verbatim quote from a magistrate Complaint:

'At Widgeton in the said County on 24 September 1995 you, being the driver of a mechanically propelled vehicle, namely a Volvo motor car ABC 123D, on a road, namely, Widget Road, being for the time being within the limits of a pedestrian-controlled crossing, the limits of which were delineated, allowed the front part of the said mechanically propelled vehicle to pass in front of the front part of another mechanically propelled vehicle in motion within the limits of the said pedestrian-controlled crossing in the direction of the limits of the crossing.'

This just means you overtook someone on a pelican crossing.

***

The Angina Monologue. Part Two. While waiting for my heart investigative operation I had severe symptoms of hypochondria. Every twitch in the left side of my chest got me concerned. Being told you have this condition must be great news because you are actually suffering from something.

Anyway, every time a felt a slight twinge in the chest region I would think I might be about to have a heart attack, which was a bit sad as I was clearly overreacting. What did not help were the people around me thought just that: that I could drop dead at any time now I was diagnosed as having a mild form of angina.

I was down for an investigative operation to examine in more detail the state of my heart and arteries. They might see blockages that angioplasty could remove. Also there was the possibility of hardened arteries leaving less space for my blood to travel along it.

It was to be a quick visit to a day ward. I was offered a pre med, which was politely refused: they are more hassle than there are worth. It is like injections down the dentist. I had my own tried and tested thumb and fingernail technique. So a tube was passed up my side. Then a dye was passed through it which if you looked on a monitor you could detect any blockage or hardened arteries by looking for where the dye was not going. I did not have a blockage or hardened arteries.

I went back to the ward and it was explained to me that I had to lie flat for something like four hours (it was like old times from when as school boy I was not allowed to move) and then I could go home. In the ward one of the nurses kindly offered me a cup of tea, which I jumped at, in the not moving at all sense of the word. As I always had to drink to protect my kidney and I had not eaten or drunk anything for hours beforehand. She put the cup and saucer up close and gave me a straw. I sipped on the straw and pulled it out again instantly. She had not allowed the tea to cool down and I burnt the roof of my mouth.

So they you have it: I was all psyched up for yet another intrusive operation, refused a pre med, used my alternative pain reduction technique and was caught completely off guard by a nice cup of tea.

The consultant popped his head through the curtains and said I was not going to have a heart attack ....which was nice. I had a diagnosis of sorts: "syndrome x". This meant I had the same symptoms as those associated with angina. In effect I still had angina the symptom but not angina the condition. Syndrome x appears to be the narrowing in the capillaries of the heart but as the name suggests it is not certain.

I was advised that if I get the angina symptom again, as I could not do any damage like have a heart attack, I should not necessarily stop what I was doing and should even continue it, using if needed, the GNT tablet or spray. The theory being that the extra pushing of the blood through the capillaries might even open them up and hopefully in the long term open up the capillaries. The very process to have helped my newly reconstructed artery.

The four hours went by, the pain in my side and the roof of my mouth dissipated slightly. It was time to leave. A friend was to pick me up and I was to stay at her place that night as I was advised not to stay in my flat on my own because sometimes the arterial blood can leak and the bruising can make it difficult to move. If this happened and I was on my own I might find myself in some difficulty.

She could not park her car near to the waiting room which was at the other end of the building. In fact it was very near the ward I was in but she had to wait in the waiting room but I was not allowed to walk so I had to get in a wheel chair and be pushed to the waiting room. When I got there I then had to walk all the way back to where I had come from to get to her car.

One of my drugs was changed as a consequence of this new diagnosis. However I was asked to take it at midday. These was a real problem for me because, apart from my little bauble, being now full, it increased the possibility of me forgetting and as a consequence make it easier to get confused when taking the kidney drugs. When I was oblivious to the heart condition I had two daily drug "drops": one first thing in the morning, the second at evening meal time. Once diagnosed with possible angina, I was prescribed several new drugs, which means I had a new third daily drug "drop": just before I went to bed. Now I would have a fourth. I queried this with the doctor, expecting to be told I would have to take them as prescribed, but he said it would be OK if I took this new drug within my existing times.

On drug packets you often see directions such as "before meals", "after meals", "last thing at night", "first thing in the morning" but I am sure if it explained why they should be taken at that time they would be more likely to be adhered to.

After a few days on this new drug I noticed, while getting ready for bed, swollen ankles. I had my usual panic, thinking my kidney was rejecting. I weighed myself and found I was my usual weight so I may not have water retention, one of the signs of renal failure. I read the possible side effects of the new drug and noticed it warned of the possibility of oedema. One of my other drugs had this but I was unaffected but this new drug, or maybe a result of the new drug cocktail had, brought on the old familiar symptom.

Many months later I got an appointment out of the blue for an ultrasound. When the results arrived I was given a further appointment only to be told that I needed another ultrasound as the first one was not conclusive as to what kind of heart condition I had. It turned out after waiting weeks for the second ultrasound and more weeks for another out patient's appointment to get the result that I had an acquired heart condition as opposed to an inherited one, the other possibility. It would have meant that the rest of my family would have to have been screened.

I was found to also have an enlarged heart muscle, which was brought about, once again, as a consequence of my kidney disease history. Another heart drug that could help reduce the size of the muscle was prescribed. I found it curious that if a muscle did not have to work as hard then it should, over time, reduce itself.

About a week after taking this new drug I woke up one morning to find that one side of my tongue had swollen over night. I thought nothing of it and by the end of the day the problem had completely gone. Then about a week later the same thing happened but this time on the other side of my tongue, the day of the Law Centre x-mass meal no less. This time I was more concerned and phoned the NHS direct line, which I had never done before. I thoroughly recommend it if you are either the type of person who never sees you doctor and just hopes the strange symptom will hopefully go away or you always see your doctor, as soon as you feel anything and turn up at the clinic where your doctor wished you would.

Being a long-term taker of daily doses of immuno suppressive drugs must be increasing my susceptibility to cancers and assumed glands swelling was one of the early symptoms. I was told on the NHS direct line that it was probably the new drug, which had never occurred to me mainly because the symptom was intermittent. I re-read the drug information sheet and at the very bottom it said, "If you experience any of the following effects stop taking the tablets at once and tell your doctor immediately (these side-effects are extremely rare); swelling of the face, lips, mouth, tongue or throat." On the NHS direct line this warning was explained. It could be dangerous to continue taking them as next time the swelling could be worse to the extent you could have difficulty breathing or be unable to do so.

I always read the information on the newly prescribed drug packaging but not really taking it all in as it lists so much. I think you should not only read it on taking your first tablet but again about a week later as it would register if you had recently developed some new symptom and then you could immediately link it to the new drug.

I went to my doctor. Which one? Well take your pick: GP, nephrologist or heart consultant. I was put on another drug that was not known as being as successful in reducing the heart muscle but it gave me an opportunity to ask why the underused muscle cannot achieve the same task itself now it had to work less. It was explained that there are three different types of muscles. The one most people are familiar with are the muscles, say, on your arms. You could stretch your arm out and after a while you would have to put it down, as it would eventually begin to ache. Heart muscles obviously are different as you cannot just stop your heart to give it a little rest unless you had your very own heart by pass machine.

The hospital has now contracted out a company to deliver the two essential drugs to each transplant patient's door. Not all the other drugs mind just the main two: steroid and immunsupressives. Each time they phone they always ask me if I have a stock. Well yes I do but I am not telling you. I want a few weeks overlap just in case your van breaks down or there is an industrial dispute or suppliers cannot get the drugs or there is scare over a certain batch and they all have to be returned even though we are promised that a new batch will be sent as soon as possible.

After my first transplant I childishly contemplated what I would do after the nuclear holocaust four-minute warning began. I would have liked piece of mind so that I could contemplate my end with all the other survivors rather than have to pop round all the late night chemists to see if they might happen to have a few thousand boxes of my kidney and heart drugs ("I've got a exemption certificate") just to tide me over, you understand, until industrial economy recovers over the next few hundred years. A bit silly really as I had just come off a kidney machine.

So each time I tell this company that I do not have a stock. If I ever did I 'd lose my cover, I 'd never accumulate any more because every day I have to take the drugs. It is not as if, next time I can explain that I have now got a stock again because last month I took a little break from them as I thought I might be relying on them a bit too much recently.

The home deliveries are helpful, as I do not have to lug large quantities home. Everything seems bulkier now, not just because I get months of supplies but also because bottles have been replaced by individually sealed drugs, and sometimes with days in the week on them. This makes it easier as far as remembering goes but I am too scared to change my tried and tested system. I have to be even more careful as I have to take two tablets that are both white and so very similar to each other.

Although I get the basic two delivered I still have to keep track of the reduced stock of all the other drugs. Sometimes I think I need some computer software including a matrix and a spreadsheet to keep up. When I run out between check ups I see my GP but he can only give me about two months worth. I often run out of different drugs at different times. I may have to create a designated stock so that they all run out together.

I wrote to this home delivery company (not so much meals on wheels but potions in motion) asking if they could deliver all my drugs. They told me that the one of the drug companies pay for this service and are looking into the possibility of expanding it. The newsletter they sent me included comments on a recent survey: "why don't they deliver all my drugs. You deliver some but not others"; "I would like all my prescription requirements met by XXX (for my transplant only ,of course)"; "As my supply gets low, I get quite anxious as to whether the next supply will arrive (which so far it has), however a call, email or fax from XXX anywhere up to 10 days before delivery would be reassuring"

My Mum's brother, my farming uncle, married and had a son. My auntie who helped run the farm had to move out of the farmhouse. She moved to a small cottage on the edge of the farmland. It had previously been a short-term holiday let in the summer months for "townies". It now needed to be extended and renovated so she could live there. It lacked running water although there was a brook with a tiny waterfall on the other side of the road. Water was put in, within water pipes you will be glad to hear, and the kitchen was extended and a shower was installed. Meanwhile my granddad had died and my grandma had moved to a cottage in a nearby town where several years later she died.

I discovered I was one of the joint executors of my grandmother's estate along with my uncle. However my auntie died two months before my grandma without leaving a will. That is she died in testate.

The estate of my grandma - I was to sort out during my busman's holiday - had a will leaving specific legacies (non land prezzies from beyond the grave) to several relatives. Her cottage and all else was to go to my mum and on her death to her kids.

My uncle kept an eye on the town cottage and I occasionally visited it. Once during a visit while staying at the farm cottage down the valley we found small quantities of money hidden away in the strangest of places that got me thinking even my grandma had forgotten about them. They were fivers found all over the place: under the mats, carpet and mattress. On lifting one corner of some carpet I spotted that familiar shaped long brown envelope often used by solicitors and indicating a will within it. As I lent down to retrieve it I wondered if it would be the same one, just another copy or it would be a more recent one in which case I might not be an executor or even beneficiary. I could not remember the date of the will I had seen but knew how to check immediately if it was just a copy. In the will there had been an error, describing the relationship between two named relatives. On opening it I went to the relevant paragraph and the error was the same, in the same place. I was pretty sure I was not trespassing and stealing.

It is very worrying when people hide wills. When someone dies and a will is hidden the relatives might not ever find it. You should always leave a will or at least a copy with your paperwork in, say, your desk to make people aware of its existence. Do the will hiders think someone will find it and then on realizing they are the main beneficiary go and get the shovel from the garden? Well if you had spotted that in their character I would not leave them anything. I get really riled by these companies who not only draft and execute wills when they are not experts but offer to store it for you, and then charge for the privilege. They call it safekeeping. In practice it is more like will hiding from the relatives.

We could not sell either cottage. According to the will my mum was allowed to live in little town cottage rent-free. But how come the instructing solicitor did not know she was married and lived over a hundred miles away with a family? We could have rented it out or sold it. Then Mum would get the rent or the interest on the proceeds of sale but the capital could not be touched until she died and then distributed between us four. It ended up unsold, unlet and I had to pay the bills such as building insurance and the poll tax. The latter involving me having to appeal the community charge band it had been placed in. All the other buildings along that stretch of road were much bigger and it was assumed this cottage was a farm house.

Then out of the blue I got a bill for over £600.00 for water charges for the previous years. It had been empty for some time but the water company's argument was that they had a policy that if you have furniture in any property that means it is occupied and therefore you are liable for water bills. I told them no one had lived there for years and the furniture remained there simply because we could not very easily move or sell it as we all lived a long way away. I was about to write to them and suggest that if I instructed a water expert to examine the water trapped in the lead pipe for years, between the sink and the road, and it turned out it could be proved that the water must have been there for years, would they withdraw the bill and pay the expert, when a letter arrived effectively saying OK then £25. So I paid it before they changed their mind.

The problem with the two merged small estates was difficult to manage, as apparent uncertainty over the farm cottage was causing interest in the minds of many other relatives. They were phoning and writing to the solicitors instructed by my grandma asking questions and for progress reports. After consulting with my immediate family and fellow executor I replaced the solicitors with myself as there was a real risk the estate could be bled dry.

Also the will's terms were awkward and it was not very nice being in a situation where you gain from your mothers death – a similar problem with many inheritances -so I decided to vary the will which is a right many beneficiaries do not know about. In short you can rip up the original will and write a new one. There are three conditions: you do so within two years of death; all beneficiaries agree to all the new terms and there is no one who is under a legal disability by which is meant no one is lacking in mental capacity and no one is under 18.

We sold the town cottage and divided the estate up equally between the five of us and got £2,000.00 each. I got paid for taking on the task, which actually saved the estate money I'll have you know! The problem that still remained was the farm cottage. You will recall my family got what was left over. At the time the will was executed my grandma could not have expected her daughter to die before her so her estate and cottage passed to my grandma and my family ended up inheriting it by a legal fluke. It could not be sold easily because although it now had a water supply it came from the farm but there was only a license (binding between present landowners) and not an easement (binding on all future landowners) so the right to the water and sewerage ended as soon as the farm was sold. Furthermore the kitchen was built on the farmland but was a problem that was easily surmountable as by then we had possessory title (squatter's rights) but the lack of an easement would allow potential purchasers to make a ridiculously low offer so we decided to let it out to friends.

   I experienced my first sensation as feeling like a landlord at a Law Centre staff - volunteer drink in a local pub. This was a thank you to all volunteers and volunteer solicitors. The latter group, after their hardworking profit cost earning during the day for their respective solicitor firms did regular free legal advice sessions in the evening. The other volunteers helped out during the day. They were usually law students who wanted to see how the average lawyers average day was like but that had to wait until they began their respective training contracts in a high street solicitors practice. Law Centres work very differently. These social gatherings were helpful because very few knew every one because all paths very rarely crossed.

   I was able to present myself as a qualified solicitor with principles who was content to work part time but on a moderate income, when one of the joint boat owners, who had been trying to track me down that night and heard where I was, walked in unexpectedly with a pattern book for the new canopy we had to consider buying because the old one was falling to bits. I was then the so-called minimalist solicitor with a blinking boat. After we decided on the exciting colour he departed.

   While I was able to attempt to explain it was small boat and I only owned a third of it a friend appeared and while settling down in the next table mentioned over the heads of the group I was with that she had better pay me for her recent visit to the cottage. More strange looks. He must have a big family inheritance. No wonder he can afford to work part time.

I tried to explain it was a very small collage that I only owned a tiny quarter of charging a cheap rent of £10.00 per night regardless of how many people visited. It was not even making a profit. In fact we were so good at not making a profit that we were making a loss.

"I've spoken to the unit and they said it would be advisable if you did not visit your Mum at the moment"

She was now in and out of hospital on a regular basis. The joint health insurance policy that my Dad had taken out suddenly lapsed. Within the small print there was hidden away a limit to the number of nights you could spend overnight at the hospital. Being ill had invalidated the policy. I know the purpose of the private health industry is to fill beds and not, unlike the NHS, keep them empty and the point of these policies is to make money for the shareholders, but whereas investors or gamblers in the market, depending on your opinion, are warned with "Their value can go down as well as up", these private health policies should have an equivalent: "Their worth can let you down as well as wind you up."

When I wanted to visit on one occasion I was advised not to because Mum had MSRA: Methicillin Resistent Staphylocccus Aureus. It was the super bug; methicilin being a cousin of penicillin couldn't kill. I was therefore unable to see her because as this infectious virus is commonly found in hospitals and I was ..er......immuno suppressed that I was more likely to catch it and also could carry it away to my renal unit and pass it on to other immune suppressed kidney transplant recipients or dialysis patients who more susceptible to picking up such a contagious virus.

Mum was now not only paralysed than one side but blind in on eye due to blood clot directly behind it. There was talk of drilling a hole in her skull to release some of the pressure. Unfortunately in the changing NHS system it looked as if she would have to go to another hospital about 80 miles north for this operation.

The new breed of NHS accountants must have calculated that money was saved by shipping scared and vulnerable and, of yes, ill patients to a specialist hospital in another area. This helped the balance sheet, in theory, but when you bring in this most irritating factor of humans things do not look that rosy financially. It could well back fire as without relatives being able to visit easily it may slow down the recovery process and the patient may end up in hospital for longer and cost money the end.

Mum was given a stark choice to make as to whether or not to go ahead with the operation but after consulting with the rest of the family decided against it. Months later after more test results were revealed we discovered that had we chosen this proposed treatment it would have been unnecessary.

"Long-term immune suppression can lead in some patients to nodules on the skin"

At one of my four monthly check ups I pointed out all the tiny nodules that had begun to appear over the last few months thankfully in places that were not public, was referred to a dermatologist. At my appointment some weeks later I was informed that the original plan to freeze them off was not possible because the little machine had just broken (" I refer the Right Honourable Gentlemen to the comments I made some chapters ago") so would I mind if they burnt them off. I didn't. Especially considering the likely wait for another appointment. Anyway I brought along my finger and thumb so I could use my pain redirection technique. Afterwards I was told I was very brave which I found kind of cute because these dermatologists deal with all types of patients but old timers like me and other kidney patients were used to procedures far worse than that.

I also had the use of liquid nitrogen to remove another skin condition as a result of many years of immune suppression This removed the first layer of your skin. I hoped it was not stored side by side in the same cabinet with nitrogen (liquid) along side nitro (glycerine)

"As you are immunosuppressed please take care when you are out in the sun as you are prone to skin cancer"

After what I had been through I was not going to get tripped up by being careless and allow a small little spot to be diagnosed as malignant. I wore hats with a brim, never went out top less – another excuse to conceal my scaring that could easily be mistaken for a treasure island map and made sure I used block 30 if I was ever out all day in the blazing sun.

So no sooner had I purchased a nice new wardrobe of shirtsleeve summer shirts after my fistula scars were slowly vanishing and my artery reconstructive showing no unsightly lumps, I had to cover up again.

There were other cancers risks to be alert to for the up and coming successful kidney transplant recipient. In the book, "Kidney Failure Explained" by Stein and Wild. It says that twenty years of yummy steroid and immuno suppressive tablets is likely to lead to cancer for 25% of us. Bare statistics again. I 'd like to know more. What's the percentage for people of a certain age? If the majority of transplant recipients had a transplant, say, in there fifties what is the statistical difference with other people of that age group. What about me. I am nearly coming up to twenty years. Is the 25% that relevant to me and after 30 years, if my kidney or I last that long, what is the percentage then. Do other family members have a history of cancers? What type of cancers. What type of renal failure. Are they excluding skins cancer that you can protect against? Are the cancers from a particular part of the body? Do they vary with the non-immuno suppressed community? Is it already fate because every day you are continually suppressing your immune system?

And more importantly what can do to avoid it. Changes in diet, mild consumption of alcohol such as red wine appear to be proffering some good news. Giving up tobacco we can take as read.

May be I'm being optimistic that my kidney will last that long but hey in the meantime likes go for the extra fruit and vege, especially those small cherry tomatoes for ridding your bodies of those free radicals, a large quantity of which are early indicators of a susceptibility to cancer.

While on my PC trying to write this book I got one of those spams. I've just changed the name of the author but here it is otherwise unedited:

"My name is Sugar and I have a story. It is not the saddest story, yet it's mine. I have been working since my father died when I was 13 years old. My mother worked 3 jobs so that my brother and I would not have to go on public assistance.

My father died from a genetic disease called Polycystic Kidneys. (http://www.pkdcure.org) This is when Cysts grow all over the kidneys and get so big that they overpower the kidneys until they cannot work anymore. All of my aunts, uncles, and cousins on my father's side have died from this disease at the age of 42 and younger. I was told that my brother Jeff would die if I did not donate one of my kidneys to him. We were the only survivors of our family because of this terminal disease and I was his only hope. Unfortunately, that is how I found out that I also have Polycystic Kidney Disease and could not help him. He sadly passed away.

I have been working as a single parent holding down 2 jobs as a waitress. Within the last 3 weeks, I have had 2 operations and have another major operation in a month. My kidneys are so large they weigh over 40 pounds and must be removed because there is no room in my body for them. Once the operation is complete, I will have no kidneys and will have to live on dialysis, while waiting for a transplant. I can no longer waitress, as I have done all my life.

To have a deadly disease is difficult enough, but to

know that I have passed it on to my only child, is an unbearable guilt. This is what my son has to look forward to shortly.

I have lived my whole life depending on myself and supporting my son. I never asked anyone for anything. In fact, if someone ever needed help from me I was always there financially and emotionally.

Unfortunately, I now have to ask for help. If you could spare any amount of money, even if only $5, it would make my life a little easier. At the very least it will help solve some financial problems so I can focus on my health. All I have now is hope. If you can help financially it would be most appreciated. If you cannot, then your prayers are more then enough. Thank you and God bless all.

Sincerely,   Sugar

For instructions on how to help Sugar, please email her at..."

This uninvited guest in my computer very probably lives in that country where nearly half of bankruptcies are due to the non-payment of medical bills. The United States of America. One of their web sites explains in stark terms the financial reality of a society lacking a health service like ours:

"Dialysis treatment, like most high-tech medicine, is costly. The NKFS spends about $2,400 a month on each dialysis patient, but needy patients can pay subsidised rates of as little as $100 a month. Approximately $40,000 to 65,000 per year. Almost everyone with renal failure qualifies for Medicare. Medicare pays 80% of the remainder. Thus, most patients pay 4% of cost themselves or about $1600 to $2600 per year. This makes it possible."

Is Sugar and her story true or is it a scam spam? I had a few questions. 40 Pounds. What each or twenty pounds each. Mine were eight pounds each when they were removed. Three operations? Have the Americans decided to burst cysts and discovered they can reduce the rate of renal deterioration or is the doctor able to claim against the insurance company before the policy expires. Such policy expiration happened with my Mum when she actually needed it.

If you kidneys were that enlarged I would guess you were already on a kidney machine. Didn't her uncle go on a machine? If not why not? Was it because of the lack of a NHS across the pond?

For a while the web site Sugar referred put up a disclaimer on their home page totally disassociating itself from the plea for money.

Thankfully I do not live in the USA because if I did my dad and I would very probably be bankrupt by now.

The website referred to gives up to date developments on suggested diet, the new drugs and techniques that are said to slow down the cyst creation and so the kidney failure process.

Things have definitely improved within the NHS over the years compared with the time I required its service several decades ago. You now get many enclosures with you appointment notice but the computer created letters leave a lot to be desired. I for instance get several letters that are identical but for three pieces of information: the date of the appointment; the department and the name of the consultant in charge who you might not actually meet. Not always informing you what is going to happen when you get to your appointment. This is fine if you have an occasional one off appointment but not if you are involved in several departments and cannot keep up with all the consultants names that sometimes change. But not always.

A friend of mine phoned me because he wanted me to read to him a letter he guessed was from the hospital. He was blind and knew his GP had made a hospital referral for him. When I looked through the envelope contents I found two letters: one informing him that he had an appointment and a second informing him that the first appointment, which he had only just been told about, had been cancelled and the second letter gave him a second appointment date.

With the enclosures was a note to say that you can get the question and answer information sheet in brail. The GP must have known my friend was blind and lived on his own. If he had mentioned this when making the referral he might have got it in brail and not need to phone me.

There is the NHS Direct help line about but what about an NHS help website. This would be for those, such as renal patients, who either did not want to speak to anyone or felt there concerns were minor and did not want to block a help line when others wanted it as they were going through a crisis. It could have a standard letter explaining on what renal failure is and be printable for patients who have had enough of trying to explain and given up talking to people who disbelieve their plight. There could even be letter specifically related to diet so that if you were invited to a meal you could send a copy in advance to the poor host cook who would be reassured they did not give you the wrong foodstuff.

On this NHS web site for kidney transplant patients they could also introduce a notice board page just for the patient so they would be able to update themselves on developments. My first one would include the following for the transplant recipient, who unlike the dialysis patient, is no longer in regular contact with the unit:

- Not to take St John Warts (spotted on notice board in renal out patients)
- To avoid grapefruit when actually taking drugs (information I remember getting once but cannot recall how or when or even whether the advice has now been withdrawn.
- To avoid anyone with mumps or shingles (on a sticker on each steroid pack)
- To take extra special care when out in the sun to avoid getting skin cancer (leaflets in a rack in out patients)
- Diet suggestions if concerned of cancer risk.
- Problems on retaking your drugs after vomiting or a bout of severe diarrhea. (Once again read this somewhere)
- Explaining why should not take doses at the same time if forgot to take last one when time to take next

- Tips to ensure you regularly take your drugs
- Reminders to get your flu jab (and pneumonia jab for those select few who have had a splenectomy)
- The name of that shampoo for your hairy ears
- Any news on non gelatin tablets for the vegetarians
- Genetic counseling for those with hereditary conditions
- A printable letter explaining it is not enough just signing a kidney donor card and sticking it in you back pocket, hoping that if you are run over then not only have you to ensure you have a clean underwear on but that you are wearing the right trousers. What philanthropist have to do is tell their nearest and dearest and their official next of kin what they would like to happen if they no longer need their organs.

Usually, when I attend out patients I do not recognise anyone from scanning the waiting room apart from someone who looks vaguely familiar from my dialysis days but then it is me trying too hard to recall someone. Then it is usually in and out. I have been meeting fellow kidney patients in other places.

I was in pub with some friends and I heard someone say, "excuse me are you...." I looked up from my seat and immediately recognised the fellow kidney patient from years earlier we had spent the night together: in adjacent single hospital beds on dialysis through out the night. Both hoping for a transplant in the morning. I could tell he was still on dialysis because his skin colour had not changed; he had not put on any weight around the face, which would have been a sure sign of steroid use, and he had a very small short in his hand. I, on the other hand had a pint of lager right in front of me. We had a chat and exchanged addresses. I made sue I did not glance at my drink or worse pick it up and take a sip to remind him what I can do that he still cannot.

I meet people who have kidney trouble, which puts me in an awkward spot in not knowing how much to tell them of my experiences. Until I know their situation and at what stage they are at, I have to be careful in case I frighten them. However if they are on or about to go on dialysis I can show

how you can get a successful transplant and can come out the other end.

In a party I was introduced to someone who had kidney trouble and it turned out she had polycystic kidneys. We spent a lot of time chatting, as she was desperate for information because in the very early stages you may visit out patients, say, once a year, not knowing anyone at the waiting room, or what is going on around you. Not knowing what to ask and to who, where the doctors have no real time unless you are ready with a set of questions. In many incidents you can be so ignorant you do not know how to formulate an actual question. Well anyway we did our usual respective party mingling and when I met with her again she told me that her boyfriend had forbidden her from talking to me any longer because we appeared to be talking to each other too much.

I'm at the Ironmongers in a small queue waiting to buy something really interesting like a kettle (I drink so much I go through kettles remarkably quickly) I noticed the man serving behind the counter. He had that familiar moon face look and I spotted another real giveaway. He must have had a very recent visit from a hospital because on the upper part of his hand there was evidence of recently removed drip.

While waiting I was deciding whether to introduce myself, I was concerned that I would make him self conscious of his appearance by the fact I had clocked, amongst other signs, his " brutalisation of the face".

During the wait he served someone who wanted to know if they had one of those tea cadies you can put on the wall and the next person wanted to know if the shop had a white empty bottle carrier. (Some body give them a real problem to worry about.) He was rushing around doing his job for these customers searching for these poxxy little futile things when I wanted to pick them up and throw them out of the shop.

I eventually spoke to him and he was fine and my hunch was correct. He appeared to want to talk about it. I wanted to see if I could extract any news from the unit.

With cadaver transplantations there is the ongoing debate about the pros and cons of opting in and opting out. In

Britain we have the opting in system. This means after you die no one can remove any organs for transplantation without your next of kin's permission. Hence the donor card system and the suggestion that you tell your relatives about your philanthropic decision. A slight improvement is the comparatively recently created register which means information is gathered nationally and so removing the existing adhoc, piece meal process. This would avoid the awkward period of crisis in an intensive unit with the doctors who would be able to remind the next of kin what their relative desired.

In recent years there has been a severe drop in transplants. This is partly due to the compulsory wearing of safety belts and the increasing skill of doctors in keeping people alive once they are in an intensive care unit (the bastards.) The British Medical Association, the doctor's professional governing body is coming round to supporting a change in the law.

Opting out, or presumed consent, means that unless you indicate otherwise when you die doctors can remove your organs to help others live. For instance two kidneys help four people: two get a new lease of life by coming off their kidney machines which provides two new spaces for two others who would have died. And that's just the kidneys. I have not even mentioned the other organs.

This means the register will be reversed with those not wanting to be touched after death being on it. This new register would be necessary for those who simply do not like the idea or have a certain religious conviction. There has always been the fear that doctors will not try hard enough to keep you alive, as they want your kidneys and other organs for their other patients. This is unfounded, firstly because the definition of whether someone is brain dead is more precise and there are always two completely different medical teams. One set for the severely ill patient, another from the transplant unit who has a patient who is longing to be unchained from a life on dialysis. Otherwise having such a conflict of interest would create a serious breach of medical ethics. For instance when my Dad gave me his kidney there was set of doctors clearly responsible for his interest and another team for mine.

When you think about it few people have any qualms about having their appendix or tonsils removed when they are alive but do with other parts of their body when they are dead. These organs are not going to last long in a coffin but will make a massive influence on living people.

In one Asian country they have adopted the opting out system but there is an unusual condition for doing so. If you have the misfortune of needing a transplant later on in life and you are on the opting out register you are not entitled to a transplant. This would be further consequence as, without an NHS, they would be unlikely to be the possibility of dialysis and even then it would not be a stopgap until a kidney became available but for life. So only the very rich would have to use it until they left that country to buy a kidney elsewhere.

On the bright side statistics from 1991 show that for two European countries, who had introduced the opting out system, there was more hope for those who get renal failure. There was a 183% increase in donors in Austria and a whopping 400% in Belgium.

John Harris, a bioethicist at Manchester University goes a bit further and thinks the option of opting out is not enough:

"..... to be brutal about this, I don't think the dead donor has any rights and don't think their relatives do either given what is at stake. You have to remember that most of these transplants, not all but most, are required to save a life. I don't think anybody could say, reasonably, that they are entitled to be the cost of someone's life in order to keep their body in tact after death. And as a matter of fact our society already accepts that principle.

We have court order post-mortem examinations, which are not a matter of consent. You cannot opt out of them. You cannot conscientiously refuse to participate. Post-mortems are performed for two main reasons, which boil down to a suspicion as to the cause of death. That suspicion maybe that there is foul play, that there is a murderer at lose or it maybe that there is a suspicion of an undetected disease or risk factor that it has important to find out about.

In other words we accept the principle that the dead body maybe dismembered in the public interest and that public interest amounts to a life-saving interest. If there is a murderer at large somebody else maybe killed. If there is a disease agent at large someone else may be killed. So we accept the principle that we are able to take bodies apart to save a life. It seemed to me that is exactly paralleled with cadaver organ donation. I think there is a very powerful case for making all cadavers the property of the state and allowing cadaver sources of organs to be instantly available without any permissions required."

"Do you want me to wake her?
"No it's Ok .I'll ring another time"

I phoned my Mum to ask how she was and her day nurse said she is asleep do you want me to wake her and said no it is OK I call again. When I did a few days later she was in hospital.

"Michael"
"Yes?"

I was alarmed at my response. No real reaction a part from a feeling of sadness

Ping .... WKQ:1+1=2

We all knew it was not far away. Now there was no longer the continual dialysis machines; the restricted diet; the feeling of tiredness and, if there was to be a transplant, the constant fear of forgetting to take your drugs and be partially responsible for its rejection.

The Law Centre allowed me compassionate leave for at least a week or longer if I needed it. I even went to work to sort out a few things before getting the train. While travelling I just hoped some jerk wouldn't say something like, "Cheer up mate. It might never happen."

Friends of mine got married in a Church of England. One had a large family and many relatives attended. The other was an orphan and had no known blood relatives. As I entered the church I noticed that one side of the church was jam packed while on the other side it just had a few members of the congregation near the front. Apparently it is traditional to arrange everyone using this strict custom.

At Mum's funeral we attended the church ceremony. As we went down the aisle there was no sitting arrangement choice for the close relatives and as the immediate family members approached the vicar at the front of the church he asked everyone in turn if we were blood relatives and depending on your answer you were directed to the first or second row. My mum will hopefully forgive me but it reminded me of Michael Palin in a Monty Pyton film asking "Crucification?. Good. Down there second on the right. One cross each" such was the inane custom. So at a most stressful time blood relatives were separated from the partners, the non-blood relatives. If you wanted to be comforted by your partner you couldn't because they were behind you and if you turned round the rest of the congregation would be looking in your direction to see how your were coping so you know you couldn't very easily turn around. All for what? Custom. "Give me that old kind religion. Give me that old kind religion." I wanted to say and do something but knew it was the wrong time and place but I am warning you now. Don't let it happen to you. Have a word with the vicar/priest in advance.

"Side effects that have sometimes been reported in patients taking cyclosporin include........swollen gums"

I mentioned to my dentist my gums were getting worse. For years I had trouble with them and would often be spitting out blood after brushing my teeth. Mum's suffered the same side effect but it was far worse. The gums would grow up the sides of the teeth. The dentist decided to refer me to the hospital. I did not have to wait too long for the hospital appointment, which I found remarkable. No real waiting list for something as relatively minor as this whereas you had to wait months to get your next heart appointment. I was told how to brush my teeth a different way and use a finer and smaller type of toothbrush. I was told how to check for plague. I returned a few times and was eventually left to my own incisors.

I now no longer go for those regular six month dentist check ups after reading about a government report suggesting that they are not always necessary. Everyone just accepts it as some unwritten law but it has as much credibility as all those "special" days to help the card industry. I 'm waiting for the introduction of the Second Cousin Twice Removed Day. The last time I went I needed to take a drug, amoxycillin an hour before, not for a filling but for a "clean and polish" because of my acquired heart condition.

On the day of the filling work, on attending the surgery there was an unusual atmosphere of activity you do not associate with dentists. I learnt that the night before there had been a break in. While in the waiting room I was disconcerted about the sound of the drill next door. It seemed far more aggressive and powerful as I remembered it. I was concerned that without any recent operations I must be going soft. This after all is just a silly little filling. Nothing compared to what is ahead of me in the years to come.

I do not go for the injection. I'm willing to put up with a little discomfort, finger nail and thumb on stand by, rather than hours later realising, once the dumbness had dissipated, that I had been chewing the inside of my mouth when I thought I was eating my sandwich.

When I was called I walked in and while acknowledging the dentist and his assistant, kneeling down in the corner of the room was a workman repairing what looked like the frame to a window and in his hand he was holding an industrial drill.

"Polycystic kidney sufferers are prone to getting blood vessel problems"

I very rarely get headaches these days but I had a bout of them recently. So concerned was I that I went to see my GP. Now you are probably thinking: go to the doctors over a silly little headache. Well yes. I never get them. I've learnt one thing: if you get a new symptom that lasts more than a few days do not ignore it. That's how patients see their doctors a bit too late and the response sometimes is a very grave why didn't you see me earlier because the condition is no untreatable. I situation that crosses over to my work where had clients seen me much earlier I could have done so much more. In our own little way we have our legal equivalent of the NHS Direct line. Both are helpful in nipping in the bud the medical condition or legal problem in its infancy.

My GP decided to make an early appointment for me to have a brain scan. With my condition I could well have an aneurisms, blood vessel problems in the brain. Luckily, I was OK. The diagnosis was something called cluster headaches.

Now I take sixteen tablets a day. I still have those little multicoloured round plastic containers, found over twenty years ago on a skip. I will never change this system while I have a working kidney as it works for me. When I explained the quantity once to someone, the response was "you poor thing." No. If I stop taking this concoction it will mean I will have stopped taking immunosuppressives and slowly weaned off steroid and back to taking alucaps and tablets for vitamins, blood pressure and iron (if I decide to take them) as I will be back on a kidney machine

Yes I may put an adult rattlesnake to shame but it is better than the alternative. My check ups are now twice a year and the sense of relief in the few days after the results showing that everything is OK is indescribable.

At my most recent check up I took the following day off work. The phone went .On answering it I heard an unfamiliar female voice wanting to speak to Michael. A terrifying experience the day after my check up as it could only mean bad news if it was from the hospital. It wasn't. It was someone from Oxfam checking if I will be attending the pre Glastonbury health and safety course, compulsory for my shift on the gate.

I went back to my PC, to continue writing this book in fact. A few hours later the telephone went again. Still signifying possible danger I cagily picked up the receiver. It was another female voice but one I recognised which was a relief. She must have thought I was in a good mood. Back to the PC. Again the phone. This must be the hospital. I do not usually get phone calls during the day in the part of the week most people I know realise I should be at work. Another unrecognisable female voice. I heard the dreaded name of the hospital but along side the word pharmacy. I was being informed the rest of my six-month prescription was now ready for collection.

**

CHAPTER TEN : Nature Fights Back.

At this stage I was about to end the book but then a curious incident happened to me on top of a Welsh mountain near where Tyr Peg is located.

You will recall that as far as my family is concerned the devilish polycystic kidney gene originated from this valley.

I had decided to spend a week in Tyr Peg to decorate and carry out minor repairs while also checking out some possible circuit walks for future visitors. On the ordnance survey map there was a clear footpath marked that took me away from the village and up and over the mountain into the next valley. I decided to investigate this circuit walk, as it would take me back down to the village and back up to Tyr Peg. Also it was convenient, as I had been invited to a meal in the next valley.

Initially all went well as I followed the designated foot path along the valley where it was clearly marked and then as I got to the top having crossed a brand new foot bridge over a small brook I was to discover that the footpath had vanished. Then I did. Let me explain.

I walked for while searching for the paths possible re-emergence as the path may have been covered with overgrowth. Eventually it got thicker and higher but I carried on walking. I was not always looking immediately where I was treading but looking ahead to see if I could see the return of the official ordnance survey footpath. As I regularly looked down at the rugged terrain along side my boots I could hear but not see several very small streams with very deep walls that I had to step over once I could gauge where they were.

But at the same time I was looking in the distance for the mystery footpath which had vanished. Then I vanished. And in doing so heard a snap. I hadn't spotted one of the mini streams.

The second after hearing the snap seemed to last for ages. Spinning through my mind I was thinking: this is it. I had broken my leg; I'm on my own and mobiles don't work up here last time I tried. The paradox was that had I been wearing trainers and not walking boots I may have avoided the damage because as I was falling I could've readjusted myself but the size and weight of the boots prevented me from adjusting as my left foot dropped into narrow stream.

I gingerly got back to my feet to see to see whether I had indeed broken my leg. I knew I'd done something and was hoping it was just a sprained ankle and the snap was caused by the break of a chunky plant stem as I fell. As I got up I could barely walk but because of the heavy terrain I knew I had to continue. There was no fence or tree or anything to support me: I just had to get to the edge of the mountain top plateau to the gate I saw in the distance. I felt severe pain but knew I couldn't stop. When I got to the gate I leaned across it taking my leg fully off the ground for the first time contemplating what I could do next. I could go back pretty difficult with the heavy terrain -- or continue, leave the top of the mountain and head down the next valley that I would be able to look down on if I kept on "walking" in the same direction. Or I could simply just hang around and try and get a mobile reception: it would mean wasting time and once I had stopped it would be very difficult to start again. The one thing I knew I couldn't do was shout or wait to see if anyone would be passing through.

I quickly decided I had to keep on moving because if it was a sprained ankle it would soon seize up. Then I had my first bit of luck. Down into next valley I noticed that there was a wonderfully long fence taking me in exactly the right direction I needed to go. I couldn't stop any longer I needed to move.

I began the gruelling journey following the fence. Although I now had some support I could now see the possibility of getting down the mountain. Getting moving again was difficult and I knew from now on I couldn't stop. The fence was sheer luck but looking in the distance I soon realised, because of the nature of the valley, I had to get on the other side of the fence because of the sheer drop coming up which was caused by the deep mountain river gorge. This was when I noticed I had not just badly sprained my ankle. As I lifted my leg over with the aid of both my hands, as I looked down I noticed that my foot was effectively hanging off the end of my leg as it was at a very strange angle. The snap was not an unfortunate plant stem but one of my bones.

I had to effectively ignore what I had just discovered and continue. I won't bore you with the very strange twists and turns in the fence but the strangest obstruction was a dead sheep entangled in the fence. Normally you would obviously walk round it but I was clinging on to the fence and so had to step or should I say hop over it. It was a very strange sight as it looked as if she was trying to escape from a sheep concentration camp and either she had hit an electrified fence or submachine gun down from one of the towers as she was that close to freedom.

After a while as I glanced down the valley I notice that not only had the fence decided to head down in the "wrong" direction and I about to lose my main support but that there was a river I now had to cross. I need to find a walking stick or in my case a hobbling stick. I then had my goldilocks moment. The first one was no good, which I painfully discovered was not strong enough as it snapped in two and sent me crumbling to the ground. The next one looked better and I had no choice but to rely on it for my river crossing. Many may classify this river as merely a mountain stream. It was clearly not very deep and in normal circumstances I would have leapt across at a deep narrow stretch but on this occasion I had to hobble through at a more wide and shallow section with my trusty, sturdy and newly acquired stick. I continued along the other side of the bank to turn and twist in the valley to noticed the river had done exactly the same thing and so I had to cross it back again further down the valley.

This stick was not that sturdy after all. It snapped and I experienced yet another collapse to the Welsh ground, landing in some pain. The third stick was just right. After a while the riverbanks widened and the valley levelled out and so I was able to hobble along rather than down and then came to what look like a dead-end until I noticed up above me and to the right a gate. I then had to do something new in the journey: go up hill. I could go straight up. I had no choice but to extend the distance by making a series of zig zags. Once at the gate, getting there by a series of criss-crosses up the field I noticed I was now near what could be described as civilisation. Once I got going into the middle of the sheep field I noticed what looked like a small road and to my left I saw something that many would have raised many superstitious types' arms aloft when they would no doubt shout hallelujah! It was a church spire. A church I recognized. I knew where I was. I did not raise my arms to the Lord and exclaim hallelujah for two reasons: not only because I'm an atheist but also if I did so I would simply fall over. Again.

Strangely the last hundred metres down the steep sheep field (getting very strange looks from the occupants) seemed more painful than the previous few miles: manly because for a long period I had no fence as support but also because psychologically I could see the possibility of an end in sight.

At the bottom of the field there was another fence I had to climb over and then there was a small bank down to a country lane. Once there it seemed like paradise: being able to walk with my faithful stick, dragging my broken leg, on a flat hard surface, without tripping over a heavy lumps of turf and not having to stare down at my feet because I could see along the tarmac lane there were no obstacles. I passed the church on my left and slowly it was getting nearer to the renovated barn where I had been invited for a meal and I was only two hours late having set off hours earlier tan necessary as it was unknown territory on my newly discovered walk.

As I walked along the driveway up to the barn I was fantasising that soon I would be able to sit down and possibly order my nephews and nieces around to get me a drink. To keep my body hydrated and my kidney healthy I was already thinking that I hadn't drunk much recently. The cars were parked but as I got nearer to the barn I could not hear anything. I knocked on the barn door and the dog barked but no humans came to the door. There was nobody in. I had been invited for a meal, all four cars were in the driveway but nobody was around.

I sat down and took my boots and socks off and examined my swollen leg and had no option but to wait. After some time someone spotted me from the next cottage and, possibly suspicious, asked me a few questions and very kindly, with the spare key, presumably because it was part of his duty to keep an eye on things in the holiday next door amazingly let me in to wait. I hobbled around helping myself to what was available and hours later everybody returned.

Initially they were apologetic as they thought their late change of plan had resulted in me not getting the message. Earlier on in the day while I was having my exciting adventure up the mountain, they had all decided to eat in the pub in the village and walk there. My brother then ran up the mountain to Tyr Peg to tell me but I wasn't there but assuming I would return soon left a message. From Tyr Peg there are two ways to get to this holiday let: down to the village and then up the next valley along the nice narrow country lane or the ordnance survey map footbath that I decided to follow that apparently not many others do. They therefore waited in the pub table window glancing out to see me pass to stop me walking to what I thought was my meal at the holiday let.

I told them the full story and on examining my leg thought I had only sprained my ankle. Asked if I could move my toes, I proved I could, and was reassured that it was just a badly sprained ankle. The feeling appeared to be: you couldn't have broken your leg. If you had how could you have got down the mountain. So by that reckoning the only way you can prove you broke your leg is to still be up the mountain. No doubt the proof would mean you'd have to take with you a big felt tip pen and a big piece of cardboard and while you were slowly dying you would draw a big arrow pointing at your leg saying "See I broke my leg. This one if you check "

In the evening I was dropped off at Tyr Peg. On the first night I awoke shivering but I wasn't cold. I thought this is very unusual and then it occurred to me: I was in shock, admittedly it was delayed shock but my body was reacting to my previous day's adventure dragging myself down the mountain. For the next two or three days I hobbled around the cottage fending for myself and my relatives popped round to see how I was and brought meals.

After a few days, as I was not getting any better, it was decided I should go to the nearest GP who was in a valley several villages away. I hobbled in to the surgery with my trusty stick I waited till my name was called and hobbled in, hearing what I imagine was a few chuckles in the waiting room behind me, not sure if they thought I was being overdramatic with my sprained ankle or found humour in the ridiculous stick. Once in the GPs room I sat down and she heard my story and went through a series of examinations and at each stage asking me "does this hurt?". I would imagine a situation like this she often heard the word "no" but never "yes" but rather "aaaaarrhh". She then very confidently told me I had broken my leg. She then wrote a letter for me to take to the local hospital, and then to my surprise opened her consulting room door and I had to walk out!

I then hobbled out past the waiting room - hearing what I imagine was the same chuckle - to my sisters waiting in the car outside. There was naturally some shock when I told them I had actually broken my leg and it was not just a sprained ankle and then on a journey back, with a few mobile phone conversations decided I should go to a hospital further away as that was where my father was heading that evening. There was then a change of car and I headed off to a distant city centre A and E department getting there just in time for the Friday night drunken idiot rush.

In the waiting room there was a loud group of people, some clearly intoxicated and either inpatient or still experience the jolly alcoholic hit that was delaying the eventual real pain they were sure to meet. I was initially called in by a nurse who looked like she wished she wasn't there, took the paperwork I had to hand over to her and immediately suggested I'd probably just sprained my ankle and was shown the door back to the waiting corridor. I then hobbled over to my seat and waited for probably an hour or more but with my experience of waiting rooms it was something I could easily cope with. Then at the other end of the corridor somebody shouted my name; I struggle to my feet and noticed that the doctor that had just called me glanced at the trouble I was having as I hobbled over to him along the length of the corridor and then he turned his back and went into his room which I presumed I had to follow him. At first glance it was obvious to me that he thought I just sprained my ankle. I sat down and we went through the same routine I had with the Welsh GP at this time he looked at me in the eye with a serious concern and said "I think we better get you a wheelchair"

So four days after breaking my leg I was actually going to get some proper treatment.

The fun did not end there. After waiting several hours in the early hours of the morning I was released leaving with a temporary plaster on my leg because I was being transferred to a hospital near my home and the plaster did not go all the way around my leg because my leg had not yet fully swollen. During a conversation while the nurses were dolloping on plaster of paris, it was suggested social services would be able to help me once I got back to my flat. How so very quaint and innocent. From my community care legal cases at work I knew I didn't stand (well that's certainly true) a chance.

When I got to my father's home he told me that he and his wife had previously booked a holiday and I was left in the house for several days although I did have neighbours visit me to check on me. I phoned the railway company as they boasted of the special efforts they make for disabled people on their trains or so I thought. I was promised over the phone that the arrangements would be made for me to have a wheelchair to the train and the disabled seat on the train. At the station car park a wheelchair came to pick me up and take me to the platform; ramp was put on the train when it was arrived at the wheelchair went up the ramp into the carriage and I was introduced to the seat that I was supposed to sit on the next one and half hours which turned out to be a double seat like any other seat and not the disabled seat I was promised to allow me to put my leg up. I then had to sit in one of the seats and pull the tray down in the adjacent seat so I could rest my leg on that. I was stuck in this position for one and a half hours. So much for the disabled service. Admittedly the ticket collector was quite shocked by my treatment and even gave me free cups of tea for the journey.

It was much better at the other end of the journey: the ramp was there; the wheelchair was outside the train can so I got my crutches to the wheelchair and was met by a friend who gave me a lift to my flat. Unfortunately getting out of the car involves several steps up to the front door and then even more steps to the top floor flat. This brought back memories of getting an ambulance back to my student flat after my first transplant when I was fearful of huge haemotemisis. Then I didn't have crutches but I could walk with one hand holding the bag and the other holding the operation scar.

I then began my first undignified trek up the building, up three flights of stairs on my bum. The next few weeks I had to do that many times in both directions. Initially my movement around the flat required both crutches. Getting my mugs of tea from the kitchen to the living room was hilarious. I had to move the mug forward to places that were at elbow height and then move past it; lean backwards, balance myself on one crutch, retrieve the mug and move it forward to the next place I could place it. By time I got to my destination the tea was stone cold! ("Which service do you require?". "Social. Please hurry : it's an emergency. I've been trying to get my tea from the kitchen to the lounge and ....gasp... got to keep going .... it's too late.... can't see any steam rising from the mug ....so cold....got to... got to.... start all over again". "Stay right where you are. Don't move. We'll be quick as we can. Have you got enough tea bags or do you want us to bring a pack?".)

A week or so later when I could put weight on my knee I was able to use a chair and move it around the flat not needing crutches.

Eventually I was able to crawl around the flat on both knees. This was luxury as the mug of teas could be pushed in front of me on the floor like a game of "push h'ppenny".

A few days after returning I checked in with the local hospital, handed over my x-rays and had more x-rays and to get my proper, more permanent plaster cast moulded on to me. I was offered a choice of colours which I found rather amusing: with all the NHS cutbacks and financial restrictions they waste time and effort introducing a selection of colours for the plastic cast. I initially thought of black as it would be less conspicuous but realised I wanted everybody to know so they wouldn't trip over my leg so I went for the traditional white ones. The downside to that was that people would scribble all over it. I managed to avoid that apart from the one occasion when only after I had noticed a friend had been writing something when it was too late to stop her. She had written: "benefit cheat".

Although I had a few offers to go shopping for me I demanded my own independence. I am afraid this is due to years of dependence so when I could look after myself, however uncomfortable and time consuming I would. I started to shop over the Internet. There is a section on the supermarket's websites shopping form for you to explain special instructions. I put "in top flat cannot answer front door broken leg. Please ring bell and step back from door and will throw key down" needless to say it was never read so I had to shout when I heard the doorbell and eventually the van driver would come into view and look around and then on looking and spotting me questioned whether I still wanted the supplies. Confusion often prevailed for some time but the driver had to come up to the top flat or he wouldn't get my signature to confirm delivery.

On one of my excursions to the hospital to have my leg x-rayed the radiologist was none other than a friend of mine who had had a career change and had visited Tyr Peg.

I put in a weekly appearance at the Law Centre, which required me having to go up all the stairs on my bum to my office.

My colleagues there were very supportive and I know I could have as much time off as I needed but it was easier to check my post and take any urgent action on a case than get someone else to do it. Also money was saved by not paying for a locum. I was solely responsible for staffing a telephone free legal advice line and ran did it from home by borrowing the centre's mobile phone.

During this time I would get the comment on more than one occasion: "It's a good job you didn't really break your leg or you would have been in real difficult up there on your own." I was.

I got there by taxis at first but then used the bus. On one occasion I got a bus from the hospital to the bus stop directly outside the Law Centre. I sat near the driver where there was disabled seating, when I came near to my bus stop I looked around for button to press and had inadvertently pressed the emergency button as opposed to the bus stop button, and by the time I had struggled to the front of the bus I noticed that the bus driver had driven straight past. When I asked for an explanation his retort was: "you pressed the wrong button". This was sheer vindictiveness because he knew jolly well I meant to press the bus stop button and is right next to him and so after a few choice words I had to get off the bus at the next one. And walk all the way back. With no real hope of success, I decided I had to make an official complaint against this nobhead of a bus driver. I eventually received a dubiously looking standard letter, to report that "such complaints are taken very seriously blah blah blah" but was told that although the complaint was fully investigated and the necessary action taken they didn't tell me anything at all about what they said or did to the bus driver (brain implant possibly) and quoted soon dubious looking phrases about privacy and freedom of information and data protection. The problem was I was never given any information nor did I feel that the next disabled person on one of his buses was going to treated any differently. When I appealed to the independent bus complaints authority or whatever they're called they said it was three months ago and therefore you're too late although when the bus company itself referred me to the appeal process they did not give me the time limit.

Eventually my leg became less painful and I was able to hop around on one crotch. I was told to put as much weight on my leg as was possible without incurring pain as that would speed up the healing process. When I spoke to my friend at radiology, who saw me several weeks later and noticed I was walking again, she commented on the fact that I had recovered quickly because I wanted to. This suggested that there were several of her patients who love the attention which I found very sad.

When eventually the plaster came off I was told that I still need crutches as without the protection of the plaster cast initially it would be more painful than normal to move. I soon discovered this and realised it was because my leg was no longer held in place and therefore there was more scope for pain. At this stage the renal unit six monthly appointments came up and I updated them on my exciting ill health career and the doctor immediately suggested that I should be checked for DVT -- deep vein thrombosis. This has become more prevalent after people on long-haul flights on aeroplanes have suffered from it brought about by not moving their limbs for several hours. A similar cause of DVT can be caused by having your leg in plaster for several months.

Although the doctors at the A and E didn't suggest this the renal doctors had. There saw it as an emergency and tried to arrange an ultrasound the next day but after the doctor and myself having to both chase the promised early appointment several times I got an ultrasound that revealed I did indeed have Deep Vein Thrombosis. (Not to be confused with the famous 1930's American blues singer.) I was then sent to a ward to treat it and was told that they would phone them up to warm them I was on my way there. As soon as I got there I was told because I was a renal patient I really had to go to the renal unit and was about to turn around and go back the way I came and walk to the other end of the hospital when I was offered a wheelchair which I was grateful for having only recently got the knack of walking unaided. After several hours waiting at the renal outpatients I was told no it doesn't matter, you didn't have to go here, you can go walk across to the normal DVT ward. I then waited a few more hours for a wheelchair back to the place I originally started from.

The next few days I had injections of warfarin which is an anticoagulant which is usually known for being used as a rat poison. I thought these unpopular rodents were particularly sensitive to this drug but apparently they just bleed and cannot stop and they run out of blood and die.

With me, and presumably other humans with DVT, it is used to very slowly break down the clot in my blood vessels whilst also thinning out the blood. Earlier on I had a scan to make sure the blood clots were only in my leg as any higher up the body near the heart or lungs the DVT could kill you.

The injections continued but during one incident I thought I was going to get reported to the hospital authorities for something I said. It was Saturday and I was working at a local festival and had managed to escape for a few hours. I arrived festooned with walkie-talkie gadgetry about my person. I was called into the room to have my warfarin injection which I entered on my crutches. I sat down but I could tell the young female nurse couldn't get at my veins in my arm very easily. It was always better if your arm can go limp while resting it on something. I was sitting on a bed with my two crutches standing up and leaning on my legs. On noticing her difficulty I innocently said, "Shall I put my hand on my crutch." I slowly realised how this could be misinterpreted and began explaining and apologising simultaneously but luckily the nurse didn't understand what I was babbling on about. And then I had the dilemma of deciding whether or not I should explain myself or just appear very strange.

The injections were downgraded to tablets and the next six months I was barred from consuming alcohol and cranberries, as they were known for being anticoagulants themselves, and if blood thickness (viscosity) was not controlled I could get into serious trouble. If I was cut my bleeding would not stop for ages as my blood would lose the capacity to coagulate or clot. If I banged my head I was told to phone 999 as I would be susceptible to internal bleeding, brain haemorrhaging. I could just see myself in the panic picking up the earpiece and accidentally smashing into my cranium thereby exacerbating the medical crisis presently in full swing. Another bang just for good measure making sure the ambulance hadn't made a wasted journey. This reminded me of my days on dialysis when I was then injected prior to the session with another anticoagulant called heparin to ensure the blood would not clot in the kidney machine before it was allowed to crawl back into my body thoroughly knackered, on their hands and knees (making sure they don't graze themselves) from going round the machine hundreds of times and managing to stay in one piece. No sorry not one piece: that would a big clot, like I'm being. I mean get back in as lots of little droplet type pieces. I think the only other anticoagulant is aspirin, which have to take every day. Full House! Do I win a prize? I was also told to come off my prescribed aspirin, which I had to remind everyone I was on.

I was given an Anticoagulant Therapy Record. This was a nice little yellow book within which I was to write down the results of an exciting new concept called INR. It took me many attempts to find someone to actually tell me what the initials stood for. International Normalised Ratio. I was told the figure was 1 and if you are ever over this figure the viscosity or the wateriness of your blood was higher than normal and therefore would take more time to clot depending on your ratio. Everyone's blood clotability varies. A close eye needs to be kept on how watery your blood gets so that it doesn't get ridiculous high so that it would never clot and like the poor rats you just bled to death. Mine was (hang on, I have to refer to my little yellow therapy book) up to nearly 3 at one time. You are therefore kept within a tight range and if at the last checkup your blood was getting too thin then your dosages went down accordingly.

I therefore had to visit my GP near enough weekly during the six-month period and phone the hospital the next day to be told what dosage to take and to immediately write it down in my little yellow book.

At one stage is called into the hospital and at my consultation in attendance there were two doctors, one who appeared to be the trainee. They appeared to be testing me on whether I understand the importance of the treatment and why I was on it. I noticed that the doctor had a page of tick boxes and the more I spoke and amplified on my knowledge he ticked more boxers at a faster rate and so I sped up to the extent I was just showing off. He then went into a tick box frenzy. And I thought hey: I may be able to get out of here real soon just by showing them I am not some sort of nincompoop Then I noticed a flourish of ticking after which he put the pen down and I got the feeling I was free to go. So I did. But I was somewhat annoyed. They could have easily have spoken to me on the phone and if they thought I was unaware invite me in for an interview and explain things. Rather than what happened where I had to experience my 325th NHS wait, or whatever number it is. Thankfully I can walk to the hospital but what about people in neighbouring towns and villages who have to spend ages and expense getting to the hospital only to be asked to effectively prove their awareness of the medical treatment. What a waste of resources and the patient's time and travel costs. I do hope I'm wrong and there's a good explanation. Let's hope it's not some kind of NHS target where a certain amount of patients had to be seen on a face-to-face basis and I was called in because it ensured that they reached their targets and they could tick more boxes.

Towards the end of the six months I learnt no test were going to be made to check if the clots had disappeared. They would simply assume they would all rooted themselves to that section of my veins by growing tiny blood vessels as a sort of mini anchor.

The renal unit, to be on the safe side, also had me checked for osteoporosis. Commonly known as brittle bones. Once a kidney patient always a kidney patient. Consequently always at risk of brittle bones. When your kidneys aren't working you take calcium tablets to try and beef up your bones because as you will recall from earlier chapters the dialysis machine takes out of your blood the good as well as the bad stuff. when you have a transplant you are taken off this drug and the risk of thinning of the bones goes. Well for a while anyway.

Guess what? The side effect of the long-term use of steroids is osteoporosis. Once a kidney patient always at risk of getting clobbered by osteoporosis. Even greater if you are female.

If I'd broken my leg in, say, the kitchen or during a very simple walking escapade the renal unit would have been even more suspicious of me suffering from osteoporosis. So ten out of ten for sending me for a check, given that I had been on steroids for several decades, having had the audacity of having had a successful kidney transplant.

On my diagnosis of having it two ironies were born.

Had I not broken my leg I would not have been diagnosed with it until seven years later but now it has been confirmed I can be treated for it. My prescribed drug intake goes up once again: one drug I take weekly but if I don't take it the right way it will have painful consequences later on in the day and the other is called Calcichew which you cannot.

Apart from drugs the other treatment to try and strengthen your weakened skeleton is to partake in what is known as "weight bearing exercises". Initially I thought that was involving weight training or carrying a caravan on my back. But it just means walking as opposed to, say swimming or cycling where it is the weight or pressure put on your bones that is being proposed. So now I have to do a juggling act: cycling or swimming for exercising my cardiovascular system to help my heart or walking to help my bones.

The second irony? Back to Tyr Peg walking up those Welsh mountains but next time I will not go alone.

The first time I had an inkling that I had cancer was when I was in the shower. I had to go to work that afternoon on one of my days off. I had a late shower and as I moved my hand up to just below my neck I noticed a lump that had clearly come up overnight. I went to the GP straight after work and his first words were: "goodness me". He said he'd never seen anything like that in the 17 years he had been a GP. In a sense that was a slight relief because it wasn't a standard symptom and therefore not a standard sign of cancer. The reception staff faxed a letter to "General Surgery" at the local hospital for the lump to be inspected urgently but several days later I still hadn't receive the urgent appointment that I was promised and so went back to the GP and this time saw my usual GP.

The first one appeared to be a locum and had sent a fax to general surgery when in fact because it was a lymph gland issue, should have been sent to the oncologist: or should I whisper the cancer department. My GP said he'd phone and sort it out and the next day I had a phone call to request I attend an oncologist outpatients the next day.

In any hospital now you will never see "Cancer Ward - This Way". A dirty word. But I guess Solsiniskin's Cancer Ward would never have had the same effect if his novel was called The Haematology and Oncology Unit to indicate to the world how life was like in the Soviet gulag.

A few yards off the main corridor at the main entrance of the hospital I saw an open plan reception area that appeared to be staffed by pensioner volunteers. I asked for the whereabouts of Level E and to my surprise one of the volunteers asked me to follow him and took me down the corridor to three adjacent lift entrances. He told me to go up one of those. I climbed in and immediately notice all the levels were numbered: no letters. I then stepped out and went up the stairs and asked anyone who looked like they may possibly work in the hospital what had happened to Level E and presumably it's accompanying upper and lower neighbours levels D and F and for that matter A, B, C and possibly G but I always got the same surprising response: "there is no Level E in this hospital"

I knew this was rubbish because on the phone the person told me Level E: E for egg. I continued going up and down the levels of the stairs and spotted somebody else who clearly worked in the hospital and got the same response: "There is no Level E in his hospital": not a more helpful " All the levels here are numbered" or, which would make sense: " Which ward are you looking for?" "What are you looking for?" The third time this happened I get a bit annoyed as I was now going to be late for appointment. After a few more minutes of aimlessly walking around the corridors I'd tried another tact and ask for the Haematology and Oncology Department. I am then directed to the other end of the "hospital" er building complex.

Eventually I find my Level E and slowly work out that the hospital is a bunch of hospitals all in one big building complex. Unfortunately it is known as the largest of the hospitals to everybody and used as a shorthand to incorporate the group of hospitals within.

These three people who clearly work in the complex assume as a new patient to the "hospital" that you know this. They clearly are at a loss as to what is going on in the other ends of the complex, just a few corridors away from where they work, to the extent they don't even know that there's a whole structure of lifts that aren't numbered but named in alphabetical order, possibly all the way to F.

I got there in time and began my first wait in a cancer ward waiting room. Sitting directly opposite was a young woman in her early twenties who some would clearly classified as a glamour type. She was surrounded by other people who could be all have been her grandparents (well not all of them but you know what I mean) and she was holding back the tears as she was reading from the booklet that must have just been handed to headed "Hodgkins lymphoma". What ever that is.

Looking around she stood out as being one of, if not the youngest and I also noticed the many and varied head attire covering the baldness brought about by chemotherapy which I was bracing myself for if indeed I was to be diagnosed with cancer which looked likely.

When I was called to meet for the first time my very own oncologist I was told I would have to have a series of tests to discover what had caused the lump. I had read up from the internet but didn't disclose this fact as I know quoting obscure websites irritated doctors so I tried to get an opinion but the consultant wasn't prepared to commit himself as to whether I had probably got cancer but told me to await the results. He did think he could get me to see a surgeon that afternoon to arrange a biopsy on the lump which was refreshingly quick.

After leaving my first consultation with an oncology consultant I has given a blood sample request form to put in a wooden box by the entrance to the room where blood is taken. There is a typed sign: "Please put your form at the back". I dutifully did as indicated and sat down hoping, it will not be another long wait. The consultant said it wouldn't be and I'd have plenty of time to go for lunch and get back to the dermatology department where I had an amazingly unfortunately bad timed check up the same day. (It looks like I am having nodules frozen off again! You will recall shortly after my first transplant I had to have tiny growths on my skin removed and the freeze off machine didn't work so I had to have them brunt off)

Meanwhile the wait gets longer and I am fixated on the blood request form wooden box because I know this system will not work well. Many people, unfortunately a large proportion of elderly and confused and no doubt very stressed, some have possibly just been given the diagnosis 30 seconds earlier. They don't read the sign, don't even notice the sign and shove the form in the box sometimes in the front, sometimes in the back. Oh dear I going to be late. Do I get up and direct them? I look round at the irritated faces of the other patients who also realise the system means that there is no orderly queue. One or two polite patients make the point to the nurses who come out of the room and take the first form at the front. We are reassured, unconvincingly by the nurse, that they are not to worry as there is a time date on it. This is clearly nonsense: the date will always be today and I simply don't believe that every doctor writes down the exact minute when the form is filled in. This is confirmed when the next nurse emerges from the door, picks up the first form and shouts out to the waiting room the name of a patient who clearly was the last person to put their form in the box but put it at the front. You think it doesn't matter. It does. I have a full day of rushing around three clinics within this mighty complex and I am hungry and it can be all avoided.

By the time I had my blood taken all I could do was rush out into the street, buy a sandwich and go into an another hospital entrance in time for my second outpatients clinic appointment of the day and wait while trying to eat my lunch.

After that appointment, I rushed round to another hospital to the General Surgery ward (I'm back to this clinic originally an error from the locum GP) and waited. Eventually I was met by the surgeon who told me they would not be taking a biopsy of my swollen lymph gland but they be taking the whole thing out as it was easier as it was too near a major blood vessel. He went off for a while, came back 20 minutes later and said we need to get it out quickly. He could fit me next Tuesday or tomorrow. I decided on the next day. This meant I had to phone my friend and tell him I will not be getting the train now and had to cancel my weekend away that supposed to begin the next day.

I would need a general anaesthetic. They told me if I could stay with someone or someone could look after me the following evening I would not have to be an inpatient.

With my mobile I phoned around to see if anyone would allow me to stay at the home the following night to avoid being an inpatient which I had been able to do avoid for several years. While being questioned by one of the nurses, which included listing all my prescription drugs yet again and giving my date of birth, my mobile rang and I was told off for having a mobile on in the hospital when the surgeon told me it was fine. On the other line was a friend who said I could stay at her home. I was thus able to avoid sleeping at the hospital the following night.

The next day I turned up at the hospital and was given an ECG scan just before which is now apparently common practice for all general anaesthetic surgery.

After the usual hanging around I was escorted to my bed given a operating theatre gown and a dressing gown, not being able to work out which was which both being of the same thickness and design. One was the usual standard gown which you put on back to front and remarkably I was allowed to keep my underpants on. Unheard of years ago. The other gown, I was allowed to put on the right way around.

The nurse then said "the anaesthetic doctor will be with you in a moment"

"The anaesthetic doctor? What's happened to the anaesthetist?"

At this stage the nurse began to giggle and explained, "Most people will not know what an anaesthetist is"

What is this?: The opening sequence to "Janet and John have an NHS operation" What will we have next: the Trolley Wolley man will soon take you up to theatre when the Knifey Wifey man will cut out the naughty lymph gland and then the Kiss It Better nurse will bring you back here.

At the operating theatre before I was put under there was no count to ten procedure but a much better bedside manner. I had a nurse holding my hand – a bit over the top for an old timer like me – who actually appeared to have one duty: putting me at my ease until I was unconscious. This unlike previous operations from years before where the nurses duties also involved looking around at everything but me. Where they were far more interested in what was being done than who it was being done to. Maybe in the past I always had new and inquisitive nurses who were going through the motions of occasionally glance over at me and asking if I was OK.

After I gained consciousness I had that familiar strange sensation of not been aware that time had passed when I knew it must have. I knew it has because I was in a different place and I felt a pain in my lower neck where my lympth gland had been removed.

My friend was to busy to collect me so she sent her partner to pick me up and I think he got a bit of a shock. Immediately identified as my overnight carer he was beckoned over to a quiet corner of the ward and given a full set of instructions. "Here are Michael s pain killers." "Make sure he does not take more than the stated dose." "Make sure he does not use any potentially dangerous equipment such as a hot kettle"

After all that we had to get to his house by walking across town by getting two buses during the rush hour. So I was running across busy roads which is not exactly what the hospital protocol had envisaged. At least if I fell and was run over the hospital trust couldn't be successfully sued.

On arrival I was fine but I toyed with the idea of taking the painkillers to ease the pain but fought against it firstly because it was a bit over the top and secondly the drug contained codeine and I remember years ago there was a scare that it damaged the kidney and I certainly was not going to risk that.

I looked through the rest of the pack that contained the drugs and dressings for my wound and spotted an advice sheet:

"The following advice is to help you when you get home:

Painkillers

You have been prescribed:
Name of medication
Cocodamal

Stitches

You have sutures which will dissolve/will need removing in _____ days. At_____.

Dressings

You have a opsife dressing. This should be removed
/~~replaced on~~ 7 days

You may get some bruising or swelling that this will
improve after a week. If the swelling or information
persists after _____ please contact your GP.

Additional information

Next appointment in one week with Dr X"

This was the appointment in which I was to be told
whether or not I had cancer but when I phoned to check the
appointment the outpatients' clinic did not have my name on
their list.

At about this time (the exact sequence of events escapes
me) I got a standard hospital appointment which on opening
the letter I assume was the recall for the oncology outpatient
clinic for the results. On opening it I was being informed that a
female surgeon who I had never heard of was inviting me in to
"Breast Surgery Clinic!" What is happening now: have I been
diagnosed with breast cancer, which can occasionally happen
to males. But no: after a phone call it transpires that as the
operation was done in the General Surgery clinic, this letter
was a standard call up which was routine after every operation
from this clinic. The female surgeon who incidentally did not
do my operation is the head consultant for that surgery team.

Crikey. Why are the NHS hospital clinics structured in
such an inane named way? I'd have preferred it if they were
simply given a raw number, like they did in soviet schools
than have this quaint ego based name labelling that as it
proved with me was totally confusing. I never did meet and
never will meet this surgeon so why even mention her name on
any letter.

As all who get treatment in hospital will know you hardly
ever see the consultant you "are under" but mostly see "one of
the team". When someone in the hospital asks you who is your

consultant they must often be met by many with an unsure look which no doubt triggers a "doh" summary of your awareness capabilities by the enquirer. Well let me tell them: most of the time it may have been written on a sheet you were sent months or possibly years ago and you still have never met the consultant.

Anyway I used this confusion to phone up for the results. I spoke to the secretary of the oncologist but she said such results were not given over the phone and I asked why not. I was told that for some patients the diagnosis can be so distressing that they needed a doctor with them to console and explain the implications. I retorted that I would be able to take it and pointed out over the phone that you could put the patient out of their misery by telling them they don't have cancer if indeed that is the result. I nearly got into a convoluted discussion about the fact that many people don't get diagnosed with cancer and so if you didn't tell them the result they wouldn't know that it must be bad news. (And then I thought maybe that's what they do do!).

She said she saw my point and then I was put through to the oncologist and after a few searching questions by him he told me straight that I had cancer. Non Hodgkin lymphoma. This thankfully avoided another long outpatients appointment wait to be formality told the news in person. I was then to await the next letter for the times for further investigations as to how bad it was. How far it had it spread. Was it treatable?

I went on the Internet to discover all the possible symptoms: first symptoms can be quite non-specific making an initial diagnosis difficult. The most common is a painless swollen lymph node in the neck, armpit or groin which steadily increased in size. Other possible symptoms: heavy sweats during the night, extreme tiredness and unexplained weight loss. On another site there were a few over possible symptoms: persistent flu symptoms, difficulty shaking off infections, fevers, abdominal pain, diarrhoea will change in bowel habit, a persistent cough or breathlessness, pain in the enlarged nodes after drinking alcohol and a persistent itch all over.

And while I was surfing the superhighway I wanted to know what a lymph gland was and what was its purpose and also what is the difference between Hodgkin's lymphoma and Non-Hodgkin's lymphoma. Apparently Mr H discovered lymphoma the disease but as more discoveries were made and research undertaken others were able to differentiate between the original form of cancer.

It is very fitting that my latest diagnosis has a name that is described in the negative. My heart condition is syndrome x : we know what it isn't; i.e. it is not angina. Now I have a lymphoma that is not the one discovered by Mr Hodgkin.

The next stage of the investigation was to have a CT scan and bone marrow test known as "asprit and threfine" to see if the cancer had spread throughout my body. Asprit is the medical term for when they suck out bone marrow fluid and threfine drags up bone scrapings into a syringe. It hurts. You have a local, which works as the needle enters the skin but after that you feel it as you cannot give your bone a local anaesthetic.

When I arrived for the bone marrow investigation (for investigation read intrusive investigation) I was escorted to a very small room where two doctors attended and then I realised one was training the other. I got the impression that the junior in the partnership hadn't done this before as he took some time before he took the plunge and put the plunger into me. Beforehand I was told that this might be "uncomfortable" which is a euphemism I have discovered means it'll hurt. It did. When it was all over I was told it was all over. Unfortunately when they looked at the contents of the needle for the trefine the senior doctor said there wasn't enough and we (we?) had to go in again. It wasn't all over.

I just wish they would tell me it would be painful because then I'll be able to utilise my ancient self-invented pain redirectional trick with my fingernail pressing into another fingernail. On this occasion I was totally unprepared and was annoyed with myself for allowing it to happen.

The CT scan was straightforward but I had to drink about a litre of some special fluid so that my insides showed up when I went into the machine.

I got a call. I think it might even have been the next day, which I was very impressed with. They had the results!

At outpatients I was worried that I wasn't. I may get the biggest shock of my life. But I was not mentally preparing myself. How often I tried to adjust I couldn't. Although I already knew I had non-Hodgkin's lymphoma I had no idea to what degree.

When I was eventually called my oncology consultant arrived with someone that looked like another doctor. This was ominous. But they didn't look as if they were going to give me bad news and I therefore relied strongly on my intuition that it wasn't. In summary I was told I was lucky (and later on in the consultation I was to gently remind them that I was not lucky: I was just less unlucky) and that the cancer had not spread and so I was not going to need chemotherapy. Not initially anyway.

They began to explain to me the treatment I had read about on the Internet but haven't paid much attention to as I was resigned to chemotherapy. While there were explaining the treatment they had in mind I was trying to recall what I had read only a few days ago. I slowly remembered that this treatment went hand in hand with having my immunosuppressive drugs reduced or even stopped.

This surprisingly was more worrying to me than the actual treatment as it would mean I might have to sacrifice my kidney to beat the cancer. With all the effort I had put in trying everything to protect the kidney and devising every conceivable routine to remember to take my drugs I was now having to really risk it all on an oncologists deciding the best way to fight off the cancer. For the remainder of the consultation I was just waiting for me to be told this.

They explained I was going to take one drug daily for the time being that was mainly used for only this type of cancer. That would now make seven different drugs a day meaning twelve and a half tablets. I would come into hospital for the next four Thursdays to take another drug intravenously.

("However this will mean....."?: No. Neither doctor mentioned I would stop taking he immunosuppressive drug that would put at risk my dear transplanted kidney). I was then told I would have radiotherapy every day for four weeks. Hence the appearance of the other doctor: the radiologist. ("You do understand that in order for this to work you will have to stop taking....."?: no)

"Is that all clear Michael? (" One other thing your present transplant treatment......."?: no)

When I thought the coast was clear I endeavoured to ask definitions of terminology of the cancer world. What is the different between a cure and remission? Obviously I knew there was no cure for cancer but I had heard the word used in such a context. Basically I was to discover a useful piece of information: there is a rule of thumb that if you can stay in remission for five years you are deemed to be cured.

I then posed the classic question about the treatment I was to undergo for the next two months. Thankfully not the "how long have I got doc" but the "what are the chances of it working". I was told about 50:50. I took that to mean if I was on the wrong side of the 50 it would then be chemo.

The two doctors left and I was placed in the hands of a nurse who was to explain the treatment timetable and as I left the room and got as far as the door- trashy TV films time- I was waiting to hear behind my back: "did the doctors tell you about your present immunosuppressive drugs? But thankfully it didn't happen and only at that stage did I feel my transplant was still safe, for the time being anyway. As an obedient patient I dutifully carried my blood test request form to the sacred wooden box having arrogantly explained how you could introduce a better system. I suggested simply asking people to put the form at the front of the box, which is the natural thing to do, and so the nurses take the forms from the back. I even got carried away with the total foolproof suggestion that they should have a little letterbox in the hardboard wall separating the waiting room and the nurse's treatment room which would stop all the anxiety. What's the betting nothing changes. What's the better that behind the polite smiles the nurses thought I was a cheeky bastard.

As I now always do, when I got home I eagerly opened the drug package carefully read the patient information sheet. It looked as if I was taking this to a reduced a certain type of blood cell manufactured in the bone but I couldn't be sure and considering I was going to have radiotherapy it hardly seemed important. There was a big list of what to tell your doctor or pharmacist if any of the questions were answered in the affirmative. Any long-term kidney problems? -- yep. Are you taking cyclosporin? -- yep. Our you taking any anticoagulants? -- yep. Are you taking any medication for heart disease? -- yep. It also warned you that these drugs may result in loss of coordination and dizziness and tiredness and not to drive or operate machinery. I always thought it was heavy machinery. Now I can't even use my computer!

Over the page it mentions the "occasional" side-effects. Such as feeling sick and suggests you only take the drug after meals. And finally it lists an abundance of side-effects that have been "reported occasionally". This appears not to have much medical authority and could be just perceived or coincidental conditions that one patient had attributed to this drug. So if you want the list, that could scare the living daylights out of you...: "Ladies and gentlemen. Roll up! Roll up! Gather round everybody. For you delight and delectation we have":

"Fever, a general feeling of being unwell, headache, vertigo (a sensation that your surroundings are spinning either up or from side to side), nausea, vomiting, anaemia, uraemia (the presence of excess urea and other chemical waste products in the blood), swollen glands, loss of coordination, weakness or unsteadiness, unconsciousness and unresponsiveness, sleepiness, depression, loss of feeling part of the body, "pins and needles", taste disorders or inflammation in the mouth, a change in bowel habits or unusual bowel movements, impotence, sexual or infertility problems, and liver problems (abnormal liver function tests, hepatitis), visual problems (including cataracts), ejaculation during sleep ("wet dream"), diabetes, boils, hair loss or discoloration, heart problems and high blood pressure, blood disorders which may be characterised by abnormal bruising, high levels of lipids (fats) in the blood, blood in the urine, swelling, and breast enlargement in men. There have been very rare reports of the presence of blood in vomit and a severe allergic reaction (anaphylactic shock). If you have these or any other side effect whilst taking this drug please tell your doctor immediately."

So, with a large dose of trepidation I entered the next episode of my roller coaster medical journey by beginning my cancer treatment and swallowed, after breakfast, the first tablet of this newly prescribed drug.

After following my own home made rule I reread the side effects a week later so that any mild symptoms could be identified early and I could look out if they got worse.

There were no real problematic symptoms. Initially. And that was just for the daily tablet. I now had to go in for my weekly infusion.

I was told that the first infusion would go in very slowly. If I reacted badly I would be kept in overnight and the infusion would be stopped and started again when the symptoms were over.

The possible side-effects were flu like symptoms which can include high temperature, chills, weakness, muscle aches, tiredness, dizziness and headaches. Low blood pressure, feeling sick and occasional vomiting, pain from the tumour or part of the body where you have cancer, allergic reactions such as skin rashes, itching a feeling of swelling in the tongue or throat, irritation of the nasal passages, wheezing, a cough and breathlessness; lower resistance to infection; bruising or bleeding (such as nosebleeds, blood spots or rashes on the skin, bleeding gums), anaemia and lastly flushing. Such symptoms are unlikely to last after the infusion session ends.

I'm able to report that I didn't have any noticeable symptoms on the first slow infusion but during this period generally - I don't know which or whether either drug caused it - but I was sleeping a lot but that could have easily have been my escape mechanism: to try and cope by hiding away via the simply skill of resorting to unconsciousness.

Being not so much a born but a self-taught pessimist, during my conscious moments I was already planning to have "short back and sides" ready for others and myself to get used to short hair on me, ready for "a skin head" and no hair at all if the radiotherapy didn't work and I had to have chemotherapy.

My first "2 hour" session lasted 7 hours. "The doctors don't understand the practicalities" , a nurse told me. I had to have an antihistamine infusion in case I got anaphylactic shock from the cancer drug. Anaphylactic shock is commonly associated with those ultra sensitive to wasp or bee stings. It can be fatal. It knocked me out: I could barely keep awake. The fear of this type of shock was also a possible side effect of the other cancer drug I took each day but hey who's counting?

When I was put on my drip I was told " if you have difficulty breathing just say". You what?. How am I going to do that if I cannot breath properly? "Miss? Excuse me Miss I appear to have difficulty breathing"

There was no buzzer or anything in the vicinity. I looked around. There was a small, very practical oversized footstool to put your nice cup of tea on. I had decided if I got the above mention side effect I would be kicking it into the nicely decorated hung ceiling. Hopefully that could attract attention. It would collide with the ceiling bringing a few of those polystyrene tiles tumbling down all over me. As far as I was concerned the more the fucking merrier.

Having not had treatment in hospital for years I noticed a big change in the taking of your OBS (observations). Regular checks for pulse, blood pressure and temperature had gone completely modern. No longer the thermometer in the gob while at the same time my wrist was held by the nurse and s/he looks at her/his upside down watch attached to her/his blouse/shirt and then put the end of the stethoscope on the inner part of my elbow while pumping up the black strap around my upper arm. Now a trolley arrives with permanently attached gadgetry, a clip is placed on the end of one of my fingers; the black strap is attached but no longer is there the need for anyone to pump it up but there was just a button to press. While the arm strap begins to tighten the little machine is taking your pulse from the clip and it is recorded it on the fancy display. A thing in the ear, as opposed to a thermometer under your tongue, is taking your temperature.

During my little journeys within the complex I had another bout of irritation over the lacklustre attempt to put helpful signs and notices up within the hospital complex. Before I couldn't get to my ward. This time I couldn't get out of the frigging building. I had to hunt high and low for sign for the level that was "way out" but even then you didn't know which "way out" it was: the locality or name of the street would help. On one of the stairwells I asked someone who looked like a technician or doctor how I can get out and it came up with the immortal line: "Which building do you want to get out of?"

This one really stumped me. Which one do you think? I hardly want to get out of that building over there. I was having problems conceptualising the time space continuum: can you be in a building within a building?
Can you be in two buildings at the same time? Eventually I came to my senses and got out of the building regardless of where I would end up on the periphery of the complex. I recognising the street, got my bearings and went home. I was starting to think that some of the side effects of these drugs were catching up with me. I recollect "confusion"; "unresponsiveness" and "sleepiness". Was I losing my sense of direction or had I lost the capacity to get out of a building or didn't understand any longer my fellow man. Apparently not, because I was still going to the Law Centre and working on my cases but no one had said "You can't do that"; "What are you talking about" or "I got your letter Mr O'Sullivan but I can't make head nor tail of it".

I did not have an allergic reaction to the weekly infusion. I was fine. The next three weekly sessions went smoothly while I was on the drip but I had strange symptoms during this time, which must be from the daily anti cancer drug.

Over the next month I had more flu like symptoms in that period then I had had in the last 30 years. They ranged on a day-to-day basis from sore throats, runny nose, cough, cold, very sore throat, galloping runny nose, cold etc. On one occasion I didn't have any of these, apart from the low-key cold but my body began to ache all over but strangely the ache tended to concentrate at different parts of my body but always at different times. And I was thinking: hey, this isn't on the list.

The first extreme ache began down my right leg which meant I had to hobble to walk about and then that leg "got better" then the ache reappeared in my back and then after holidaying there for about 20 hours retired to my other leg and then disappeared. It lasted for about four days during which I was near enough bedridden.

At one stage I got really worried and phoned a friend because if it got any worse I would be in real trouble. This resulted in a doctor visiting on a Sunday. My obs were taken and she gave the impression there was nothing to worry about. My other concern was dehydration and the possible damage to my kidney and as soon as I was mobile again I drank loads.

The week before I was to start radiotherapy I was called in and asked to present myself at the main reception. My name was ticked off from a list, and I was told I would be called "soon" I was called along with five other names from aloud public address system and we were told to go to the lift to the basement where the radiotherapy treatment took place. It was a strange sensation: walk into the lift and waiting there along with other people clearly going through different stages of cancer treatment.

The following feeling I felt will be distasteful to some and so I warn you now. It was if we were on the way to the gas chambers and when the lift door closed behind me I had the peculiar sick fantasy that Zyklon B pellets would falling from the roof. When we arrived at the basement I was hoping there was no sign on the wall opposite as the door opened: "to the showers".

We then arrived at the basement reception our names were once again passed on and ticked off from the list. Presumably the waiting area was too small in the basement so this eerie process was to prevent a bottleneck of patients.

Directly opposite me was a big board with the types of treatment down one left column: and a notice which read: " if you have to wait for more than 30 minutes you will be informed".

After staring at it for a while I worked out how it worked: alongside the six or seven various treatments if you are going to wait more than 30 minutes each would say so. What confused me however, alongside two of the treatments it said 30 minutes!

After one hour I couldn't take this false promise any longer and so got out of my seat and went up to the reception and made my point. Went back to my seat the receptionist ring through, who then got up and went to the board and wrote 45 minutes. It was now over an hour, 60 minutes, and I haven't yet been called and so the very least it should have said 75 minutes! As an old-timer as far as NHS waiting rooms go I was not getting too peeved off about the delay but, really, either introduce a working reassuring system or don't use it all.

How I was eventually called and the raw material for my face masks was dunked into a tank full of some sort of fluid and then put over my face. The idea being, I guessed, was that it was to solidify and then, I assumed, stupidly, as it happens, layers of protective metal were to be added. Apparently to protect my face and neck from the radiation. I was then told about the risk of side-effects of having radiotherapy: an under active thyroid, destruction of some of my saliva glands and, wait for it, throat cancer.

I was told it was very likely I would get a sore throat at the very least, particularly towards the end of the treatment and I might have difficulty swallowing and therefore might not be eating solids. Those little jars of mashed up baby food were suggested. So far I had not lost my appetite so I would have needed about ten jars for each meal. I can imagine the accusatory glances when I took them all off the shelves when mum discovered there were none left for her little one. You got quadruplets? Is there a baby food shortage?

Go on. I bet your dying to know the full panoply of possible side effects of radiotherapy:

Radiotherapy will nearly always make people tired (fatigue). Possible side effects: hair loss in the treated area. If the radiotherapy is directed at the neck area there is possible sore mouth or throat; some food may taste different to normal.

Initially I was surprised that the side effects of radiotherapy were far less than the drugs but then when you think about it the drugs introduce an unlimitless potential cocktail of chemical reactions and so the possibilities are wide ranging. Radiotherapy, on the other hand, is a more straightforward process of damaging, or killing off, parts of the body.

At about this time I was given an exciting four page patient information leaflet entitled "About Your Radiotherapy". In it there were clear paragraphs with headings such as "Can I Bring A Relative Or Friend With Me?" And "Will My Treatment Hurt?" But no paragraph headed "What Are The Possible Side Effects". When I asked about the side effects there was surprise that I had not been given the leaflet. When I explained I had but there was nothing in it on the topic I was told something would be done about the clear omission. (Yeah right)

What did annoy me while the mask was solidifying on my face was I was never told how long it would take so I naturally assumed a few seconds. As I lay there I didn't want to ask, and move my mouth, as I didn't want to mess up the mould.

I was in an awkward position: being told to have chin up in the air. Was I also having x-rays taken? I didn't know and couldn't ask. It took about five minutes rather than the 30 seconds I was expecting.

Maybe they normally tell the nervous cancer patient, going through the first radiotherapy treatment procedure, before they plonk the masks on but this time they must have forgotten. Plonkers. (Hey I found another word on my pc – "Language : English (UK)" - that they will not accept as a word. Plonkers.)

Over the years when I didn't understand something medical I have been asking different doctors the same question. On this occasion it paid off. I asked the radiologist the chances of this treatment working and he said 90% in my favour. This clearly contradicted the 50-50 I was told earlier. I was soon to discover my error: the radiotherapy was talking about the chances of killing off any cancer cells that had not been removed after my lymph gland was. However when the oncologist was talking about 50-50 he was referring to my chances of being "cured" ie going into remission for at least five years.

A few days later the actual radiotherapy was to begin. But would it work? ."We'll have no talk like that."

This was the common retort amongst friends and colleagues if you ever dared to let slip by questing what if the treatment

didn't work. OK you move on to chemo but what if that either?

You don't get guarantees from the medical profession in case they are proved wrong and you can turn on them which is perfectly understandable. However I think they go to the other extreme . Just like in law when your client asks if they will definitely win their case. In either profession you can never be sure but for me the medical profession go too far the other.

There is a middle way which is not a kop out. Reducing the anxiety by not putting up such a self protective defensive shield can be achieved by, for example saying " In similar cases to this in the pass we have succeeded." Or "In my opinion I will be amazed if you don't win through"

Being told not to think pessimistically or rather not being totally optimistic immediately blocks you off from talking about it which can be devastating if you simply need to talk it through with someone.

Of course people will say this because if this discussion was opened up they would not know what to say but in their embarrassment they fail to appreciate how they have cut you off from a discussion you need. You are then left to dwell on it on your own. This results in you getting trapped in a mental loop of disrepair when another person can say something that can snap you out of it which is so easy to do by the most simple counter suggestion to extinguish what is going on in your own head. The patient guides also seem to bypass these issues in the same way.

It was to involve the whole of March. It was bad timing. I had planned to go Tyr Peg for my spring vegetable planting. I had ploughed up the little lawn and last year had successfully grown potatoes and made damson wine from the little damson orchard over the fence in a field now owned by the new owners of the farm, once owned by my relatives. They allowed me to pick the damsons each year as they don't use them. My uncle had originally planted the orchard but each year the damsons were left to rot.

I wanted to grow more vegetables because there was no shop in the village and as I didn't have a car, usually arrived there by public transport, I wanted to be self-sufficient. Otherwise I would have had to walk about 6 miles to next the village, which had the nearest shop.

This little cottage in North Wales was my escape from the town as it was a million miles away from my hospital(s); my GP; my pharmacy and everything else associated with my health conditions. (It even has my secret stash of prescribed drugs so that I never have to return if I miscalculate or decide to extend my visit). Nant Farm and Tyr Peg have memories for me when I was younger when at the time I had no idea what the future held with regard to my ill-health. The irony here being that it was "them hills" where my ancestors came from, lugging with them, over centuries, the polycystic kidney gene and where I recently broke my leg.

The rustic way of living even though it was for a few days at a time was refreshing. Walking to the next village for provisions, which was around trip of three hours, was nothing when you compare it with what previous generations had to do in the past, and as many still do in other parts of the world, just to survive. It was strangely cathartic.

So was chopping logs for a fire that had to be done or in the colder months it would simply be too cold. It was always 100% success chopping logs and such success is quite rare in what most people do these days. Apparently there is an old Chinese saying: "he who chops wood gets warm twice".

I've heard some months later that the North Welsh water supply was infected with C difficile and all the water companies customers had to boil water before drinking. We at Tyr Peg weren't customers. We don't have mains water. We survive on a mountain spring and so with all that modern technology allows: easy transport to the next village and the modern heating systems, they couldn't drink their water without boiling it first on their modern cookers.

When I think about the only bit of good fortune I can recall ever having is this unjustified inheritance due to a legal fluke but once again, the irony being it was in the valley that was the source of my health problems. Obviously I am not including the comparatively short time I have been on the kidney machine before having a transplant but I would submit, Your Honour, that doesn't count. It would be like saying you were lucky that you didn't break you leg in two places. Less unlucky doesn't count as being lucky. And don't you forget it.

Hopefully, if the month of intensive radiotherapy worked, I could plant vegetables when I was in fit state to make the trip, albeit a month late. And if I was still OK in the autumn I could pick the damsons.

That year I had planned to extend my one little cottage industry to damson jam; damson chutney, damson pickle; damson ketchup; damson "cheese". Then I could supply products to the rest of my family to show them that Tyr Peg was worth keeping as well as adding to the whole TP "experience" for paying visitors. But first I had to get through this cancer.

"It's day one in the NHS radiotherapy waiting room and Michael is bracing himself for another long wait in the cancer patient household knowing there is a months worth to come." Yippee.

How do people survive waiting while not bringing anything with them and glancing through a 5 year old copy of Woman's Own? Admittedly if you bring someone with you you can chat; if you are nervous you sit there looking nervous. Me? Goodie Two Shoes. I bought copies of articles from some legal periodicals to read as I had a lot of catching up to do. After a few minutes I would look up, nervously, looking at other people on their own looking nervous and people with a friend trying to have a conversation. Clearly these were the new comers. I guess for session number whatever you were getting bored but by then you were feeling ill or tired and concerned as to whether all the treatment would actually do the trick. I then went for an old newspaper lying around that was only a day or so old.

In one corner I couldn't help overhearing two middle age men suddenly recognising each other and unbelievable asking each other how they were! ("Fine and you"). They had not seen each other for decades when at the time were both working on a building site. How very sad that their next meeting was to be about when one was about to start cancer treatment and the other was presumably in the middle of his.

Every time I was called I got a cheerful smile from the radiotherapist nurse. I was at first a bit taken a back by this. Why are you so jolly? I've got cancer. I somehow thought everyone should be more serious for us patients with the Big C. But I was wrong. What would it achieve? Cancer is just another condition. It is no longer as always seen as a terminal illness, which was my preconception.

When I went in to the room where the treatment was to happen on the shelves there were several, what I can only call death masks.

Each session lasted about 5 minutes. Before you lay on the board below the massive radiation machine you were always asked you date of birth and address even into the third week of daily visit when by then everyone recognised you.

When you lay down your own specially moulded mask was fastened really tightly over your face and then everyone hid so they would not get a dose of radiation yourself, which would really mount up if you worked there. They were at the controls to make sure it was pointing at the exact spot on my body.

It was then that I found out the mask was not to protect your face from radiation but to stop you moving. It worked. It really was like being nailed to a coffee table. If there was a fire and they forgot to release you you wouldn't stand a chance.

After the first few sessions I was given some cream and warned that soon my skin in the general region of the left of my neck, from up to my left cheek down to just above my left nipple would get sore and my hair in that region would all fall out. The only visible, but hardly that visible, spot would be where I shaved but that would aggravate the skin so I was advised not to. So the absence of hair would be visible under my chin to the left. But compared to hair loss for most cancer treatment involving other forms of radiotherapy or chemo it was nothing.

When that region did eventually get sore I bought a strip of silk to place between my shirt collar to ease and reduce the friction. But what happened to all the other symptoms I had been promised? I wasn't complaining. Just waiting.

One day I was directed to a radiotherapy simulation machine as I was not laying correctly on the real one. I was told they were going to put a small black blob on my chest. This was to make it easier to line me up on the real machine. I was asked if I consented to this. Why would I object to that? Because you will have this tiny black blob for the rest of your life. Good job I asked.

Nowadays the NHS are obsessed with consent forms. Not the consent concept but the form. They are not that interest in informed consent. In passing you will hurriedly be told what is going on, with a form pushed in front of you, not being shown all the words and pages above. Just sign the form and cover our backs. For what its worth I think they are in the clear even if you don't sign it. If you have an appointment and turn up I think the courts will accept the NHS defence of consent with all the corrobative evidence to hand. But consider the following two incidents that happened to me that I have already told you about.

Remember the shock weeks later when I learnt my spleen along with both my kidneys had been removed. I didn't remember reading just before I signed but you bet it was covered in the small print with words to the effect that surgeon can do anything s/he feels is necessary.

And the form I had to sign while near enough asleep after my pre-med on the trolley on the way to theatre when I had my arm artery reconstructed, and then only after reminding them that I hadn't signed it yet.

Also lets not forget the heart consultant who did not even know the state of his latest batch of photocopied forms. The front page refereed to the back page that wasn't there.

This is not any criticism of the doctor, nurse or admin worker in front of you. They had their job to do and targets to reach. Informed consent should have been given to you well before the last professional you see before the op. Maybe stuff to read in your hospital bed the day before or sent to you at home or directed to an NHS web site page. Not plonked in front of you when you know the doctor's time is precious. There is an assumption that you would simply sign it. You would feel guilty if you asked for 5 minutes "time out" to read it all and possible ask questions and ask for clarifications when you know you are keeping him or her from seeing the next patient. It even feels worse when the doctor handing you the form is doing the op. Does s/he think I don't trust him. Will s/he take it personally? Will s/he recall my hesitancy tomorrow?

Not a very good or possibly even an appropriate analogy but when the police interview the accused to find out the truth it ends or rather begins with the police looking for a signed confession so that they can get on. Police guidance will not tell you the main purpose of the interview - not "interrogation" - is to get a confession but to find out information. So by the same token the NHS consent form pantomime is not to quickly get the thing signed but that the patient is able to provide unrushed and informed consent rather that just consenting to sign the consent form.

On one occasion the mask wouldn't fit. It was the right mask but the headboard that it was supposed to attach to underneath my head was the wrong one and had to be replaced to everyone's embarrassment.

Towards the end of my month of daily radiotherapy I was walking through one hospital to get to another when I found a quicker route and noticed several people with broken arms. Then I turned the corner and there were another group of people with broken arms. They all appear to be walking away from the hospital not in any real discomfort but chatting and joking. I couldn't work it out. How could this be.? The coincident was too great. Were they all in a crowd during a Mexican wave and a low flying plane flew by, a tadge too low flying? Or was it that they were all at a bus stop and all put their hand out to stop the bus but it just flew by. Maybe a lecturer got irritated by class of perfect students and finally flipped when they all put their hands up yet again so he grabbed his cricket bat and let rip? No, none of these. I eventually worked it out. They appeared to be a group of medical students who were practising on each other on how to make and experience having a plaster cast but strangely they were walking home. Let's hope it was to let them see how disabiliting it can be albeit with no pain. Hey how come no one elected for the broken leg. It reminds me of the politician who decides to live on the doleful for a week and even then they can't make it.

They fail to appreciate it's not a bit of fun but having to survive in that condition week in week out, month in month.

I was having none of the symptoms that were near enough guaranteed and was starting to worry me. Was the big expensive looking monster directly above me firing blanks. Had they forgotten to add the radiation? At last symptoms. What a relief. Discomfort. If it ain't hurting it ain't working.

I got myself a sore throat but not one with the classic symptom of difficulty swallowing food or saliva. Although I had very mild discomfort if I swallowed saliva or "burped" internally. However trying to cough, clear my throat was a different matter. Once I tried to cough I triggered off a five minute coughing fit and I often ended up retching and very occasionally actually vomiting. I therefore fought off the desire to clear my throat and put up with it.

Expecting the sore throat to really kick in I was advised to buy soluble paracetemal to gargle with and those little tins of baby food for when it got so bad I couldn't eat anything else but it never happened. Although for a short while I lost my voice.

Towards the end of the month a met a nurse, who I recognised from the ward where they had removed my lymph gland, on a very quite stairwell which was becoming my back way escape route from the complex. She asked how I was which was refreshing, firstly because she recognised me and secondly, she remember my ailment. I gave her the latest update. I told her they found I had cancer. She then proceeding to tell me her mother had the same type of cancer and after her treatment she was doing fine and this all happened decades earlier.

If her mother had been on immunosuppressive this would have been uplifting but, as she wasn't, hardly encouraging as every day I continue to take tablets that caused the cancer in the first place.

Incredible a few sessions later I met a renal doctor that I knew in exactly the same place. He was teaching medical students in this hospital. He also had some encouraging words to pass on. This back stairway was quickly becoming my very own personal Get Well Stairwell.

While I was waiting for my penultimate radiography session I had a short consultation with a doctor I had never met before. She examined me and to my surprise felt the lymph gland either side of my neck to presumably compare and contrast. I queried this as my lymph gland had been removed. Apparently, I like everyone else, have loads of them so I guess she was looking for differences which would indicate either my clear side was more enlarged than the side that had a lymph gland fewer, which would indicate the cancer had spread or that side was till fine but the cancer side was more enlarged which would indicate another lymph gland had swollen up and the radiotherapy to kill off all the possibly lingering cancer sells around the now missing gland was all a waste of time. Thankfully she did not discover anything untoward.

When we spoke she implied the radiotherapy is likely to get rid of the cancer, for now anyway. I thought this because she spoke of follow up outpatient sessions. My next check up, she explained, would not be for several weeks because my body needed time to allow it to recover from the trauma. I likened it to wait a while before it a heater stops putting out a heat after turning it off. She said that would be good analogy.

I asked her about something in the inventory schedule which was now coming to an end, that had been troubling me. Every few weeks I was scheduled to have "Review and Sarcoma......" and then it ran out of space on the page. I was rather patronising told that I would know if I had sarcoma. Later I discovered it was painful form of bone cancer but even so what's half a title of a type of review doing on the edge of my inventory list when I have not got sarcoma?

At my last session I was given cream for when skin blisters and weeps occur. These symptoms were near enough guaranteed in the weeks after the radiography ends. I was told the symptoms get worse when it stops as the body knows the road is clear to start the road repairs. However I am also told from different quarters that is all rubbish so I keep on asking different people amongst the "oncology community" until I can work out the truth. I think I've cracked it and I am not referring to my skin.

A months worth of radiotherapy is about as much as the human body can take before a new series of side effects, notably directed at your skin, begin. So you would have these new symptoms if you continued with the treatment after a month but because you don't people make the wrong conclusion.

Having said all that, and got it clear in my head, or so I thought, it didn't happen to me . Throughout the radiation attack on my body all I got was the cough-'til-you-spew and the need for some fashionable cravat and, of course the mandatory hair loss. For a while I lost my voice but I didn't have a throat that was sore. So I've got all these creams and soluble paracetamal that I didn't need. A waste of money I was very glad about.

On my last radiotherapy session I was given a letter, handed to me not for me but of me, sealed with "For your GP" written on the front of the envelope.

"Lymphona. Intent: Radical/~~Palliative~~

Expected short-term effects from this treatment are:

Many people feel tired. Their skin in the treated area may become red, itchy and sore and may break down towards the end of treatment. Aqueous cream can be used to moisturise the skin, hydrogel dressing and antibiotics may become necessary if the skin is broken. Mucosal surfaces may become sore, dry and ulcerated. Infection when candida is a common problem. Taste may be disturbed. Good mouth care is essential. Mild and frequent mouthwashes can help, as can analgesics such as aspirin or paracetamol. The dryness in the mouth can last several months and may be permanent. An artificial saliva spray may be useful. Prompt treatment of any infection is important and prophylactic anti-fungals can help. Swallowing may also become difficult , which can be relieved by soluble paracetamol. Occasionally stronger analgesics are required. If the larynx was treated, the voice may become hoarse or husky but these changes are temporary. Any hair in the treatment area will fall out after two or three weeks and usually grows back within two or three months."

Taste disturbed? Does that equate with a sudden strange desire to wear, say, pink trousers with a clashing red top, or worse buying a second-hand hollowed out elephant foot wastepaper bin. For me it was not so much the dryness in the mouth but that occasional metallic taste.

Although things were looking good as far as kicking the cancer into touch for the time being - remission - were concerned, I had been warned I was due another one of those painful bone marrow scrapes. However I had to wait about a month to allow my traumatised body to settle down. The heater had been turned off but we all to wait to make sure no heater was being omitted.

I attended my outpatients appointment well over a month later. After yet another NHS long wait I spotted my oncologist and radiologist but was called by a complete stranger. We had a provisional discussion as we had never met before.

I showed him the letter I was given by the hospital to pass on to the GP. I wanted to know the difference between "radical" and "palliative". I was aware that palliative in palliative care was for those with terminal medical problems. It turned out that palliative is to control untreatable cancers and radical involved an attempt to treat them.

He examined me for lumps in the six lymph area. I made a mental note of precisely how he was checking for I knew I would be self examining for the rest of my life.

He booked me in for another painful bone marrow test but this time I was offered sedation. Last time, had been the first ever time, I had a bone marrow sample taken, I had been warned it would be comfortable which I now know is a euphemism for painful but never offered sedation. But by accepting would mean I wouldn't be able to eat or drink anything for four hours before and I would have to stay in the ward afterwards until the sedation wore off.

Now knowing what to expect and in the hope I wouldn't have a novice doing it I refused sedation because it wouldn't have taken a whole day out of my life I think I would be unable to cope with the 30 or 40 seconds of pain because I had my lifelong, unique, self-taught pain distraction technique. Also the day coincided with the law centre colleague's leaving do.

At the end of the consultancy, it was pointed out that everyone in the ward was talking about me. Strong character? Awful dress sense? Bubbling personality? No. The fact that although I was one of those rare transplant recipients with non Hodgkinson lymphoma as a consequence of long-term steroid use, but that it had been caught at localised area and not found all over my body. Consequently I was a rarity and "lucky". I was quick to point out I wasn't lucky but was less unlucky.

As I left I was given the standard sheets requesting blood samples to be put in the box which today was miraculously empty. Soon after I was called, I had my blood taken but as the needle came out of my arm I heard my name shouted out in the waiting room. I did an embarrassed wave to indicate I was already in the treatment room having treatment and the nurses were all surprised as usually you only get one blood sample request sheet. How was I supposed to know that getting two sheets was unusual?

So far, apart from the blood tests, I have had no conclusive tests since my diagnosis and cancer treatment. The only sure way to find out whether I was in remission was to have that bone marrow scrapes. Or as it is normally known: a bone marrow aspirate and trephine.

These days the common advice for all surgery and intrusive investigations is to ask lost of questions as regards the doctor's experience. Have you done this before? How many times? What is your success rate? The only problem is that you have to instigate this unofficial enquiry but if you do it on the day it is unlikely they will suddenly call in another doctor from next door, simply sitting there twiddling his or her thumbs while holding on to his stethoscope who is more experienced and so the operation will be delayed, possibly for weeks.

The assertive, lucid, more educated middle class person is more key to ask all these questions whilst the frail, elderly and very ill or less assertive would not dream of this line of questioning and every time get the novice. Sometimes, at the risk of being accused of being a martyr you should just get it over with.

I attended the ward for the bone marrow test. I noticed the doctor who supervised the trainee from last time but he wasn't there. Eventually a woman doctor introduced herself and I was told this time it would not occur in a private treatment room but behind a curtain in the open plan ward.

I was beginning to regret refusing sedation because if I shouted out in pain the whole ward would hear. I braced myself but this time at every stage of the slow insertion of the needle, the doctor looked up and asked if I was ok as opposed to last time when the trainee thought he was pricking potatoes for the oven. As I soon realised I had someone who knew how to do and told her just to tell me when it is over.

As I was leaving I asked how and when was I going to get the results. The doctor went off and eventually came back with a card – indicating the appointment was already on the system although I had not been told - on which she put in my next outpatients appointment, which was the 10th June. The next Tuesday. As it was Friday I questioned this, as I would have thought the results would not be back by then but she assure me that most of the results would be. I queried whether it would be better to phone first so as to not waste a morning waiting if the results were not ready but she said I should just go so at least the oncologist could talk things through with me.

Tuesday morning I presented my self to reception at out patients and with a slightly embarrassing squirm the receptionist told me they had got the month wrong; my check up was for the 10th July. Rather than just walk away as, I guess, I was expected to do I made the point that I am now expected to wait a month to see if need extra treatment, like say chemo or find out whether I was in remission. The receptionist went to get a nurse who apologised and gave me a number to ring the following week but I was warned that I would not be told the results over the phone. I phoned a day after the date suggested and promised I would be phoned back in a couple of days. No return call. A few days later I phoned again. Given same promise. I pointed this out. It was then explained that with the new system it was difficult getting into the computer to print out the results (brilliant new system) but would get back to me all together now: in a couple of days.

Glastonbury festival was approaching. My week to do my team leader gate stewarding but still no message or letter from the unit. Then I got the noravirus to take my mind off things which had me bedridden. It is startling few days of projectile vomiting and the like. I thought I had caught it from the hospital, being immunosuppressed, but my GP disagreed but said I had passed the contagious stage and
"Yes, Michael you can go to the..." festival.

When I returned from the madness of Pilton I phoned the unit again from work but before I got the "in a few days" routine I recited the full history and it was explained that one of the oncologists may have been handed the print out of the results and they had not got back to me but I would be phoned back that day. I was. I was told there was nothing in my bone marrow. I asked if that meant I was in remission and told she didn't know but the oncologist said that I would be pleased with that. This meant, I thought, I was in remission. I knew I would not get the full confirmation until my outpatient appointment which was the following week.

At a moment of great relief it was sad that the secretary was not trained up enough to be able to say yes you are in remission which would not be much of a training course considering this patient (ie me) after the last 6 months had worked out the basic. It looked as if these results had been in the computer for possibly weeks and I only discovered the results after persistent pestering.

And then it hit me- in remission. The best position any cancer patient can be in and it's possible to get ever so slightly in a better position as every day passes: staying in remission. Just like transplants. Well at least in the initial years anyway. I then got emotional. I seem to take bad news on the chin every time but not good news. May be I'm not used to it. I had a flash back to when I got my memory back after my enlarged kidneys were removed. Such a relief.

I had to escape from work. That afternoon I was down to chair the law centres staff meeting involving 14 people. Trying to keep control of it is always difficult because there's no hierarchy, no managers and you simply can't put your foot down. Everything has to be done by persuasion. Decisions are usually made by consent.

In fact the last time I was chair I was told I was good at it and managed to control the meeting well when it was a very difficult meeting. This was slightly embarrassing because most of the time I was looking out of the window thinking: will I beat this cancer? And then suddenly come round and have to move the meeting on.

When the meetings go on for more than two hours it meant that I have to make up that time after my usual hours that day as it is Wednesday afternoon and my end of the week and things couldn't wait till on Monday. That was why I also tried to hurry things along.

This unjustified praise reminds me of the time and I was in school art class when I was seven. We were all told to draw a figure of someone in the sun. I spent so much time on particular aspects of the painting that when the teacher began collecting each pupil attempts and picked up mine, I panicked as i realised I hadn't put the arms on. Then when the teacher presented all the offerings of the class I noticed she had my picture in her hand and then when she started to say she wanted to show everyone my picture I thought I was to be humiliated but to my absolute amazement she began to praise it. She pointed out the originality of the picture: of the person standing in the sun "with his hands behind his back"

I arrived at what I hoped was cancer outpatients for some time, sat down and immediately spotted a recently installed tv on the wall on the most inappropriate channel you could imagine: Hot Hits. Everyone barely in their twenties, still all convinced they were physiologically invincible. Who probably think The Big C is a DJ and that oncology is a posh word for bird watching

As I looked around the waiting room there couldn't be a bigger contrast: everyone a lot older than the characters on the monitor, facing the hard reality of life that those youngsters were completely unaware of.

I had a great view and the whole room so notice at once and for the next two hours that no one- repeat no one - was looking at the monitor. Most were trying to read fighting off the inane conveyor belt manufactured sound.

Why doesn't one of the clinic's workers every so often ask "I is anyone watching this?". Why didn't have the courage to say: "Is anyone watching this shite?"

The system is that you are called by a nurse and invited into a consulting room. In fact you don't wait to be invited: you are up quicker than a dog who has just heard the word "walkies". Once in the consulting room you wait again but his time it is for a maximum of about 5 minutes. On this occasion I used my mobile to cancel my lunch with a friend as I couldn't make it any longer although having an appointment for 10.00 am I thought I could.

When the doctor arrived, after wagging my tail ferociously, I pointed out at the outset of the consultation, which was supposed to be a happy one, that I was really pissed off having to wait so long when I saw patients arriving after me having been called before. He sympathised and even suggested that I make a complaint. He accepted it was unacceptable.

In passing I asked him about a strange symptom I was getting and as he was a doctor I thought it was worth a chance rather than spend hours waiting to see my GP. I told him about this strange effect I was getting every time I put my chin down to my chest. It was like an electric shock shooting through all my limbs. He nodded, understanding immediately what I was describing as it turned out it was a rare side-effect of the radiotherapy. It was the condition normally associated with people who have multiple sclerosis.

Its call L'hermittes syndrome or barbers shop syndrome, the former name presumably because of the French doctor who discovered it and the latter because of a barbershop you are often asked to bring your chin down to your chest so they can shave the back of your neck during the once fashionable short back and sides style.

While examining me he told me how to check for new lumps on the six main lymph gland sites of my body and consult the unit as soon as any appeared, thankfully not having to go via my GP.

I was in the clear. Well in remission for the time being anyway. I had an outpatients appointment in three months time.

Several weeks later I was still getting these electric shock, I went to my GP he suggested I come back if after three months I am still getting them as it might be something else like a trapped nerve.

Meanwhile in another hospital not that far away I was having more frequent kidney check ups than usual to ensure all this cancer nonsense was not effecting my faithful transplant.

My function had slightly deteriorated. This may have been due to the cancer, the cancer treatment or not related to either as function can fluctuate from time to time. What is important is the trend. The previous set of results showed an improvement since the drop in function. The next check up after that was important: the trend could carry on improve or begin to noise dive again indicating possible rejection. And I could get to these results the day after my check up over the internet. There was a further slight improvement. It looked as if my kidney was going to survive. For the time being anyway.

The three month cancer check up had arrived. I waited 45 minutes and thankfully the television was down low with subtitles and I sat well away. When I was called in after the preliminaries, of how I was I met another person from the oncology unit, I mentioned that my "barbers shop" syndrome was still with me but that it appeared to be reducing. I mention the fact that I was constantly checking my lymph gland site areas but was told this was very common and to just put one day aside each week to check. Dead easy advice to give a bit more difficult to comply with. The examination did not indicate any lumps although I noticed another part of my anatomy was being checked out where I not know there were lymph glands. On questioning the doctor she was also checking for enlarged spleen and liver. I was about to tell her she may have some difficulty locating the spleen then she told me she had read my notes and knew that I had no spleen. I didn't have an enlarged liver but with all such consultations it needed to be checked as this indicates the possibility of lymphoma.

And so I was given my piece of paper requesting blood tests to be put in a wooden box. All to do now is have my blood taken and try and get out of the building. When I was on dialysis and much younger than nurses often comment on how good my veins were and that is why I was often asked if the trainee nurse could have a go on me because putting the needles in those veins then were comparatively easy. These days my veins were not that good and the nurse often have to look all over both my arms to find a site even taking into account the much smaller needles than the dialysis ones.

Eventually on this occasion a second more experienced nurse joins in and I continue to use my "thumbnail pressed into my finger" technique to redirect the discomfort. No wonder the veins are hiding. They're sick of it. As would any self-respecting blood vessel be.

I direct them away from the sections of my arms especially where my old fistula was and my artery was reconstructed. Explaining this I get a question that over the decades I often heard beginning when I was an 11-year-old boy to now: "you have been in the wars haven't you?". All I need to do now is get out of the building.

Even after familiarising myself with the exit route months earlier I still got lost and I noticed the temporary signs were still there but this time with lots of scribbled graffiti from irritated patients. "Becoming permanent" directly on the words "Temporary Notice". On another one: "Been over a year now" hurriedly scribbled in the corner.

Hopefully on my return, still free of symptoms or lumps, when I next return in four months time, it would be interesting to see whether or not there is a new permanent notice, which may prevent people getting lost. Or will I see someone walking up the stairs from the basement all in rags, now the remains of apparel clearly far too large for him, weakly placing his hand on my shoulder trying to speak. After persuasive requests to repeat louder, I bring my ear closer to him " level E .... where's level E.. trying to find level E"

Another kidney check up arrived. In the morning I got up but didn't take my drugs because for the mornings of check ups you cannot take them till after your blood is taken.

After the usual palaver of blood tests, urine samples an the taking of my weight I saw the consultant. I've never met him before and told him that the cancer was till in check but I wanted to know what happened to the results of the heart check I had requested last time because I had noticed a distinct deterioration. I had had cardiogram four months ago and still not had the results.

He thanked me for reminding him and told me that over the last few years my heart had deteriorated and after a short conversation it materialised that I no longer had just syndrome x but what he termed heart failure.

I obviously was a bit put out by this. I asked him what is the clinical term. I had, or still had, syndrome x but what is my new lucky catch? I wanted to know so I could look it up. He repeated that I had heart failure "just like kidney failure". Surely he meant heart disease, not failure. If you have kidney failure you function has stopped and you need to go on a kidney machine. If you have heart failure the heart pump has stopped and you are invariably dead. What is it? Syndrome x + y? Sydrome x squared? Syndrome (x + y) all squared? No still heart failure, not even heart failing.

I asked him why, considering I had asked for my heart function to be checked, I wasn't told the results. He said there was no point in letting me know because there is nothing they can do about it. He did say, however, that I should be put on statins which I had heard about but could not really understand why years earlier I wasn't on them already. It was a comparatively new drug for people with heart disease. But on leaving he hadn't prescribed it so I presumed he was going to write to my GP as the bill would end up with the GP's health centre as opposed to coming out of the hospital's coppers.

I waited few weeks to give time for the letter to arrive and then saw my GP, when at the same time I could get a few drugs I was running out of but he had not heard anything. I reported what had happened and he sad I had fallen through the net but he would sort it out. About a week later my GP phoned me at home and explained my new heart diagnosis was not something I should really worry about as it was not severe and very common with people with a kidney history. After a short discussion as to how my symptoms had got worse he agreed that I have tests.

In the post arrived a "Choose and book" confirmation letter and thankfully my GP didn't get involved in this NHS choice pretence. Which hospital would you like to go to: your local one or one where it would take a day to get there? Choice? Not informed choice. Just choice. Which room in the ward would you like to convalesce in: room one, room two or room three? I don't bloody know ?

The letters ends: "Please read any enclosed information if any publiohod material is enclosed with this letter, it has been sent to you because it contains useful and important information that you may need to know before arriving for your appointment"

If? I could wallpaper my living room with these standard enclosures. You get them each time you have a hospital appointment. Stuff that now goes straight in the bin: Information guide (site map, directions, ads like the transplant donor scheme and funeral directors); Patients information :welcome to the (hospital); Pre registration form for accurate and up to date information (ie a questionnaire with a second half on ethnic background, presumably to check if I am still white British); The hospital free bus shuttle and the Patient information service stuff on your clinic.

I bet you if I chose a distant hospital I would only get the local bus service shuttle and not the train information to get there.

I attended for my heart test, saw a consultant and more tests were to be organised.

**

A few weeks later I went to see my GP on what on the surface looked like an ailment that had nothing to do with my chronic conditions although the GP I see has always got to the possibility that it might. Assuming it didn't I was given a prescription for one tablet to be taken once a day for a month. This is very unusual for me and I left his consulting room with my prescription note with just one item on it and walked through the waiting room clutching my little piece of paper thinking this is what most people in this room expect to get: a total cure for a temporary ailment and then they will be as right as a rain once again.

OK they have to pay their £7.20 prescription charge or whatever it is. I never know how much these days because of my prepayment certificate that I have to pay for each year but there is news.

I have recently heard that cancer patients now get free prescriptions. Oh dam: I'm in remission. However even if I wasn't this news is not that good if you have other ailments.

Off the top of my head let's suppose that a patient also has a kidney transplant, osteoporosis and a heart condition. The many prescribed drugs you had to take over the year would mean you'd have to buy a prepayment certificate anyway so the fact that you were a cancer patient would not help you financially at all. Having said that however they appears to be a vague promise from the present government that all patients with a long term chronic condition will in the future have free prescriptions. I live in hope.

I got a letter from the hospital which had enclosed the usual panoply of literature telling me how to get to it. The appointment rather unusually was eight o'clock in the morning and I was expected to be there for at least two hours. It was one of my work days. That morning I must have underslept as I got there very early. I strolled down some very empty corridors to the x-ray department and presented myself and supplied the letter and the questionnaire that I was told to bring along. In fact I was told to post the questionnaire in advance but in another sheet in the envelope I was told I didn't have to and you could bring it a long to the appointment. It asked questions such as "is it possible you might have metal in your body (e.g. shrapnel or bullets)" or, I might add, a forgotten pair of forcipes ....left by surgeon that s/he had forgotten to remove after an op.

I glanced down at the side of the appointment desk and I thought I saw a "MR I. Patients" sign. Was this a memorial sign for a regular customer who dropped dead on that very spot? To commemorate the life of a regular customer, just like those signs on park benches? No. This strangely spaced sign said "MRI Patients". I was one of them. I didn't have time to read the notice as just then the receptionist took my paperwork and checked on the computer and said where I could sit. Just a few minutes later two female radiologists or is technicians arrived and I was to follow them. I was the first patient of the day. We left the hospital building and arrived at a mobile home. We were now outside the front of the hospital. Next to it was a portacabin. In there we chatted. Usual stuff : name, rank, serial number, what was you date of birth (it still is), address, have you been shot recently, if you weren't were you able to avoid any shrapnel etc. I then discovered I was now going to go into the MRI scan for an hour.

I warned them that I would have to go to the toilet first if I was going to be stuck in this MRI scanner for an hour. The other half of the portakabin had a toilet and unfortunately there was no lock. It wasn't a case of clinging on to the door because the toilet section was long and narrow and unless you were elastic man you chanced it or sang.

I had been in such a scanner before but the shock of only then realising it was to be for an hour was my own fault. On the leaflet I was given with the original letter, which I didnt read, it was explained that I might be.

MRI stands for Magnetic Resonance Imaging if anyone is taking notes. This is a safer way looking into the body without using x-rays.

The large dome magnet is large enough for the patient to fit underneath. The leaflet states you will hear gentle noise and that its important to keep completely still. You have a squeezy alarm placed in the palm of your hand and you can listen to music and CD. You need to remove any magnetic objects such as jewellery, keys, money, submachine gun, hand grenade etc. It also tells the patient to return the questionnaire as soon as possible. It refers to the letter that says you can just bring it on the day but this leaflet says for the first time that you need to return this questionnaire to confirm that you will be attending. With the letter was a sheet saying, quite rightly, if you are not coming but with all these contradictions you can understand why some patents don't.

"Occasionally some patients may need to have an injection of a special dye which helps to improve the quality of the image" How long will this take? "This depends on the area of your body that is being scanned. Most examinations take 10 to 30 minutes but a few take and take up to an hour". Well guess what? I need an injection and was in it for the full hour.

There was yet another sheet with the letter telling you how expensive the use of these scanners are and that there were only three in the region of the country. I was also told to confirm I would be attending. The opposite of what you are usually told. Yet more potential confusion. Rather than throwing loads of different pieces of paper in with the appointment letter why don't they just put in the original letter, in bold, an instruction saying that if you don't confirm by a certain date it will be cancelled .

My appointment was really bad timing. Several months earlier I had agreed with a friend to buy tickets for the Chelsea- Tottenham football game and the only day it was possible for me to get my ticket with him was that morning which meant I had to be get on the special ticket line at nine o'clock in the morning but I was stuck inside the bloody scanner.

My valuables were put in a locked cupboard and I was given a gown to put on with opening at the front which makes a change. I lay on the bed in front of the MRI scanner and warned of what was ahead. Unfortunately it was said in a way that you felt like a small child.

When you are rolled in don't move, keep your arms by your side; you will be told to breathe in and out and do what is asked at once; have you brushed your teeth? Are you sure? You will hear funny noises, here is the button to press if you have a problem, put these headphones on because it's quite noisy in there. Who's been a good boy then?

I was transported into what to me looked like a torpedo cylinder from one of those World War II submarines war films but to others a nightmare scenario for claustrophobics. Then the excitement began. "Breath in take a deep breath, breathe out, all the way out and stop breathing". You would then hear a funny sound and then after that five seconds you were told to "breath away".

This seemed easy enough. The process happened again but this time when you were expected to hold your breath the time had doubled which you were not warned about or ready for. Consequently on a few occasions I couldn't manage it but all ended with "breathe away"

From inside this torpedo cylinder you could hear what sounded like the submarines engine room. And the noise resembled a small ship passing by giving the classic hoot. I was warned about the noise but not what felt like a blast of air on to my chest.

By now I was getting slightly irritated because I had one of these massive old-fashioned headphones on that I was told was to deaden the noise. They were never exactly on my ears from the time I lay down because due to their bulky rims they were pushed forward to my temples. I was trying to find a way to adjust them but couldn't. Previous attempts to bring my hand past my chest failed partly because of the narrowness of the confined space and partly because of all the stuff attached to my chest. I didn't know if I was at risk of messing up the results but I eventually moved the headphones back over my ears. I suddenly realised the actual instructions were coming from the headphones.

On one occasion I was on the verge of getting the giggles. When I heard "the voice" with the usual breathing instruction the radiologist appeared to be in mid conversation but not with me but with someone in the other compartment of the Portocabin. She forgot to say "breath way". Not that funny but many seconds later she was back to remind me to carrying on breathing. Being a kind of guy that tries to use his initiative I had beaten her to it having already decided to carry on breathing regardless of what an NHS employee told or didn't tell me to do. I was able to control my giggle risk in time for the next scan a few moments later. God knows why she didn't just say once from the outset that when the noise ends each time you can continue breathing because that is what happened each time.

When about 10 minutes of the hour remaining I was rolled out from under the scanner for, needless to say, needle time. A doctor was waiting with a syringe. As I popped out the radiologist said I was a very good boy .... sorry, was doing very well.

Being absolutely still for nearly an hour left me with pins and needles in my left hand but I was able to flex myself in the hope they would go only to be ready for more needles.

The doctor headed for by right arm and I put him off as that is where my reconstructed artery was and so he went to my other arm to inject some fluid which was to act as a comparison between previous tests before I was shoved back under the scanner.

My veins didn't want to play and they blew at several sites until one didn't. Once injected I was rolled back in and the series of tests began again and then I was rolled out, left to put all my clothes and, partially dressed, walked into the other section where there appeared to be a party.

There was about seven people in the second small compartment with a big colourful sign saying "happy birthday" with an appropriate cake on the side desk but thankfully everyone was drinking just coffee. Feeling like a gatecrasher I collected all my belongings and rushed to the law centre in the vain hope I could still get the tickets rubbing at my arm only to discover that the vein that had not blown now had as a bruise was coming up. It had only just made it but would I ?

Yes. Once at my desk I was lucky to phone and get the tickets but on looking at my desk diary realised I was to chair that afternoons staff meeting.

In the following week waiting for my next set of heart tests I heard two interesting things about my local hospital.

On the local television news there was a warning that no one should visit the local hospital if they are suffering from diarrhoea and vomiting symptoms. This immediately brought to mind the noravirus which I had just before my annual stint to the Glastonbury festival and nearly had to cancel. Rather than risk getting it again I reminded my self that next week I will definitely stop at that dispensing hand cleaner and not touch anything.

In fact I think I'll go and pinch a few bottles from the various entries to the hospital and have a bath in it. On a more serious note I have heard recently that asylum seekers who are not allowed any kind of support arer actually stealing these bottles and drinking them to make themselves ill so they can get a bed for the night.

The other bit of news I got from the media was from a national radio channel, BBC3, that played music especially made for patients were under the MRI scanner of that very hospital.

The following week I had to return to the heart department but wasn't allowed to eat anything during the four hours immediately before my appointment or drink hardly anything. As I walked towards the entrance of the hospital I noticed that the MRI scanner that last week was coupled to a lorry had vanished. Presumably, to prevent this expensive piece of equipment being stolen, it was stored in a garage at night. I was arriving at 7.30am. My appointment was for, 8 o'clock. I must have underslept.

I walk along the now too familiar corridors and presented myself at the reception at the heart clinic and noticed that Mr I. Patients' notice had vanished. Did I just dream last week's session? No my arm was still slightly bruised from my vein blowing.

I was directed along a more private corridor and at the very end advised to take a seat and after 10 or 15 minutes was asked to following a nurse. A doctor was waiting to take an ultrasound of my heart. The plan was to pour me full of adrenaline to get my heart pumping so that the ultrasound could see the blood flow in my heart. They wanted to see where the blood was not going and why.

As is now very common the attempts to get the needle in my vein took about 20 minutes as several of my veins blue. And so, which was now very common, the needle ended up in top of my hand. They try and avoid the hand as a site as it is more painful than middle of my arm which now seems to have had its day for visiting needles.

We were now able to start. I had a part of my chest shaved, stickers attached which each had little metal nodules which in turn had wires attached

The adrenaline slowly want into me while my blood pressure was regularly taken and the results read out by the nurse. Sometimes this drug sends your blood pressure up or sometimes down. Mine went down and had to monitored closely. I was given two squeezie balls to ... er ... squeeze quickly in each hand to try and increase my heart rate. I got iller and iller and felt sick. The doctor monitored this to know when to stop. My blood pressure was still being read out by

the nurse. Another submarine analogy. "Depth 1000 feet, ...
1500 feet.... 2000 feet......"

Eventually the doctor stopped the infusion. He was
hoping to get more adrenaline in to get a better picture but my
symptoms indicted he had to stop earlier than he hoped.

During this process I shouted out twice. Not in pain but
when the nurse and then the doctor began walking away from
my bed with one of wires accidentally and temporally attached
to their clothing which would have caused me to follow if I
hadn't pointed it out. During this time we also had visits from
his medical underlings asking him questions about other
patients.

While I was slowing recovering as my blood pressure rose
again he explained I didn't have any abnormalities in the
heart. So I now know I had a normal damaged heart. You've
got to take your good news while you can. However the fact he
couldn't speed up my heart to the recommended level without
me becoming ill was obviously not good news.

As we were getting on I was able to extract some
information on other aspects on the state of my heart. I was
previously told that as I had syndrome x : angina the sympton
but not angina the condition. I now learnt that although I had
thickened walls of the heart this is not as bad as thickened
walls of the arteries. Heart attacks come about due to a
blockage caused the part of the arterial walls breaking off.

Contrary what I had been told before he told me that I
indeed had angina the condition but not the more life
threatening. I tried to distinguish these two types of angina
and the doctors seem to accept my definitions of primary and
secondary angina.

While I appeared to be hearing something new compared
to my other discussions with previous heart consultants I try
to fathom out which of the two recommendations I had
previously been given that contradicted themselves should I
follow. Years ago I was told if you feel uncomfortable and had
a tight chest to stop doing what I was doing and "listen to your
body". An another doctor in the past had told me it's a good
idea when you feel uncomfortable in this way to keep on going

because that extra bit of pressure on pumping of blood through your system can actually open up the arteries, veins and the capillaries which might slightly improved or prevent further deterioration. This doctor suggested I should go for the latter and we spoke about using the ENT spray even before I exercise as I would possibly be doing this without pain.

**

My various chronic health conditions appear to be stable. I now know from here on in it cannot get any better. I now have several medical ticking time bombs. All due to one small poxy little defective gene.

cancer

I'm still in remission and have check ups every three months when the consultant checks the six main sites to see if there are any painless lumps. I still get aches around the area where the radiation took place; my hair is back and hardly get a barber's shop attack. The consultant checks for an enlarged liver or spleen or even an average size spleen because you may recall decades earlier I had it removed). Blood is taken. Eventually. In the intervening three months it is up to me to report any lumps. As regards cancer generally I just read that a genetic "master switch" has been discovered which could allow cancer to be turned off in the body. Hope they get all the funding to be able to expedite this research.

However when I belch there is always that metallic taste which I now may have for the rest of my life. So one more favourite pass time bites the dust as I loose some of its enjoyment. The one thing that gets to me is in the news when they report someone dies of cancer they never say
which type. I want to know to be reassured in my pathetic and total non statistical or meaningful way whether it was my type or not.

kidney

364

I'm still not yet back to my six monthly checkups. It became 3 months to keep a close eye on my transplant since my cancer and the slight drop in function that occurred. Incredibly they are in the same week as my cancer three-month check-up. Hopefully the kidney one will move way into the distance as my function continues to stabilise.

My consultant told me the transplant will out live me which probably means it will be the cancer or the heart condition which will get me in the end. If anyone had said that a few years ago I would have got irritated. I haven't forgotten how the treatment my Mum had when she was getting strokes as it may well have caused her transplant to reject. I was always told transplants always reject in the end. It is just a question of when.

Recently I had a dream. The surgeon returned to my bed. Not sure if it was my bed or one in a hospital he had a knife and took out both kidney. I didn't feel a thing this time. He removed my working one and my Dads and reassured me he had a brand new one for me and that it was in the deep freeze and he was just going to get it. So then I knew I was in hospital because my fridges small frozen compartment was full as it had a half packet of frozen peas in it that were about 6 months old. Anyway I was concerned that someone else would have taken it (the new kidney, not the pees) by he time he got there. Very strange.

Heart

Because I have a chronic heart condition and osteoporosis I'm always left with a dilemma. For my heart I need cardiovascular exercise or it would simply get worse and worse. I've had the problem of how far to exercise when the discomfort begins but it looks like I might have the definitive answer now at long last: listen to your body but push it ever so slightly beyond the pain barrier.

However my normal exercises such as swimming and cycling no long tick the boxes not after the osteoporosis diagnosis. With this disease it is recommended that you partake in weight bearing exercises. You need to walk or jog or ramble and so cycling and swimming is not enough.

Most of my attempts to exercise are outside but I always end up having to stop walking and pretend to look in shop windows to recover my breath or even stare down the chain on my bike because I can no longer cycle. Otherwise the embarrassment of the funny looks wee too much for me.

That's why I bought Wii Fit which is a game associated with indoor exercise pretending to be doing outside sports while standing in front of the telly. My purchase is essentially a health and fitness regime that allows you to go at your own speed. It assesses your gradual progress while most of the time you are standing on a aboard On one test I was 10 years younger than I am and on another 10 years old! Regular mini workouts means that not only can you reduce your age as you get better, but also help exercise my heart and reduce weight by putting the sports version of the game's "bat" in your pocket when you jog and put pressure on my skeleton when on the board.

osteoporosis

I am ultra careful I don't slip or trip and risk breaking a leg bone. I still take that special drug once a week. The one you have to take first thing in the morning on an empty stomach and seat upright for at least half an hour after drinking half a pint of water because of the discomfort incurred otherwise.

Recently I heard that a drug company succeeded in challenging the government's decision in the High Court to allow GP's to now prescribe, in preference to this drug, a more expensive one but without patients having to go through this parlava.

tyrpeg

This cottage still sits on the side of a mountain like it has done for the last three centuries. Recently I have been investigating the history of it. In the village it is now common knowledge that the oldest of the two pubs was built in part by the remains of the one the Spanish Armada ships wrecked and washed up on the North Welsh coast. This could mean that that tyr peg may have been made in part from the same boat beans.

I've also discovered the literal translation of the word: Turnpike. I've even discovered where the word itself derived from. In this part of the world pitchforks were called pikels or pikes. Before the days of electronic coin machines you relied on farm labourers who halted the traffic as it arrived at the paying point. The two stood on either side of the road with their hike across the road held out at waist height and when their colleague received the charge they turned their pike down allowing the vehicle or farmer with livestock to continue on their journey.

Well I think it is interesting. A booklet now for sale in the village reads:

"Ahead the turnpike road continues to the pass at Milltir Gerrig. long ago farmers from the Tanat Valley would carry corn over the mountain to sell in Bala. The little toll house (Tyr-peg) is about half a mile up the road. Three pennies was the toll for a carriage and pair, two for a cart load, one penny for horse or donkey, ten pennies for twenty cattle and five for twenty pigs, lambs or goats."

Also I have discovered what was known as "Rebecca's Rebellion" provoked after the roads had installed turnpikes along the mountain roads because the local farmers were incensed that they had now had to pay to take there produce to market. Rebecca was the leader and used to the smash up the little typ pegs across mid Wales.

The boat still bobs around in the jetty at the local marina. The government has recently proposed legislation to extend the drinking and driving offences, normally restricted to the roads, to the canals and rivers. However I hear it only is going to apply to boats over 20 foot or so. less. Therefore when I'm next on it singing shanties and drinking shandies and the police boat puts on its alarm and bombs along the canal at 5 miles an hour plus I may have to saw the front of the boat off just to be on the safe side.

Shortly after my cancer treatment ended I took a friend and his young four-year-old daughter out on the boat and [after the chronic and not acute. Lets not dwell on the possibly others that have yet to enter stage left and stage right that no doubt will arrive due to the aging process..............]
trip he explained to her what cancer was. He told me a few weeks later that in the middle of the family breakfast she suddenly asked "Is Mick dead yet?" No not yet. What doesn't kill you makes you stronger.

................TO BE CONTINUED

****

THANKS TO JQ

m.osullivan@virgin.net

24 BELMONT ROAD
BRISTOL
BS6 5AS
ENGLAND

LULU WEB SITE TO BUY COPIES OF THIS BOOK:

www.lulu.com/shop

THE BEGINNING OF THE BACK OF THE BOOK

The A to Z of Fun and Games

Angina?
Blethitis-bilateral nephrectomy-broken leg-barium meal.
Conjunctivitis-Cancer.
Dislocated finger
Epstein bar virus-examination-endoscopy.
Fistula -fluid restriction …
Gallstones-gallstone removal
Haemodialysis
Immunosuppression
Jaundice
Kidney failure-transplant
Lymphoma-liver-leg break
Memory loss
Nora virus-non Hodgkinson lymphoma
Osteoporosis
Perforated eardrum
Q in the GP surgery - very long
Renal failure
Syndrome X. cloroids-splectomny

Transplant
Ultra filtration
Various other viruses cos constantly immunosuppressed
Water restriction
X-syndrome X.-x-rays....
You lucky bastard!
Zzzzzzzzzzzz...........................Z – animal transplant?

FREE PRESCRITIONS? GO TO:

Selection of WEB SITES in no particular order – DIP IN!

www.kidneypatientguide.org.uk
www.eurodial.org
www.globaldialysis.com
www.ikidney.com
www.kidney.org
www.kidney.org.uk
www.kidneydirections.com
www.kidneywise.com
www.nephronline.org
http://www.bbc.co.uk/news/health/
www.nhsdirect.nhs.uk
www.nlm.nih.gov
www.renalreg.com
www.surgerydoor.co.uk
http://tjktsc.tripod.com
www.bmj.com
www.uktransplant.org.uk
www.kidney.org.uk
www.nkrf.org.uk
http://www.pkdcure.org
www.internethealthlibrary.com
www.quackwatch.com

END